# *An Irish Boy*

Collection of memories of

*John Joseph Byrne*

written by
John Joseph Byrne and Kevin Byrne

Copyright ©2018 John Joseph Byrne

All rights reserved.
This book or parts thereof, may not be reproduced in any form without express written permission.

All images are copyright to their respective owners.

ISBN xxxx

Book design by
Edward Sturgeon

Printed in Great Britain by
Scan Tech Group
17 Burgess Road
Hastings
East Sussex

# Preface

John Joseph Byrne was born on the boarders of Northern Ireland and The Irish Republic in 1913. His Mother and Father died when he was five years and he had the misfortune of being taken in by the Workhouse in Newry, then experiencing a very brief introduction to The Christian Brothers Organization. He was essentially given to the charge of a farming family with a small holding some distance from the Village of Omeath in the Irish Republic. He was to endure several years of slavery, torture and degradation at the hands of these, his captors.

He eventually escaped their cruelty and found friendship and safety firstly with neighbouring farmers, then with a middle class family within the Village of Omeath and from there he makes his way in the world by employment in Northern Ireland. He has a turbulent army career both before the Second World War and in some of the most violent battles during that war.

Meeting, then marrying, the love of his life Grace Brimfield during the war, he is introduced to family life and the joys of normal existence. He has three children and a very loving extended family.

Grace tragically dies at a very young age, as does his daughter. Kevin, his youngest son encourages him to record in writing his very diverse life experiences, partly to help him cope with his loss. This helps him greatly but it is to be noted that he received virtually no formal education. So for this reason he dictates much of the text which is indicated in inverted commas; his narrative has been virtually unaltered; it is largely in his own words. Additionally to these memories from much research descriptions have been added to add context and colour to various events; also historical excerpts have been introduced to clarify chronology of his life experiences.

John's long lived life spans the incredible change in society from before the First World War in rural Ireland through the inter war years, the Second World War, then the post war austerity of the 1950's, the liberal developments in society of 1960's, then the class transcendent consumerist society of the 1980' and1990's. It represents a time capsule of each and all of these periods which is important not to forget.

*In memory of
John Joseph Byrne*

*"Setting eyes on Grace for the first time
at Lugwardine at 12pm; by the time
I got home it was 13.50 – I felt I was yours".*

**The Passing Years of My Life**

# Contents

## Part 1

Chapter 1: Early Years .................................................................................. 1
Chapter 2: Christian Brothers ....................................................................... 7
Chapter 3: Mrs Taylor ................................................................................ 15
Chapter 4: The Brothers and the Father..................................................... 33
Chapter 5: An Escape ................................................................................. 45
Chapter 6: Some Friendly Help .................................................................. 53
Chapter 7: A Belated Childhood................................................................. 63
Chapter 8: The Omeath Taylors .................................................................. 71
Chapter 9: Mac Mannus ............................................................................. 77
Chapter 10: Dancing Nights ....................................................................... 83
Chapter 11: Early Adulthood ...................................................................... 89
Chapter 12: Kicking The Bucket.................................................................. 99
Chapter 13: Joining The Army .................................................................. 103
Chapter 14: Passage to Liverpool and the End of Training ...................... 111
Chapter 15: My First Leave in The Army .................................................. 121
Chapter 16: About to Journey Abroad ..................................................... 127
Chapter 17: Brief Notes on My Experiences in Hong Kong,
  Shanghai, India, and Afghanistan......................................................... 137
Chapter 18: The Journey Back to a Very Different Europe ...................... 157
Chapter 19: Back in 'Blighty' .................................................................... 163

## Part 2

Chapter 1: Off to join The Paratroop Regiment........................................ 173
Chapter 2: Arrival in Hereford and Discovering My Beloved Grace,
  Winter 1942 .......................................................................................... 181

# Part 2 continued

- Chapter 3: North Africa .................................................................. 189
- Chapter 4: First Leave in Seven Months ......................................... 195
- Chapter 5: The Battle of Arnhem .................................................... 201
- Chapter 6: Stores ............................................................................ 211
- Chapter 7: Norway ......................................................................... 215
- Chapter 8: Civi Street ..................................................................... 221
- Chapter 9: Holiday in Ireland ......................................................... 225
- Chapter 10: Back to Work .............................................................. 229
- Chapter 11: 'Squatters' ................................................................... 233
- Chapter 12: Melvyn's Arrival ......................................................... 235
- Chapter 13: Weston Beggard .......................................................... 241
- Chapter 14: Wiggins' ...................................................................... 249
- Chapter 15: Rosemary and Melvyn Leave for London ................... 253
- Chapter 16: We Move to London ................................................... 261

# Part 3

- Chapter 1: Moving to London ........................................................ 265
- Chapter 2: Highbury Fields ............................................................ 277
- Chapter 3: Finsbury Park ................................................................ 289
- Chapter 4: Kynaston Road, London N16 ....................................... 293
- Chapter 5: Kevin ............................................................................ 297
- Chapter 6: Melvyn .......................................................................... 303
- Chapter 7: Rosemary ...................................................................... 307
- Chapter 8: My Retirement .............................................................. 311
- Chapter 9: Home Owners at Last ................................................... 313
- Chapter 10: Miscellaneous Events .................................................. 317
- Chapter 11: Moving to Hastings, 1984 ........................................... 319
- Chapter 12: Trip to Irish Free State ................................................ 323
- Chapter 13: Trying to Cope with Life Without Grace .................... 329
- Chapter 14: France ......................................................................... 333
- Chapter 15: Arnhem Visit .............................................................. 339
- Chapter 16: Christmas in France .................................................... 341

# *An Irish Boy*
## Part 1

*In memory of*
*John joseph Byrne*

"*Setting eyes on Grace for the first time at Lugwardine at 12pm; by the time I got home it was 13.50- I felt I was yours*".

**The Passing Years of My Life**

# 1

# Early Years

*John Joseph was born officially in 1913, although the date is not truly known as the Records Office in Dublin was burned in the troubles surrounding Irish independence on 30$^{th}$ June 1922. Several birth certificated were obtained during a visit of his elder son Melvyn Byrne to Ireland in the early 1970s' on a family holiday; the most appropriate or at least the most pleasing one was chosen. The similarities to fathers' recollections were responsible for the choice of birth date and spelling of surname. It was necessary to obtain a birth certificate in order for foreign travel to be possible. John had not been out of the United Kingdom since his return at the end of the Second World War.*

*These early recollections must have taken place at the time of the Great War and formation of the Irish Republic, 1915-1923. His recollections are largely in his own words. Following the tragic and premature death of his beloved wife Grace his younger son Kevin gave him the idea of recording his fascinating but tormented life. This was to prove a great therapy for him in the forthcoming years as well as a fascinating but gruesome insight into the evils of life on Irish borders in the early 20$^{th}$ Century.*

"The first faint memories of my father and mother were when I was about three years old. I can see myself being carried on his shoulders quite a lot and my mother clinging to his right arm, him giving her support. There was one time, a special time after lots of similar glimpses that I recall when I must have been looking quite starved a baker came out of his shop and looking at me smiled and gave me one big cream bun. The taste of a whole big, sticky cake was a joy not to be repeated much in early life. I managed to get the jam all over father and mother's faces; they didn't seem to mind."

"My Father and Mother lived in Newry, County Down. They were very poor, both father and mother worked at the docks unloading coal from the barges that arrived from England. They used baskets lifting coal up onto the dockside, this was very tiring work. The dust was dreadful and both were to die an early death from emphysema."

"Where we lived and what they did with me whilst they struggled to feed us all I remember virtually nothing. I know I had a sister who was near enough my age."

"I do have some fleeting but fond memories prior to this of my mother singing beautifully whilst working at a small hotel in Warren Point. I remember vaguely her passing from room to room carrying linens to make beds ready for guests. Her voice echoed along the corridors of what seemed a huge building reciting old and cheerful songs from a lost past. I can only imagine that by the time she ended up helping father at the docks that this job must have come to an end."

"My childhood has been very sad in many ways. I look back to think I was never given a present of any sort in my young years, unlike the children of today. But I feel no bad feeling for the young ones of today, in fact my own children I have tried to give as many presents and other things as possible, in part to make up for what I lacked in my own youth. My life has been like looking for, as they say, needles in hay stack, for my Birth Certificate or any form of identity to those years; I never found one to show what my right age was. They say it was all down to the troubles in Ireland."

*Chapter 1: Early Years*

"I was to find out from friend years later that my father had been sent to a sanatorium. He had collapsed in their lodgings and mother had got us two children to run call for a doctor. We had little money but the doctor being a good man had summoned a cart and had him taken to the sanatorium. He would die a quick death from his lung disease. He was so thin and under nourished that he had been beyond hope when he had arrived there. Mother soon after lost her mind. She was put into a mental institution but was to die heartbroken two months later. Of my sister I know nothing apart from there was mention that some people from the North took her into their family; I would never see her again."

"My memories of the events that followed are few and far between. I now know that at that time children with no relatives were sent to the work house. I recollect two tall laddies in brown dresses and big hats taking me to a large grey building and passing me onto an old man with spectacles and a large open book. I suppose they handed me into his charge. I had no one else to care for me."

"While in the workhouse I used to play with children of my own age group. Boys and girls were dressed in little sailor's uniforms with large white collars, we would just run around playing simple games to amuse ourselves. We didn't have all those nice things children have now. On one such day a group of us were playing dressed in our innocent uniforms just outside the work house porch and a Black and Tan soldier came into the workhouse yard, grabbed my hand and thrust a revolver into it then forced my fore finger into the trigger. He squeezed my hand and a shot burst out into the yard sending the children running to hide screaming. He showed me how to shoot people, (me aged five)."

"The work house was a cold, dark place. We slept in high metal beds in rows in long tall rooms. We were made to say our prayers by the bedsides, then lights went out and all was dark. When we thought it safe we would get out of bed and tip toe to the doors to check the coast was clear, then we would make up little imagined games playing at being priests or nurses, or shop keepers. Sometimes we would hear a footstep on the stairs outside and we would run and get back into bed in case it was the old man with the big book."

"The older people lived in some of the larger two storey buildings either side of the central block and set back from the central court yard garden, the men to one side the women the other. In the central block the 'idiots' were housed. Also within this central larger building were the dining hall and chapel. The older inmates I am told have not paid their rent or owe money to the church or to the shop keepers in the town. Some live here because they have been removed from the streets so they do not spread more diseases. They must have done very bad things. Their rooms were not like ours. Many of them never leave and have been here for years. The dormitories are small with dark stone walls with little furniture. They have bare floor boards and there is no heating or artificial light. Their clothes were not as nice as ours. Some more of the inmates live in the old stables around the edge of the work house and in semi-derelict single floor sheds. These were converted into dormitories during the times of the great famine years ago. But they are still used for the sick and very poor people. Although the men and women sleep in separate chambers they are allowed to eat together in the dining hall. They are given tin plates."

"Some 'tramps' they are called, come in the early evening and leave in the morning. Their clothes are ragged and they are very dirty. The thick rancid treacle smell around their part of the building is horrible. But I am told that these are the lucky ones and those who don't make it in for the night can end up in one of the numerous tenements dotted about the town paying one penny to hang themselves over a rope for the night."

"I am told that the Nuns march upright along these dormitories and throw a potato into each bed."

"We children never go into that part of the building behind the main block. We are scarred someone will pull us into there. What terrible things can they have done to be in such a place?"

"To us children work house was not really bad; I did enjoy playing with the others in the yards. We also used to play in the area of ground between the old grave yard and the new vegetable garden. The Elders caste a blind eye to our impishness most of the time. But on occasion we were ushered back to the playground to keep us under control."

"There were some young women there who had children of their own with them. The very young babies would slumber in wicker baskets or wooden boxes lined with linen while their single parent mothers worked in the laundry cleaning the sheets and clothes for the work house and medical wards. The other children were dressed like us and played with us in the yards and vegetable garden. There was a sense of freedom roaming around the grounds at play investigating the nooks and crannies of the muddle of buildings and yards. But I was to be there only a couple of months until this pattern was broken."

*An Irish Boy*

# 2
# Christian Brothers

Early one morning, much earlier than was usual, a nun entered the chamber and woke us from our slumbers. I and two chums were taken to the door to our dormitory and confronted by the old man with the big book. The nun affectionately smoothed down our hair and looked to the old man who announced authoritatively that we were to go to school. We had to clean our teeth, wash quickly, get dressed and make ourselves ready to leave the work house, and then go to the dining hall for a very quick breakfast.

We had time only for some cold porridge and yesterday's tea from the urn when we were called into the hall that led to the porch to meet a fat lady with a heavy brown dress down to the floor and long dark shawl over her shoulders. A wide, round bonnet with a frayed brim sat firmly on her head.

"This is Mrs Carroll", said the man. "Follow her and don't get into any mischief." She was not a bad lady. We were not frightened by her. We had seen her on several occasions before walking around the corridors in the main building of the work house. She had a solemn but not unkind manner, when I think back. We marched behind her keeping pace with the hems of her dress, forward into the town from the southern outskirts with its open plots of ground the town gradually encroaching these. Then into some wide cobbled roads flanked with stone pavements with tall grey buildings either side. Many of these had advertising bill boards some smart some tatty. There were some decaying army posters partly covered with more recent ads. I remember her pointing to a white building with a shop below and saying that was a library, be good children and the priests will teach you how to read and be good Christians. We followed on up Hill Street and further past very tall buildings four, five and six storey in height. The deep red bricks making up their mass looked daunting to us small boys. There were lots of horses and carts and ladies with fancy clothes about their business and scruffy men in soiled working clothes who were loading and unloading sacks and crates onto the pavements. We proceeded up Boat Street and then into Upper Chapel Street. We were now skirting the northern outskirts of the town. Buildings were thinning out and getting lower in stature.

We approached a handsome residence which could well have made a fine gentleman's home. It took the shape of a large country style house with central entrance and good proportioned high arched windows to the upper floor. Passing through the wrought iron entrance gates we made the short approach to the building. Mrs Carroll took us up a wide flight of off white stone steps to the right hand side of the building. We then were taken down the side passageway made rather dark by the height of the tall gable end which seemed to tower above us and then to a smaller rear Buckingham green door. She pushed open the door revealing a dark service vestibule, poorly lit and full of dark colours. There we were greeted by a short and somewhat rotund cassocked priest in his later years. He had little hair on his head and looked quite a funny figure. He spoke to us three children in a high voice in a considerate manner. "Children" he said, "It is time for you to start your study of our Lord." He thanked Mrs Carroll and said that the children would be ready for her to collect at five thirty that afternoon at this door of the establishment as was to become our norm.

## Chapter 2: Christian Brothers

We knew nothing of the Christian Brothers at that time, but later we would learn that they were a dedicated international order. It had begun centuries before as the Cistercians had constructed their abbey in the twelfth century. They had begun their teaching at Upper Chapel Street in 1851 and from here would move several times in eighty years. They had no state sponsorship and wanted to be free of the National School system so they could promote their religious credentials.

We three very small boys were led up a narrow and steep back wooden staircase with small plain square banisters and a thin round banister rail. We clung to each banister to pull ourselves up the steep climb. Reaching the first floor landing, the priest threw open a small service door and to our surprise we emerged onto a long wide corridor. Its whitewashed walls had no windows. There were tall doorways with fan lights to both sides spaced well apart. The ceiling was curved not flat and had metal light fittings dotted at intervals along its length; single gas burners were alight from each lamp. The boarded floor had simple brown varnish and was polished highly at the edges but through much traffic the main thorough-fare was dulled and crazed. At the end of the corridor was a flight of six steps the width of the corridor going down. At the bottom was a small landing with a door either side.

The priest opened the door to the right and pushed us in. In front of us were thirty or so boys of various ages, some tall, most short like myself and small in stature. I would say that the youngest would be about my age or even less and the oldest probably thirteen maybe fourteen years. They wore dirty white shirts with frayed cuffs and collars; many had woolly jumpers adorned with holes of various sizes. Most had short pants and boots in grades of decay. Like me they mostly had brown curly hair, some clean others matted. Their hands and faces generally were unwashed. Black fingernails abounded. Our smart little sailor's uniforms seemed to make us an object for their disdain.

As the priest ushered us in a low row came up from the ensemble. Some papers flew across the air. There were three priests in the room. All were somewhat younger than our escort. "Silence," shouted a rather fat, red faced man. He appeared to be the head priest in the classroom. "You may go Father, leave us with our charge". He left, the door closing with an emphasis that signalled a change in our situation.

The class room towered above us with dark brown stained timber boarding forming the pointed ceiling. To one side was a Gothic arched window with stained glass in its upper section. The walls were whitewashed as had been other parts of the building; they had a simple dado rail in dark stained wood as their only decoration. I noticed that there was a raised platform at the front of the rows of desks which was the stage for the masters to torment us from. The desks were simple wooden planks forming the tops and narrower planks the benches attached by chunky rails the framework.

Obediently the boys sat down and a hush fell over the room; all eyes focused on us tiny figures including those of the three priests.

"What is your name boy?" the round faced priest bellowed at the boy nearest him. "Come over here and spell out your name."

Nervously the boy replied "John Cowpar." At this the classroom erupted. At that moment a blackboard rubber was sent hurtling through the air and a howl spat out of the immediate silence. There was a dark skinned red headed boy probably about ten years of age in the middle of the room clutching his ear. A small trickle of blood meandered down his neck.

"Keep quiet or else you will all have a taste of my belt" spelled out McCabe.

John Cowpar froze before the priest unable to repeat his name. "Cowpar take yourself to that bench in the second row boy" instructed the priest.

"Colin O'Connell and John Byrnes sir", I coughed up failing to wait for the priest to enquire again.

"Which are you boy" he gestured to me.

"John Byrnes, sir" I replied trying to be as polite as any well behaved five come six year old could allude to be.

"Is that Byrnes with a Y or Burnes without a Y?" he said with great emphasis.

"I believe the nuns at the workhouse say its Byrnes with a Y sir, they told me how to spell it and that it was important to remember it was my name" I replied.

"Good boy Byrnes, go with O'Connell and take a seat behind Cowpar in the space in the third row", continued the red faced priest.

This time the class remained in silence as we three very small boys took our assigned places in front of the ragged ensemble.

I was not to find out for many years until my adult life the importance the priest had attached to the spelling of my name and the reasonable reception he had given to me on that first day of school. The day seemed long and tedious; religious instruction was followed by hours memorising Catholic Catechism. The three priests would walk up and down the rows of desks making sure we were not distracted from our task. I wonder if they knew that we three new arrivals were so young and from such background that we were only pretending to be reading these books for fear of being found out that our names were our only knowledge of the written word.

Midday came and the senior priest shouted in an authoritative way for us to get up, close our books and form a line in single file in the corridor outside.

In a muddled and very hasty brawl the entire contents of the class evolved into a formal single file row as the priest had directed. We were then processed back down the rear staircase we had climbed that morning, but this time turning abruptly to the left we descended a further flight of stairs I had been unaware of that morning. It was the semi basement floor and below the entrance hall. The staircase opened out directly into a large room, rectangular in shape; probably about forty feet by twenty. Compared to the generous heights of the chambers on the upper floors the ceiling here was flat and low. Two windows were in front of us. These were plain and had clear glass with no ornamentation. The walls were dressed with dado and dado rail but this time they were whitewashed above but had grim dark green distemper on the dado itself. There were rows of seminal type tables in wood flanked by simple long bench seating. To the left hand wall was a not inconsiderable sized al-cove with three nuns serving from great pots.

There were some fifty or sixty children already in the room seated at the meal. They were not distracted by our entrance and continued to engage in consuming their food.

Our neat line presented itself to the al-cove and the nuns who duly gave us a chunk of bread and a bowl of stew. We took up any available places and joined the other children in Lunch. Some food may have been flicked person to person; but as we were all very hungry most of it ended up in our bellies.

Fifteen minutes later and again in an orderly fashion we retraced our paths to the classroom. The afternoon took much of the same format as the morning. We seemed to be settling into a regime of religious subjugation.

As discussed that morning at five thirty we were delivered into the charge of Mrs. Carroll who was already waiting by the rear school door. She took my hand with the other two following a couple of steps behind and we negotiated now familiar streets through the bustling town towards the southern suburbs and our home The Work House. At that time I didn't know the reputation of that establishment. A strange feeling of security and belonging was trying to attach itself to a part of my brain.

*Chapter 2: Christian Brothers*

The following days passed in much the same format. We three boys found the school, its religious leaders, also the fellow classmates and the repetitive subject matter a bit dreary. It was a distraction from our games in the work house yard; but it was nice not having to see those sad soles hovering around the gates all day hoping for a respite for the night from their plight.

It must have been two weeks or more into our involvement with the Christian Brothers School. It was about half an hour into morning classes. None of us could have foreseen what was about to erupt. The round faced senior priest McCabe seemed to have a dry cough and looked particularly red faced. He appeared a bit hot and bothered you might say. He was hovering above a little boy in the middle of the room. The boy I would guess must have been an infant of similar years as me. Looking over my shoulder I noticed that the boy had scribbled a cartoon image of a round faced fat man onto the desk under his Catholic

Catechism Book. The priest's mouth frothed and spat out some unholy words I didn't know the meaning of. From around his cassock he tore a heavy leather belt. Grabbing the infant up from under his arm in one hand lashing out with the leather belt with his other hand the boy was sent hurtling across the room ending up in a heap on the floor near the teaching platform. The boy was shrieking with shock and pain. I have blanked out the events that followed from my memory. On the march back to the work house that night with Mrs. Carroll we three boy knew that all was not right with Father McCabe.

The following couple of days saw an atmosphere of hush remain over us children as we hoped to gain reassurance that the spectacle was an isolated incidence. We had experienced a brief taste of security of a sort and hoped it would continue.

*An Irish Boy*

# 3

# Mrs Taylor

It must have been a midweek day, possibly a Wednesday or a Thursday, certainly not a Sunday as I knew Mass in the Work House chapel had only been two days or so before. As usual in the grey early day light coming through the windows I could see the rain pouring down, over flowing from the gutters outside our dormitory. Most of the children were running around, playing innocent games. There was a mildly fun atmosphere abounding for such an early hour. The man with the big book came into the dormitory as he always did. We children stopped in our tracks and stood attentively at our metal bedsteads. We took our usual turns to use our simple bathroom facilities, then dressed and spick'n'span were filed down to the dining hall. We had our customary rations of lukewarm porridge and tea and awaited a call from the man with the big book to take us to the porch and thence to Mrs. Carroll.

"O'Connell, Cowpar and Byrnes" we awaited to hear and then to follow through to the porch. "Byrnes", I was to hear. "Byrnes, come over here" instructed the man with the big book.

My two friends and I looked at each other and all got up to go.

"No, just you Byrnes", the man said.

I got up from the bench and stared separately at my two chums. They gave a similarly surprised and vacant expression back to me. I walked over to the man as usual carrying his big book under his

*An Irish Boy*

arm and he shuffles me out into the hall and towards the door to the porch. Stopping just outside the dining hall he pauses here and gestures towards a small bound package wrapped in grey crumpled linen on the floor by the dining room door. Gesturing to it he says "these are yours to take with you".

I am dumbfounded by all of this and unaware of what is ensuing. He gestures more fervently towards the package on the floor; so I stoop forward and pick it up. Looking up from the package I notice inside the porch door a large, sinister rounded figure.

About five feet seven inches tall and certainly tall enough to tower over a six year old undersized for my age Mrs. Taylor stood to the left hand side of the porch door leaning bullishly against the dado. On this dreary overcast damp day the lack of natural light made her dark form appear almost black. She wore a brown bonnet that disguised a severely weather worn complexion. A great shawl draped down to her waste, or what one could call that part of such an oversized form. Below down to her invisible ankles abounded a mass of murky material resembling well-worn sackcloth.

In later life I would make the connection with her and images from the Gestapo.

The Master of the Work House opened his big book handed Mrs. Taylor a charged pen and pointed to a place to make her mark. She duly scribbled a meandering 'Mrs T'; he placed the book on a small table to dry then gestured to me to come forward. I remember his words to this day "he's yours to take away" he quietly mouthed "you should bring him back here every six months I tell you, and be sure ye do".

Reluctantly I was pushed out of the porch door to follow Mrs. Taylor through the vegetable patches, through the playground and past the approach to the work house gates. On we walked through the southern suburbs of Newry along Edward Street and thence to Edward Street Station. I had never been on a train before. In my excitement at the vision of the steaming iron giant I forgot

## Chapter 3: Mrs Taylor

temporarily the dilemma I was now in. I had been evacuated from the work house dining hall completely by surprise, then to be handed over to this apparition by the Master of the Work House. She had grabbed my collar to tug me the first few hundred yards then I had followed obediently as if knowingly acknowledging my position of servitude. We had progressed onto the platform and boarded the stationary train and all without one word passing between us.

The front of the engine reminded me of a face with a big red mouth and funnel bellowing smoke as if coming out of someone's head. In the middle of the furnace was a hump and behind that an open cabin where men were working one stocking coal the other pulling leavers and blowing the whistle. Smoke gushed out from above the funnel and from under the wheels. A wagon carrying coal was attached to the engine and a procession of carriages followed on dressed in a fine green and black livery.

Mrs. Taylor pressed her hand into a waste line pocket and produced a small purse, from this came two tickets obviously prior purchased, these she handed to a guard standing at the gateway to the platform.

She twisted the handle and pulled open the door; knowingly I climbed in ahead of her and sat down on an upholstered bench seat. She sat down opposite me and we both starred out of the window. I gave her the occasional glance to see if she might break the silence. The train got up steam and pulled out of the station on its short journey to Bridge Street Station. After a three minute stop at this station the journey commenced and to my amazement I viewed the eighteen arches Craigmore Viaduct in the distance to the north of the town.

The single track ambled its way firstly along the Newry Canal lined with huge wharf buildings with goods of all shapes and sizes being hauled up and down on great metal hoists. I had seen glimpses on my walks to and from Christian Brothers School of the docks and its crafts moored up being swarmed over by stocky men in cloth caps and high boots wearing dungarees and overalls. I had not viewed the extent of the activity in that area with the masses of barges laden waiting to be unburdened or the great sheds alongside the water ways storing their bounty. Some buildings were four and five storeys high some right on the waterside others set back with loadings bays and pathways in front.

Next the train passed alongside a wide pool of water Albert Basin full of boats of all description waiting to pass further upstream or to dis-barge at the warehouses lining its jetties. This basin then narrowed into a navigable water way still identified as Albert Basin. The commercial buildings thinning out; I was aware of great change to the scenery. To the north side of the basin the water was edged by a wide mud bank travelling some miles; beyond this were fields leading onto woods thickening into The Narrow Water Woods. At distance sloping up to the sky were The Mountains of Mourne. I had some distant recollection of these from the days my mother had been happily working at the small hotel in Warren Point. It gave me a warm feeling for a brief moment. Turning to the other side of the train I saw an equally lovely vision of The Fathom Forest. The day had become mild. The rain had stopped and rays of sunlight met the shimmering water with the trees of Fathom Forest merging their greenery with the water's edge. Only the occasional barge interrupted the wading birds astride the river banks. The Albert Basin had become The Newry River.

The trees of the two forests made a sea of green against the back drop of the emerald mountains. The soft grey sky was dotted by soft floating clouds. Gradually the trees thinned and to the north of the Newry River which widened into Carlingford Lough I saw the small town of Warren Point. The pretty whitewashed seaside guest houses were the threshold to the mountains and to the wide estuary of the lough. The grey stone quayside underlined the simplicity and understated comfort of the bay windowed dwellings. It was a happy place containing some of my only contented and

*Chapter 3: Mrs Taylor*

cherished although fleeting memories on this soft grey late autumn afternoon.

The train rolled on cutting a close path to the water's edge. It crossed a bridge over a small inlet; the waters from the lough trickled into the narrow stream and mixed with its boulders and grasses. We were passing the extent of the harbour opposite at Warren Point. The pretty view of the holiday town was slipping out of clarity. The lough widened considerably forming a great body of water. The odd boat navigated the mouth of The Newry River. To the south side of the train the trees again were thinning and the occasional cottage nestled within its parcel of ground amongst the woods. I could feel the momentum of the train slowing. We were going to stop at a station? More cottages grouped themselves nearer the tracks and a roadway came into alignment with the railway line. We pulled up abruptly at the sole platform, very short and extremely narrow such that the train had to align the carriages with it and the engine and coal wagon stayed forward.

Mrs. Taylor raises herself from the bench seat; the twenty minute journey had ended without her ushering a single word apart from checking curtly on my name somewhere towards the outskirts to Newry. Twisting the handle she pushes open the door and bundles her great form clumsily on the platform. I follow behind and slam closed the door. The whistle blows and with a puff of smoke the train continues on its journey.

The station block looked more like one of the cottages I had seen on the approach to the village. Donning two chimneys its shallow thatched roof capped a single storey stone building with white washed walls and three windows. Pretty window boxes sat on the sills. The doors at either end of the building were closed so we passed through a gate at the end of the platform and she thrust the tickets into the hand of a uniformed guard. He lifted his cap but she ignored the gesture and pushed past.

We progressed towards what appeared the main street. There were I would say only a handful of lanes in the village of Omeath. As the train had pulled into the railway station I had made out a long granite walled promenade forming the frontage of the village to Carlingford Lough. The main street and the promenade were connected by three or four narrow twittens. Ten or so houses were assembled about the convergence of these roads. These were mainly two storeys in height and had a variety of shapes and sizes. There were three small shops; a butchers with its pig and rabbit carcasses hanging around its doorway along with some poultry. There were two other shops offering a mixture of general produce and one also baking some of its own fare. A blacksmiths operated out of a shed in an alley to the south side of the main road. Their roofs were gently sloping, some of thatch, some of tiles but the odd one had corrugated metal to keep the elements out. All had white washed walls with neat timber windows; many had wooden porches to help gain protection from prolific the rain. Low stone walls, again white washed, lined the lanes and protected the pockets of foliage and vegetables from the passing thorough fares. A narrow path ran along one side of the main road for some distance.

The odd passer-by would turn and look at me. Me a well turned out child with boots, good trousers and collared shirt with jumper, carrying my parcel under my arm following behind this person, Mrs. Taylor, apparently a well-known member of the neighbourhood. She was acknowledged but received no pleasantry from the village folk. Some of the women in their long off-white dresses cleaning their porches or escorting their infants would physically turn as if to snub her.

We continued on along Main Street and in barely a few minutes of walking the houses started thinning. The gardens became larger in size. All the buildings were now single floor cottages again with gently sloping roofs and whitewashed walls with tiny windows. The gardens contained lots of potatoes and other root vegetables.

*Chapter 3: Mrs Taylor*

Most had either a few goats chewing at scraggy grass or a pig or two housed in little sheds adjoining small pens. The occasional established tree broke up the symmetry. The road began to climb slightly then to bear to the right. In front of us was the grand vision of The Cooley Mountains pointing up towards the sky. Large ranges of steeply sloping hill pasture covered their accent. They were divided only by occasional irregular tumbled down stone walls and rock outcrops. We were still very near the edge of the lough with the road carried on a steep bank above the water's edge. I marvelled even at such a young age at the beauty of the scene.

Mrs. Taylor gave my shoulder a tug and grasped my attention. We turned to the right and into a narrow track away from the semi made up road of Main Street and onto a rough dirt track lane. It went steeply up hill and after a straight half mile it began meandering to left and right. It was lined with dry stone walls interrupted by bramble hedges of various heights and thickness and then thickets of trees and bushes. The journey was wearing on Mrs. Taylor as well as me. She began breathing heavily and her weight made for unsure footedness. She would make the odd curse and look back at me, her shawl and bonnet making much momentum in the breeze that was picking up. I kept up but made sure to stay a foot or two behind.

The track turned awkwardly to the left and stopped dead at a primitive wooden gate flanked by dry stone walls in poor state of repair and in almost imminent state of collapse. She pushed the centre of the gate which had no fastener; she bustled through and I followed. Inside was a small field of patchy grass enclosed again with stone boundaries in dubious state of repair. Many clumps of weeds adorned the area as well as boulders and stones scattered here and there. In the centre of the field was a squalid single floored cottage; if it was lime white washed it must have been a long time ago. A centre door in two halves had a small window either side. The thatched roof was in poor state of repair and had sections missing. A single squat chimney stood to the left hand side of the roof. A small plume of smoke emanated from this.

I could make out to the right of the cottage and well set back was a two floor barn in very bad condition. It was dressed with splintered wooden planks many missing; it was covered by a twisted and rusty corrugated iron roof. There were openings to upper and lower floors with a ladder accessing the upper level. Bales of hay were half hanging out of these. Further away from these two buildings was a primitive stable with two half doors. This again was made of wooden planks but had a steeply sloping thatched roof, much of this lay bare or thinning much of it brown in colour and rotting. An elderly mare stood with its head poking out from within; its mane tired and matted. Surrounded by stones and thistles to the right flank of the stable was a muddy pond fifteen or so feet across. This would provide water for the animals and birds. On the side of it engulfed in high wild flowers and grasses stood a stout but well decayed metal hand pump which drew the water from the well. It was mounted on a crude stone base and was brown with rust. A broken down cart and rusty plough were partly disguised by the foliage.

There were three children running around playing behind the cottage. They must have been similar age to myself or a little older. I could hear them shouting and stomping around. I felt disturbed to see the raged condition of their clothes. The three boys were in brown short trousers with plethora of holes and repairs; their shirts had no collars and on top were holed jumpers; their boots were worn and down at heel, severely scuffed. Unkempt curly hair was matted above dirty faces.

I followed Mrs. Taylor straight into the house passing through a small vegetable patch in front of the door where some wiry cabbages, turnips, swede and potatoes were growing in muddy, boggy soil fenced off by strings of barbed wire. Inside the door was one large dark room. This went up to the pitch of the roof and had

*Chapter 3: Mrs Taylor*

no ceiling just the underside of the thatch. A single chimney stack in stone passed up and through the roof, at its base a great opening housed one huge round pot with three legs dangling beneath it and some crude cooking vessels. The pot was hung on a metal cradle fixed into the fireplace on either side; under it burned a charcoal fire. I would guess the room was about forty feet by about twenty, a good size and with no ceiling gave the appearance of much space. The floor was just bare clay with straw scattered about and four or five hens were freely running around in and out of the makeshift wooden furniture. The two small windows let in very little light and the smoky atmosphere stank of stale fish and old meat and potatoes. Apart from the primitive provincial handcrafted items that were in place of table and chairs there was one big chair with tall rounded back also two wide metal beds to the right hand side of the room one much larger than the other. Bundles of sackcloth lay on these beds unmade and very unclean. Cobwebs abounded and a film of dust filled the air. Some meagre belongings hung on hooks and nails around the walls. The only other piece of furniture was a wooden chest with two drawers and three shelves above. Three photos in thin metal frames, some bowls, plates and some knives and spoons were randomly arranged on these.

Next to the chimney and connecting into its flue was a small brick formed bread oven. Its rectangular opening housed a metal rack for cooking soda bread, potato cakes and the like. Above it were two wooden shelves supporting earthenware jars with muslin cloth sealed by earthenware stoppers. I would discover these were for pickling and also for storage of the home brew. Some clay pipes were dotted along these shelves.

A wooden crucifix with a metal Christ hung in the middle of the long wall of the cottage with a picture of Virgin Mary to the right of it. The only light would have to come through the two tiny windows and later when lit from the candles that were lying on a plate in the hearth.

*An Irish Boy*

Whilst I was taken in my new environs Mrs. Taylor had taken some salty herrings from the pot and put them on a plate. She passed this to me and I sat upon one of the mock-up seats and started to eat these with my hands. I was hungry after the journey and downed them in a minute or so. Just at that moment an even older woman came through the door. She wore no bonnet but had shoulder length grey straggly locks. Her pointed nose centred a weather worn face. Her shawl was of kitted wool in dark colours, it part covered a dress which must have started off light brown but was encrusted with dirt and had a multitude of darning. This was Mrs. Taylor's mother.

No words had been ushered for all this time except when she asked my name on the train. I piped up and softly said "when do we have dinner". A severe strike across my face was the reply from Mrs. Taylor. It knocked me off balance and confirmed my feeling of dismay which had been ebbing up inside me all day. Having finished the herrings the mother pushed me out of the door and into the vegetable patch where I was set to work sorting out a pile of potatoes to be given to the pigs to eat. In a bucket of chilly water I had to wash these outside the door to the house then put them in the pot on the fire to boil before giving some of them to the pigs. I was still dressed in my little sailor's style uniform; already showing signs of dirt. I was numb from fright and terrified about what had become my new life with the Taylors. My face was sore.

The pigs were in a make shift pen at the rear of the cottage. That is why I had not seen them on my arrival. They had filtered the earth inside the wooden pen into mud and were wallowing contentedly in it. They scoffed the boiled potatoes down as if they hadn't eaten for days. I felt some empathy with them as all I had had that day was cold porridge and some herrings.

I went back to the front door and put down the bucket I'd used to feed the pigs. At that moment the three boys came to the house, I expected them to say hello and invite me to play like my palls at the work house. Instead they pushed by me picking at my neat collar and gesturing to each other sniggering at me and just passed into the room. The two women sat them down on the flimsy furniture and divided up the remaining contents from the pot on the fire and fed the boys. The old woman gave them some tea which had been stewing in another vessel in the grate. Then picking up another tin cup poured some of the tea into it and brought it to me by the front door. "Take this with you and make yourself a bed in the barn loft. Make sure you bring it back here in the morning" she said. These were the first words the old woman had ushered. Knowing what to expect if I made any reply I turned and walked towards the ladder, climbing this into the upper floor of the ramshackle barn.

It was now almost dusk on this late autumn afternoon. The wind that had picked up on arrival at the small holding had now become strong with that bite that surrounds those lower pastures on the early slopes of The Cooley Mountains at that time of year. The cows on the hillside were settled for the night. The air was damp and as I crawled into the barn loft through the unprotected opening, the room felt unforgiving and lacking any comforts. My belly was virtually empty. The pigs had had more sustenance than me. Drafts blew through the missing or broken boards. How was a six year old child like me expected to make a home here? The day light almost gone I pulled around some bales of straw and tried to get warm and drank the cold tea. It was at this time that even at such a tiny age I felt desperately betrayed and wondered why god had dealt me such a cruel fate. I wished I could depart and not suffer more evils of this world.

I must have fallen asleep through a state of exhaustion. How long I'd been asleep I'm not sure but I was awoken suddenly by the sharp cracking noise from a twisted floor board bending and almost breaking under pressure very near the entrance to the loft. I sat bolt upright in fright and as I focused on the light coming in from the moonlight outside I saw the figure of a young man climbing up into

*An Irish Boy*

the loft. Heaving himself awkwardly up he threw himself through the opening. He made three consecutive jolts in my direction then raising his two arms above his head he then collapsed in a heap two yards from my makeshift straw bed on bare boards.

Seconds later he belched huge breathes out of his mouth accompanied by loud snoring. He was completely still and tranquil in his inebriated state. I had not till then seen a man blind drunk before. On occasion some of the priests may have shown signs of over indulgence; but as for this man he was in a state of collapse. He was blissfully unknowing in his induced slumber.

His hair was brown and neck length, he was unshaven and despite his clearly young years his skin was windblown and reddish. Both hands were calloused and work worn. He wore a tattered waste coat over rough striped collarless shirt. His heavy trousers were patched and severely muddied. His boots were clumsy with thick but worn soles. I was to share this tormented room with Mrs. Taylor's brother.

After staring for hours at this frightening figure hoping he would not awake, or at least not till daylight, I fell again into another deep sleep of exhaustion.

I woke in excruciating pain. My head was hurtling around in circles in the loft in and out in a swaying momentum. A deep pain pressured into my forehead. I got up then fell back on the floor out of balance with the shock and severity of the blow. Coming to a little I saw a large brown boot lying by my side. This had been pelleted at my head. Looking at the slumbering figure of the drunken youth who had passed out near me some hours before I was amazed he had not stirred. To my horror standing upright inside the entrance to the loft was a similarly attired man. He was two, maybe three years older than the former. His clothes, height complexion were all very similar. He exuded evil in his demeanour.

He gave out an exalted laugh, a vile grin spread over his face as he acknowledged my agony. "Get up you lazy wretch", he shouted

*Chapter 3: Mrs Taylor*

at me ignoring any compassion for my predicament. He then walked over to his younger brother and gave him an affectionate kick in the ribs. Grunting and spluttering the younger man sprang to his feet with momentum from the wake- up call. The two of them gave a fleeting glimpse back at me then scampered out of the opening, down the ladder and bounded towards the cottage front door for their breakfast.

It took me some time to settle into the pain that was issuing from my head. I still had had no food since the previous meagre rations yesterday. I was very cold after the night in the loft of the barn. I got up courage and went to the front door of the cottage. I pushed it open a fraction and saw the whole family gathered around the fire side. The two brothers, three children, grandmother and Mrs. Taylor were all there assembled for breakfast. They all held tin plates on their laps filled with porridge. They were helping themselves from the kettle in the grate pouring murky tea into metal mugs.

The old woman came over to me with a plate of porridge and grudgingly passed it to me. She also handed me a mug with tea. Despite the desperate situation I remember that luke- warm tea and the sloppy porridge slipping down inside my empty insides. For a moment I felt some warmth. The ensemble ignored me as I sat on a clumsy box seat inside the door.

A few minutes went by and the old woman turned around and said "remember this well, tomorrow you are not to lie in your bed half the morning; you must make the porridge and the tea ready for us when we rise. You are not here for us to wait on you. Who in God's name do you think you are?"

The two brothers, Shamus and Pat, (the older one), got up dumped their plates and mugs on the floor by the fire and brushed by me as they walked out of the door and then onto to the fields. The three children, Tim, Mikey and John ran outside and resumed their games at the back of the house.

Mrs. Taylor and her mother raised themselves and took me by my arms and pulled me over towards the fire squeezing my bony little arms till they pained.

"Now look well at this fire, John Byrnes", Mrs. Taylor spouted; "there is wood and sacks of charcoal in the barn beneath your bedroom, you make sure that each morning you get a good fire going before we rise."

She showed me the huge pot that had the left-overs from the porridge.

"You will have the porridge ready for us and be sure the kettle is well full of tea. Our hard working men need a good breakfast before going off to the hills."

She showed me the rudiments of where things were and how to prepare the necessary things both for the family and for the various animals and fowl. I was only approaching the latter part of my sixth year but I used all the powers I could gather to force all the information in as far as I could.

Next we went outside to the pigs. I had been shown the store of potatoes and root vegetables in the cottage from which I would feed the pigs. I was instructed as to the regime for the horse, the goats and the chickens. Given the time of year supplies had been gathered to go through the winter period but it was clear that these supplies would diminish as the winter beckoned. We looked at the sparse vegetable patch protected by its barbed wire enclosure. I remember thinking that there was not much left there worth digging up.

"Next week you are to clear the rest of these and set them aside indoors for the winter," I was told by Mrs. Taylor who was now frothing at the mouth through the effort of moving her huge form around yard in the course of my induction.

Going back into the cottage I was given the job of tidying away all the utensils, emptying the pot of the remaining porridge, (which duly ended up in the pigs, not me), then cleaning the huge

*Chapter 3: Mrs Taylor*

pot. I was to fetch water from the well and fill the pot. Next for yet another task I was shown how to heat water on the fire then take the pot away from the fire and wash some of their filthy clothes that were stacked up in a dark corner and also strewn across the beds.

I believe they had been planning for some time prior to picking me up; there were all manner of threadbare garment and household linen awaiting my labours. I had to perform the task of fetching and heating the water many times; then using a wooden 'dolly' I would manipulate the clothes until most of the dirt had fallen to the bottom of the pot. The smell of stale sweaty materials and rancid threads filled the one room house for hours that day. Steam filled the air. I was to peg the rags on string hung between some of the trees near the stable.

The day crept motionlessly on towards the dull, damp breezy evening. The children returned as they had the previous day; boisterously running in and out awaiting their 'stew' and bread which was being served up that evening. They still seemed oblivious to my presence. Not one said a word to me. The grandmother had been adding chopped up vegetables and mutilated lumps of dissected meat to a pile on the makeshift table. When the last of the washing had been hung on the line the pot resumed its main purpose as a melting pot for anything and everything that could be thrown into it. The pot was back in its position on the metal cradle and was bubbling away.

There was commotion and a big thud as the door threw open and the figure of Pat followed by Shamus leached in. Shamus crashed onto a seat by the fire, but Pat made a move in my direction. For no sane reason he took off his belt and flung it at me. The buckle ripped into the side of my left leg. I screamed but he picked the belt up and did it again. I ran to Mrs. Taylor and crawled under her skirt. He sat down by his brother and they laughed long and hard. The three children hissed; Mrs. Taylor and her mother said not one word.

Next morning I made sure that as soon as the first rays of light crept over the Cooley Mountain tops I was up. I silently bypassed any encounter with the sleeping brothers; made my way down the ladder across the yard, past the barbed wire vegetable patch and through the unlocked door into the cottage. All were soundly sleeping. The mother and grandmother were in the big metal bed; the three children top and tailed in the smaller bed, all were covered in sack clothes. A couple of frayed and holed white sheets I had washed the day before were their only comforts.

Remembering well my instructions from the previous day I set about organising the porridge and the tea, I had prepared a good fire and still no one had stirred. First to awaken were Tim, Mikey and John. They jumped out of their slumber and threw themselves at the porridge settling down cross legged near the warm fire. Mrs. Taylor then her mother snarled as they erected themselves into upright positions against the metal head board. Even these two witches seemed taken aback by my endeavours. Not expecting any gratitude or praise for my work I quickly made sure that I had some food and some of the tea. Relieved to take in some nourishment I continued to make ready the breakfast for the arrival of Shamus and Pat. They duly emerged, hung over by a sufficiency of the home brew the night before. They seemed a little subdued and in so much posed less of a threat to me than if they had been on top form.

I was to accompany them to the lower mountain pastures that morning. We were to round up some of the sheep that had been foraging there for some time on the meagre grasses. These were to be brought back for clipping and confinement nearer the small holding as the weather was soon to break.

*Little was I to know that as we made our ascent to these wild meadows and into the rugged hillside in my new boots and sailor's uniform from the Work House that these would not be replaced. In the years to come I would be running around this rocky terrain*

*Chapter 3: Mrs Taylor*

*below the mountain tops in bare feet in all weather. The soles of my feet would become so blistered from the cold that seventy years later they would still split open in cold weather. My trousers and shirt would have more patches than cloth and my jumper more darned holes than not. There would be many other children running around in the hills.*

*They also would be in rags and dirty, but none as bad as mine were to become; and I would be the only one without shoes!*

*An Irish Boy*

# 4

# The Brothers and the Father

*My destiny for my formative years tragically had been set. The Work House had through some ghastly chance of fate charged me to this tormented family.*

The brothers were animals; or rather animals would not behave as they did to me. Pat was the worst. I would accompany them onto the hill tops, they would get me rounding up sheep or looking for a stray cow, or on the lower slopes digging up potatoes from the frozen soil. They took no food for me and took great delight in my suffering.

It was now mid-winter; up on the lower slopes of the Cooley Mountains the soil was full of frost and hard under foot. There had been a light coating of snow the previous night. There was a fair and nagging wind blowing but I was used to this by now. The mountains looked beautiful bathed in the cold white light. All the synonymous greenery had vanished and instead the rock formations and bushes made abstract fantasy scenery. Most of the livestock had long been taken back to the fields near the small holding. The odd sheep or cow absent from a neighbouring herd ran amuck as did the many wild goats in their search for sustenance.

I had done my usual early morning chores and after finishing with the feeding of the pigs I followed the brothers, keeping a good twenty paces behind, up through the small holding's pastures then onto the lower hillside slopes. One of their cows was missing and we were to spend the whole day looking for it. It was on heat and had run off after a bull. Shamus and Pat had gone high onto the eastern pastures. They had taken a jar of the home brew with them. They often did this; they said it helped keep out the wind. I decided to keep well clear of them as they get crazy when they have too much of the juice. I ran around the rocky slopes in search of the cow. Morning turned into late afternoon and the rain that makes Ireland so green set in. It was a cold biting rain. My bare feet ached as I ran across the damp soil. I could feel some of the blisters open up and start to eject small amounts of blood. My tattered clothes let in the wet and provided no protection. My pretty sailor's uniform and boots had given in very early on. Their remnants were complemented by bits of sackcloth I had sewn in to keep them together. My feet had been bare for several weeks.

As the light faded I crept home socked to the skin. It had been some hours since the brothers had disappeared from view. Entering the cottage I saw them sat beside the fire drying out their clothes, very much the worse for drink. Mrs. Taylor shouted at me telling me to go to the other side of the room. She produced a belt and whipped me around my legs. I don't think I have ever cried so much for mercy. What the brothers had said or what had got into her to do such a thing I know not.

If she was not beating me up Pat would get involved out of sheer malice. I tried to crawl under her skirt to get away from the blows. That night I didn't get any food. When they tired of tormenting me with their belts and boots they fell asleep. I think the mother had been on the drink that evening too. I crawled back to the barn and pulled myself up the ladder into the loft. I gathered the sack clothes around me and settled down amongst the straw.

*Chapter 4: The Brothers and the Father*

An hour or so later I heard the two of them coming across the yard. Mounting the ladder they staggered into the room. I had got on my knees as soon as I heard them coming and pretended to pray. Pat was about to come and attack me again then Shamus his brother grabbed his arm and said to my amazement "leave him be Pat, he's saying his prayers". The two of them threw themselves onto the misshapen bundles that formed their beds and immediately fell into an alcohol induced stupor.

The morning arrived and I had not woken up before Pat. My head pounded as I opened my eyes in peril as his boot hit me on the side of my head. I had jolted up abruptly only to be knocked back to the floor with force from this big lump of leather.

Jumping to my feet I scurried around Pat's legs and catapulted down out of the loft door and down the ladder. Despite my weakness and undernourished state I had managed to get away from the morning's beating. My legs were bruised and had many cuts from the buckles on their belts, I was so hungry. Despite Pat having risen earlier than me I found that the remnants of the previous night's party were still slumbering. All must have had a good dose of the home brew. Even the children were fast asleep when I silently opened the cottage front door.

I had made a plan; I'd steeled away secretly five hen's eggs the day before from the hen house. I had hidden them in a hole in the stone wall of the rear of the house, a place I would frequently find great use for in the future. I warmed the pig's breakfast up, adding the eggs to the boiling potatoes and in so doing gave myself a good meal of boiled eggs. It was my saving; I gulped them down well before the demons raised their ugly heads from their drunken slumbers.

The children and brothers got everything they wanted to eat. They would have soda bread, potato cakes, meat and veg; all I was allowed were two potatoes each meal and some porridge and tea for breakfast; this I would have to eat normally standing by the window ledge. I was never allowed to sit at the table. I would have any scraps and left overs which the children discarded.

Now well into my incarceration at the Taylor's, probably between one and two years, so I would be seven to eight years of age, Pat had been going out with a girl from the village of Omeath. I don't think you could call it dating, but I remember him going out in the evening once or twice a week. He would make some attempt to smarten himself up, if that was at all possible. He would shave, wash his hands and face then put on his Sunday best. Usually he'd be gone for two and a half to three hours, which, allowing for the good two mile jaunt into the village, would allow a couple of hours with his girl.

It was mid-summer, the days were long and the nights short. I remember this time being the least uncomfortable period of the year. The family were less cruel to me. Food seemed a bit more plentiful. I could collect fresh swede from the field which I could eat whilst young and raw without them knowing. These were grown for the cattle, I had to gather them and cut them up then store them away for winter feed for the cattle. All livestock were fed by me. I would also gather hay and straw for the animals for extra fodder. During these months Pat had desisted in his attacks on me. My cuts started to heel and the bruises became less dark.

It was a bright but late midweek afternoon; the weather had been warm and dry for some weeks, which is very peculiar for these parts. I had been sent to a field some distance from the small holding to dig up potatoes. I heard a commotion coming from the direction of the stable. The old horse was stamping about and making a terrifying noise. The old woman and Mrs. Taylor and Shamus were running around the yard pushing the children away from the scene and appearing in utmost panic. I spied a thick plume of smoke emanating from the brow of the thatched stable roof. Just at that moment Pat threw himself out from within the horse's accommodation and grabbing the horse's mane pulled the creature from there out to the yard. Running towards the yard they shouted for me to get water from the well and bucket it onto the roof. But by now the thatch was full inflame. The fire devoured the simple structure its thatch roof collapsing inwards onto the fragile wooden plank walling sending the burning wooden boards crashing down onto the ground in wheels of fire.

Pat had had another argument with his girlfriend the night before. Her father had made it absolutely clear that there was no way she would marry into the notorious Taylor family. He had set into me on his return apparently for no reason. I had been in my bed and he had woken me up with his belt and laid into me with his boots. It had been a vicious and cruel abuse. That following afternoon I thanked God that I had been well away picking potatoes or else the Taylors would have blamed the fire on me. As it happened in his anger he had taken that afternoon to playing about with matches and it was the stable that suffered his fury this time.

He made his way up to our joint dormitory in the loft of the barn. He was to stay there for three months. He remained in his straw and sack cloth bed rarely speaking apart from the odd word to Shamus about his loss. For my sins I would have to take his food to him in the loft the whole time. For me it was some respite from the interminable bullying from at least him.

My days were morning to night totally filled with work. I had little to no break from the ardours. After dark the whole family except Pat were in the one room cottage. Two candles and the peat fire were the only source of heat and light. In the evenings I had to keep this fire alight. The kettle would be on the fire all the time and I had to operate the bellows. Now and again I could take some tea from the kettle.

Now Pat had taken to his bed it fell to me to help Shamus with some other duties. The stable needed rebuilding, the cottage and hen house needed white washing. Lime had to be spread on the fields. The latter was a particularly hazardous treatment given I had no shoes. The lime was deposited on the ground in little heaps, after it rained it needed to be spread over the ground at speed using long handled shovels. The rain would melt the lime into the ground but it felt like I was standing on small fires and my feet and hands would burn and get chapped and bleed.

It had been Pat who had looked after the horse. That sad old mare got little better treatment than I did. It had lots of tasks on the small holding; the obvious pulling of the cart taking goods to and from market in Newry and other smaller places nearby. It towed the plough during sowing of the different crops. It needed to be shod quite often and for this I would journey to the blacksmith in the back twitten in Omeath. My first visit to the blacksmith I discovered the Taylors hadn't paid for the last visits. I took the horse back unshod so they gave me a few shillings to take back to have new shoes fitted.

Some days later the family needed to get winter food for the cattle I was to accompany Shamus on two visits to Newry for this. Now the horse was freshly shod it was harnessed to the rickety cart. I then helped load potatoes onto it. We went to Newry to trade these for animal feeds.

Two days later the butcher arrived in the morning. I had just finished feeding the pigs and they were happily rolling around in the mud. Mrs. Taylor and the butcher went into the pen and stuck a metal hook through the jaw of one of the pigs. Together they pulled the poor creature out of the pen, the screams were vile and it writhed in agony as they meaninglessly tormented it towards the front of the cottage. To my disgust they forced me to help hold it while its throat was cut. A bowl was held under to catch the blood. This was to be used later. I had tended this pig for a year or two and had seen it develop into a beautiful intelligent creature. It seemed to react to me when it saw me, now I was part of its brutal demise. It took some time to die and the sounds will haunt me always. Next the butcher hung the pig upside down, used boiling water and

## Chapter 4: The Brothers and the Father

scraped all the skin. Next day I returned to Newry with Shamus and the animal was sold.

Mrs. Taylor had three small boys but in more than two and a half years I had not seen who had provided her with them. I must have been well into my ninth year of age before the husband, who I had heard worked away arrived.

I remember well the pleasant spring morning. Pat had risen from his bed a month or so before. Even so he was still a bit subdued after his three months in bed. Whether he had got over the rejection of his girlfriend's family or not I don't know but a thrashing, at least from him I hadn't had for some time. This was good because despite Mrs. Taylor's preponderance with punishing me, both the old woman and the younger brother Shamus tended not to get pleasure from my pains. Once again my wounds were heeling. The cuts were drying out and the bruises lightening in colour.

The stable had been rebuilt and the horse was reinstated in it. I had helped Shamus white wash the cottage and the outbuildings. No way could the scene be described as idyllic, but looking across the yard, past the white washed cottage, up towards the woods then the sparse but emerald green Cooley Mountains on this sunny morning, the hedgerows and trees foliage returning after the long winter months, 'pretty' at the least could describe it.

Looking down to the lane beyond the gate I saw a figure. It was that of a tall man probably in his late thirties but clearly through hard manual labour looking fifty or more. He wore a long trench type coat, grey collarless shirt under that, rough trousers and great lumbering boots covered in mud. Making keen progress he entered the yard and briskly approached the cottage entrance. I was by the fireside cleaning potatoes as was the norm ready for the pot for the evening meal. Looking up at Mr. Taylor as he strode into the house I said "afternoon sir", and went about the preparations. Mrs. Taylor was sitting in the one chair and had awoken after an afternoon snooze. She appeared shocked at the new arrival. Getting to her

*An Irish Boy*

feet she looked her husband up and down and greeted him, not too affectionately. He put his arm around her as far as was possible given her stature. She pulled away not even having embraced her partner after his long absence. He did not seem perturbed just sat himself down on an old trunk and started puffing on a clay pipe he produced from his pocket then lit.

"Look at those boots John Byrnes" she said gesturing at me to clean the mud from her husband's boots. I got up and got a good rag and water then cleaned the mud from these. Taking a dry rag and spit, I polished the boots kneeling in front of Mr. Taylor making sure to shine them well. I looked up when I felt finished to see if they wanted anything more. He lifted his right leg and with his great boot kicked me fully in the forehead. It was such a kick that the blood shot out and I screamed in pain and shock, my head flung upward by the impact came in contact with his face. His narrow black eyes buried in furrows of wrinkles and grey anaemic skin pierced my eyes. Blood ran down my face. The two evil creatures laughed and laughed. I stood motionless numbed with fear. What may come next?

"Wash your face and go and stand in the corner over there" was all that came. They needed to keep me there so that no one else would see what they had done to me.

Two hours or so must have gone by; I had long previously fallen to the floor and had been sitting cross legged awaiting the end of the ordeal. The two figures had soon after my attack disrobed and had been performing some type of grotesque ritual in the larger bed. Finishing the consummation of the ritual Mr. Taylor had dressed and without words to either his wife, or to me his object of torture, had left as suddenly as he had arrived.

Mrs. Taylor slept for a while then rose. A most aggrieved expression sullied her face. She simply shouted over to me to go outside and fetch in the milk from the cow. Wiping my face with a wet rag once again to try to remove the semi dried blood; I went out to fetch the milk. I was to hear the following year that Tim, Mickey and John were joined by Margaret.

Nothing was mentioned of this event. Children and the two brothers seemed oblivious to Mr. Taylor's visitation on Mrs. Taylor. The grandmother had made herself scarce for the whole time. The nasty cut to my forehead healed itself, the skin knitted together, but the scare would be a permanent reminder. In modern times such a wound would automatically necessitate a visit to A and E and probably several stitches. For me it was a make shift compress administered by myself. No one even noticed it the following day, and the perpetrator of the crime certainly was not going to draw attention to it.

Pat had now resumed some of his jobs about the farm. He still hadn't recovered from his loss and his mood swings resumed still severe and savage. For me it was very unfortunate. I had to accompany him up to the hill pastures tending the different livestock. I also had to help him on the fields adjacent the small holding ploughing, seeding the crops and tending the soil. This was very bad for me having to be near him so much. The three months he confined himself to his bed were the least punishing of the time at that dark place.

Three days after that violent episode we were returning from a day ploughing in the lower pastures; I was tethering the horse before putting it away for the night. Without any warning Pat had picked up a plank of wood from upon a pile that had been part of the stable which got burned. He ran up from behind and smashed the plank into the backs of my legs. I collapsed in a heap beside the mare. The horse was rearing up in panic. It broke away from its harness and ran crazed around the yard. I rolled around in pain unable to control myself. A few minutes later I began to get my senses back. The impact was such that shooting pains travelled all over my body and I couldn't put weight on my legs.

"You've broken my leg", I shouted at him. But he just stood

and starred. I didn't say any more. He always carried a revolver and in that frame of mind he may well have used it. He was always shooting at the wild cats in case they took the chickens and when he did so he would always finish by pointing the gun at me. I was just an animal to torture in his eyes.

My leg had not been broken; my collapse to the floor took much of the impact away. It would leave me limping badly for weeks afterwards. But in just two days I was to receive worse.

It was late in the evening and the children were asleep in the smaller bed. I was standing near the fire trying to make out some texts from Catholic Catechism. I had learned a few words at the Christian Brotherhood School and some texts we had been taught parrot fashion. It was meant to be part of my training for Confirmation. Mrs. Taylor and the old woman were seated and almost asleep with the heat of the fire. Shamus had gone to bed.

Pat took the book out of my hands and told me to recite the chapter I had been looking at. It was one of the texts I had learned parrot fashion, this was lucky to some degree. I recited the text and he insisted I repeat this. I did so four or five time. It was late and the day had been hard and very lacking in food. I started to fall asleep standing up. He placed a stick of fire wood into the fire and burned the end of it. He then put it into my small hands. The skin on my palms singed and let off a horrible smell. I screamed. He took the burned wood away and told me to repeat the text. I coughed out some more text. He put the burning wood in the fire and once again held my hand as he forced the burnt wood back into my palms. Shrieking in agony I fell to the floor. The blistering skin burst and blood eased out. He must have been frightened by what he had done. He stopped and went out of the cottage and to the bedroom in the barn loft. I went to bed that night with nothing to put on my injuries.

The next day I was in the barn on the lower floor, arranging bales of straw that were left over from the winter. The two brothers were up on the lower slopes; my injuries were such that they could not get any use from me. The children and the old woman were in the field behind the cottage out of ear shot. I saw Mrs. Taylor coming after me with a whip. What in God's name did she want with me now I thought after all the traumatic events of the last few days? She thrashed me for no reason three or more times. It drew blood. I yelled out loud but didn't move, remaining half bent over rigid with the pain, so injected with trauma at this enduring cruel punishment.

When she left I walked as fast as I could a mile or so from the house. I was in a ditch a safe distance from danger. I curled into a ball and sobbed, I was crying out in desperation. I had met many children during my time on the mountainous slopes and I had met the odd farmer or farm hand. Most adults knew of my condition. Most steered away from confronting the issues but you could tell in their eyes and the subtle gesticulations of their faces the acknowledgement of my suffering. One man, a Mr. Morgan came across me on this particular day.

"Who's been doing this to you boy", he said, aghast at the sight of my legs and the palms of my hands and my forehead.

"You must go to the policeman in the village and get him to go to those Taylors" he pleaded.

He gave me some bread and some water he fetched from a nearby stream and he used his handkerchief to wipe away some of the blood. He comforted me for a while until I stopped sobbing. I pulled myself up out of the ditch and I shook myself until the intense trepidation eased.

*An Irish Boy*

# 5
# An Escape?

I made my hesitant way back to the small holding and to the barn. Mrs. Taylor came out of the cottage and called for me to come over to her. In her sadistic way I knew she just wanted to give me another beating. This time fear turned into anger.

For a couple of years I had trained myself with a make shift sling to kill birds and small rodents with stones. I had become very proficient at this and could kill a small bird at twenty to thirty feet. I had got much practice on my mountain patrols tending the cattle and sheep. Mrs. Taylor was some distance from the barn entrance. As I emerged from the dark opening she stopped in her tracks. This nine year old boy who hours before she had mercilessly whipped for no reason and had been crying and submissive, a crippled child, now stood upright in front of her head held high. I carried my sling one stone ensconced and a couple of pockets full of ammunition. The sling was charged and ready to release.

"If you come near me I'll cut your head off with a stone" I bellowed. As if bewildered she made two steps forward and said nothing.

I released the sling and the stone sped forward at great momentum I knew only too well. I had rehearsed for this moment hundreds and hundreds of times. It projected through the air at impressive velocity. My intention was to give a warning shot.

It shot past the side of the old witch's ear making contact only in so much that it moved the tips of her hair. She did not flinch She knew this was a warning. Completely stony faced she waited not for a confirmation of my accuracy and intent. She simply turned and walked back to the house into the cottage doorway slamming the door closed behind her. I knew she intended to wait there until the brothers returned. Then my life would not be worth a penny. I made a pact with myself I would never set foot in that house again.

I took the advice of Mr. Morgan. I walked briskly to Omeath all the time thinking of my plight. I had nowhere to go to live. I knew I was very young. I had a vague idea that I was approaching nine years of age although marking time was something that could only be gauged by the passing of the seasons. There had never been any interest in giving me an identity, I had been there to work and be abused. I had no family, no protectors. I retraced the route I had taken so many times on my errands. This time with not even the security of knowing I had a bed back at the small holding. Leaving the country trail that led to the place of my detention I progressed onto the Main Street that gave the lengthy introduction to the village. The long road skirting the lough, I contemplated the majesty of The Mourne Mountains lifting up from the grey waters. The emerald slopes merging with the soft blue skies on this bright day. A sense of escape began to come over me. I didn't know what to expect from the policeman but I felt I must be almost free of the cruel clutches of the Taylors.

As I walked into the village the odd passer by acknowledged me in a way I had not seen previously. Gone were the looks of disdain that I would have got if accompanying a member of that Taylor clan. Instead their faces gave kinder compassionate glances with looks of concern and even sympathy. There were two senior aged laddies standing on the pavement talking together as the pavement commenced on its early approach to the village. They looked straight me in the face.

## Chapter 5: An Escape?

"My poor we lad, what has come of you", one said.

I explained briefly some of the proceedings of the last week to their shock and horror. Almost aghast they took me by the hand and straight down the main thorough fair into the heart of the village and thence to a white stone house with tiled roof. They escorted me straight past the front door into the building. In the front room was The Special Constable.

This kindly looking middle aged man was fitted with a peek cap with metal fittings and badge. His slightly portly build was dressed in a fitted uniform of jacket and trousers; a strong leather belt held his jacket firmly together and he wore heavy leather boots. He had a neatly trimmed small moustache. The two laddies took me in and sat me on a bench that was under the window inside the front door. I had seen these laddies on occasion before on my trips into the village. They appeared to have seen my demise over the past few years and were well aware of the reason behind it. They spoke at length to Special Constable Hutchinson. He seemed deeply troubled with what he learned. He called to a woman in a back room to make us all tea and get me some bread and jam. He could see I was very malnourished as well as having been badly abused.

A little over an hour passed and the Constable bade the ladies good bye but said to them that he did not know exactly what to do with his dilemma. I was in the charge of the Taylors and it was to them he would have to take me to see what they would undertake to do. Not having a guardian if I did not go back to the Taylors I would have to go back to the Work House.

The two ladies had left none too pleased with his lack of resolve. Their protestations were to no avail and he eventually bade them a swift retreat or else he would have to forcibly evict them from his establishment.

Half an hour later Mr. Hutchinson had coupled his horse to a small cart at the back of the building. Reluctantly I joined him on the plain wooden bench seat riding above the two large wheels. The

47

*An Irish Boy*

last thing in the world I wanted to do was to go back to that prison and to that hated family. I knew that Mrs. Taylor would never let me escape punishment so severe for my threat on her. Leaving the last isolated cottages on the edge of the village the cart hurtled faster than I would like towards the partly made up extremities of Main Street. Without slowing much we turned into the rough track heading towards the Taylor's. Twisting left and right we abruptly halted in front of the gate to the small holding. The horse almost bolted as the last bend had led us too swiftly to the ramshackle barrier.

The Constable climbed down from the cart. Opened the rude gate and guided the horse through and then around placing it in a position so it was facing the exit to the small holding leaving the gate well ajar. Perhaps he was prepared for a non-too pleasant reception. Almost instantaneously the door to the cottage swung open and to my horror out poured the Grand Mother, Mrs. Taylor and Shamus and Pat. They resembled an angry mob, a rabble. If steam could have been coming from their heads it certainly appeared to be.

"Where has that rascal been", the old woman said. "He tried to kill me this very afternoon and I'm lucky to be alive", said Mrs. Taylor.

"You hold your tongue woman", shouted Mr. Hutchinson.

He continued: "this starving retch you have tortured and conducted your evils ways on for three years or so. I give you this chance to take him to the Work House tomorrow or else you will all pay for your cruelty. The whole village knows what you have been up to and we won't pass a blind eye to it any more".

"Frick off to you", I heard Pat slur.

"Get you in 'err Pat my dear", intervened the old woman and she pushed him back into the house before he put his hoofs in any deeper.

"Tomorrow at 9am you will take the boy to Newry, and that's a must!" said the Constable.

He mounted the cart in which I was still seated gave a light tug on the reigns touched the brim of his cap in the direction of Mrs. Taylor and off we sped through the gate around the tight bend down the meandering trackway and away, away!

It was with a great sense of relief that I held myself to that seat as we departed the Taylor's. Twisting and turning down the track the stone walls and hedgerows evaporated in a way I'd not seen before. It was as if the Special Constable was also trying to escape, perhaps he knew the extent of the menace of that family; he may have been aware of Pat's firearm and its frequent use. He didn't slow until reaching the civilized partly made up Main Street.

As if afraid of the consequences Mr. Hutchinson did not offer me a bed for the night. Returning to the police house his words to me offered no comfort or security.

"Find yourself a place to stay for the night, John Byrnes, and tomorrows take yourself back to the Taylors and they will take you to Newry and back to the charge of the Work House. You will find they will look after you, you will be better off there", he concluded.

His wife grabbed his arm and whispered something to him out of earshot to me.

"No", he said dismissively, "we can't do it for him or else we'll have all the wretches from the mountains on our doorstep!"

He slowly closed the front door on my small face. My short figure in tattered garments covered in injuries, totally forlorn and let down. Just as I felt I'd escaped I was on the street without a place to sleep and no food.

Although a spring early evening it was none too mild and showed every sign of a shower approaching from the other side of the lough. The light was beginning to fade. The pretty cottages in the village showed dim lights through their windows. Some had smoke issuing from their chimneys. The shadows on the water of the lough darkened. What was I to do for the night?

*An Irish Boy*

Three years previously a while after I'd first been taken into servitude at the Taylors I had taken myself on my own to the village school. The establishment was run by a very religious man, Mr. Coleman. He and his wife had one daughter and two sons. Mr. Coleman had seen me going up and down to the village on the cart with the brothers for some weeks. One day when we were passing he had stopped the cart and said to Shamus that I should be sent to the school. He uninterestedly agreed. He had merely wanted to get the man off his back.

For the first year or so I would attend no more than one day a month. Educationally it was of no help at all. Apart from Catholic Catechism I remembered nothing as the gaps were too great.

The little school house was outside the village on the southern fringes. It was a single storey white stone building with solid slate roof. It had doors at either end of the frontage accessing two rooms inside, one for infants the other for older children. Surrounded by high conifers it was quite secluded from its neighbours. The schoolmaster's house was twenty feet away across a gravel yard. It was a two storey building of some size, much more recent in construction than the considerably older school. It dwarfed the small school house. Its pointed gables stood well above the low flung school roof. Internally, as the case in parts of the Christian Brotherhood School, dark green dado bordered the rooms. Long benches and small desks of crudely hewn wood filled both rooms. To the right of the yard were the toilets, two simple huts with wooden seats over buckets.

I made my way past the house of the Corefields on the village outskirts. These were probably the only friends in the area of the Taylors. It was the time of evening that the bread would be put on the window sill to cool after baking. Passing speedily past their house and relieving them of their cooling bread I at least could fill my belly with something. I headed to the toilets adjoining the school house. Closing the door quietly I settled down for the night filling myself with the freshly baked bread, sheltering from the nights rain. This was my first night out of the cruel hands of the Taylors.

Knowing that I could not rely on help from Mr. Hutchinson I made my way early the following morning to the Taylors. I approached the gate to the small holding but did not pass through staying at a safe distance. I shouted and shouted for them to come out, for them to take me back to Newry and to the Work House. For half an hour I repeated my cry. They did not come out. Maybe they had heeded the words of the Constable?

*An Irish Boy*

# 6
# Some Friendly Help

Mr. Morgan had shown me such kindness only the day before so I decided to go to seek help from him. Feeling slightly reassured that I had done the right thing by going to the police on Mr. Morgan's advice I felt sure that upon returning to him he would look after me and all would be well.

Mr. Morgan, I knew, had a small cottage in the lower pastures of the Cooley Mountains two or so miles away from the Taylors. I had never been there but had met Mr. Morgan out and about on the hillside tending his sheep and goats. For years he had only too clearly witnessed my injuries. At first he thought I had just had accidents falling over rocks and such like. As time went by he had become suspicious of the continued cuts and bruises, he had often given me some food and had said I looked starved. More recently the nature and extent of my injuries could clearly be seen to cause him great distress.

His cottage lay in a remote position above Omeath on the way up the Cooley Mountains on the route up to The Long Woman's Grave. I followed the meandering lane from the Taylors down through the unmade-up bye way to the main road, Main Street. From there running briskly along a short stretch of the highway taking in the wide vista of the lough, I left Main Street and took the track up the slopes above the lough in the direction of The Long

Woman's Grave. Climbing sharply the view of the lough extenuated into a vast watery mist with mountains on either side sweeping up into the cloud on this spring morning. The fertile pastures planned out below wrapped around the village, dotted with small copses and larger woods.

These rocky slopes I knew provided a hard existence. I had roamed over them my latter childhood years herding the animals, tending crops and gathering potatoes and other foodstuffs. Mr. Morgan did the same.

Set just below the bank to the right hand side of the track, below a tumbled down stone wall protruded into view a chimney stack. With it's plume of smoke drifting into the blue grey air I knew this must be Mr. Morgan's cottage. There were no other buildings anywhere else to be seen. Looking over the wall bordering the track I saw a tiny cottage clinging to the steeply sloping bank. The hillside dropped rapidly below given a sense of peril to its position. Never the less its location offered a stunning view over the land to the body of water in the distance. A tiny rectangular pocket of land attached itself to the right hand boarder of the lane. Screened by the remnants of the stone boundary wall it offered little protection for anything to grow.

I stopped and took in his domain. The cottage seemed to have been part of a larger building, possibly twice the length of its current structure. To the western side was a walled enclosure in the form of a single room but without a roof. A sizable inactive chimney stack stood proud above the ruins. It had two window openings and a doorway but no timber frames remaining. It was used to house his one pig and hand full of chickens. The eastern section which was standing complete with roof was a one roomed dwelling with one window and one door. Its thatched roof had been partly made over with corrugated iron sheets. This must have formed the lesser part of the much larger former dwelling.

*Chapter 6: Some Friendly Help*

I passed through the open gateway from the track. Knocking at the door Mr. Morgan shouted out from inside his house a warm hello. I was filled with contentment. I had taken my young self out of captivity and danger and had come to meet my friend. He would look after me.

He opened the door and came outside into the daylight. He was a strong man used to hard work but obviously of latter years. He wore his usual rough trousers, boots and collarless, grey shirt. He smiled kindly to me and said "you've come away from those Taylors at last me lad".

I agreed and told him of my night spent in the school house. I told him about Mr. Hutchinson's visit to them but that he could not help any further, that he had made great haste to get away from that place.

We went inside the cottage. It was almost as bare as that which I had been used to at the small holding of the Taylors. There were perhaps a couple more items of furniture and a few more worldly possessions within his abode. The chimney to this part of the building was not as well-proportioned as was the derelict one in the adjoining section. Its hearth was also smaller and housed the usual great pot and kettle and selection of vessels. Above it the chimney stood high stretching up to the pitch of the roof. The one small window let in a ray of light as did the open door. A long wooden table with five stout rounded chairs with arms flanked its sides. A tall dresser of some size stood against the longest wall of the cottage. It had six wide drawers below and three sturdy shelves above. It was laden with photos, storage jars, pots, tin cups and plates. There were no make shift improvised items of furniture to be seen. As for debris and rags and chickens running in and out, there were none. Pictures and photos and religious symbols there were on the walls but these were few in number.

Mr. Morgan pulled up two of the chairs to the fire side; we sat down by the lighted fire. It was cosy and warm, the spring morning had been nippy and the night in the toilet of the old school house cold. He poured two large mugs of dark tea from the kettle in the hearth. It was warm and comforting to my lips. Next he produced some soda bread from a metal box which sat on a high shelf putting it on two tin plates we sat back and enjoyed the peace of the morning.

He had chatted to me many times on the mountainous slopes but I knew little if anything about himself or his family. He was to now tell me of his wife who had born him a son and therein died in childbirth in that very room. He told me of the death of that son just two months later; that the doctor from Carlingford had lost a wheel from his cart on the way to them in the bad weather and the boy had suffocated before he was able to get them.

It seemed that twenty years before his father and mother with his three brothers and sister had left the small holding and had gone to Liverpool and from there onto Glasgow. His parents and grandparents had made it through the rigours of the latter half of the previous century with the Irish Potato Famine and the disease and extreme poverty that followed but had decided to do the best for the children and seek a new life elsewhere.

Mr. Morgan had remained, still a young man intending to make the most of what they left him. But with his ensuing personal tragedies he had given up, let the small holding collapse into what it was now. He could support himself and make out his own meagre existence. "John", he said, "I am so sorry but I cannot keep you".

His words entered my head as a softly penetrating knife. My moments of comfort and security were cut in two.

"You can stay here with me for a week, but then you must make your own way lad", he followed.

My seven days with him were the best seven days I could remember. I had no fear of random acts of senseless punishments being meted out by the sadistic Taylors. I had ample food and drinks. Although I bedded down at night on straw covered with sackcloth I was safe and warm on the floor by the fire in his house. I knew that if the brothers came to find me he would protect me.

Throughout the week I helped about the place. I repaired some of the broken walls to the road and mended some fences. I tended the animals and tidied the yard and field next to the house. We got on great. He enjoyed having a young lad to talk to as he had spent much time on his own over many years. If only I could stay on with him to look after me; was my all-encompassing thought throughout my time there.

He had warned me throughout the week not to get too at home. I would have to leave the following Monday morning. He said that I should go back to Newry and take myself back to the Work House as the Taylors should have done. They would then find a new foster family for me who would be in a better position to bring me up than he was. After the terrible treatment I had received they would be sure to find me a better home.

Come Monday morning he roused me from my slumbering at an early light. Filling me with sufficient breakfast and some food for the day we walked down to the village to meet a friend of his who was to go to Newry that morning on his horse and cart to market some of his produce. I was very sad to leave Mr. Morgan and I was very sure that the Work House would not find me any better family than they had found for me before.

His good friend Paddy chatted to me on the journey to Newry. Paddy I had seen before in Omeath. We had not spoken before but he was the sort of person with whom you felt at ease. He was a short, plump, quite smartly dressed 'forty something', which to me appeared quite old. Very chatty was his personality. He joked a lot. Mr. Morgan had filled him in to some extent on what had happened over the past week or so. He told him about the attacks and beatings I'd received and how I had escaped and gone to the police for help. Paddy had been aghast at the submissiveness of Constable Hutchinson to the Taylors. Mr. Morgan had asked him to take me to the Work House. He had given him some sort of note to give to the Master of the Work House explaining my predicament and requesting they find me a new family.

The route back to Newry was not long by any means; barely half an hour, maybe forty minutes. It was one I had journeyed many times. Leaving Omeath, heading into pastures with views of the lough to the north, the long straight road skirted Carlingford Lough and the Newry River heading for the Fathom forest. Then with the forest to the south and the Newry River to the north the river becomes the Albert Basin and thence the docks. Captivating was the scene as always; dramatic and unreal. We would leave behind the small, silent and sleeping village and head through undulating and varied natural landscape ending in the industrials harsh and noisy environment in the Newry docks.

"John Byrnes", said Paddy, "you are nine years of age are you not?"

"Nine going on ten" I said emphatically although I was not sure whether I was possibly still even only eight years old, I had no way of knowing.

"You are just a lad, but what you've been through makes you many more years than your age, doesn't it boy?" he continued.

I was not going to dispute that by any means.

"What I'm getting at lad", he said, "is do you really want me to take you to the Work House to find another family? How do you think you could manage on your own? Do you know of any people who might help you in Newry or there about?"

I shrugged my shoulders and coughed a smile; I certainly didn't want to go back to the Work House; that to me would be tantamount to being sent back to the Taylors.

We agreed he let me off at the docks. Whatever I would do I would find a job and no matter where it be I would find a place to stay. If need be I could beg; I had seen many people I felt were better than me doing so.

*Chapter 6: Some Friendly Help*

He pulled upon the reigns and brought his cart to a stop amid the kerfuffle of the dockside traffic. We both sat silently taking in the scene for a minute or two; then looking me full in the face he patted me on the back and bade me a very knowing good bye. I dismounted briskly and then turned back towards Paddy giving a very generous wave as he departed leaving me once again all on my own.

The docks were their usual hustle and bustle. They were filled with small crafts manoeuvring between ships laden with goods. Men scuppered to and fro purporting their services and transporting their wares. Carts filled the streets and alleys and horses and donkeys deposited their produce. I was captivated like never before by the activity. In the past I had been under orders from one or other of Pat and Shamus. Not a minute to be able to take in the visual amenity of the place.

I hurried around the environs enjoying my freedom. I chatted to some of the boys who were milling around looking for either jobs or for no good. I ate the food Mr. Morgan had prepared for me; I drank from the water fountain meant for the horses. It was great. The afternoon was young and the day mild and dry. The world was not all bad.

I felt an intense pain in the back of my head. The pain instantly took hold of all my body. The pain powered itself at express speed to the front of my eyes. I collapsed and all was dark and silent.

I opened my eyes in a blur I could make out the unmistakable surroundings of the Taylors house. I was on the floor in front of the hearth of the fire. The hearth was glowing red hot. Apart from the glow from the heat of the fire the room was subdued. Pat, the old woman, and Mrs. Taylor stood above me towering over my crippled shape slumped on the floor. Pain stabbed into my head as if daggers were being inserted. I rolled around unable to collect my senses.

They walked away and sat down on their shabby makeshift seats, except for the old woman who seated herself on the only chair.

It seemed as if hours passed, I didn't move. The old woman stayed put. Mrs. Taylor and Pat remained as they were. The fire died down slightly, candles were lit. The pain reduced to a dull ache.

The old woman put a tin mug of tea by my head. I still didn't move for fear of what was to come.

"That whack on the head I thought you'd done it Pat, this time" said Mrs. Taylor seemingly amused given my new state of consciousness.

"If you go to the police again or try to run away, next time you'll be crucified" spouted Pat venomously. "We'll enjoy it" he continued.

The evil trio departed to the yard for whatever reason I did not know.

I realized that Pat had come up behind me whilst I was distracted in the docks must have hit me hard over the head with something that made me pass out. Then he had thrown me into his cart and brought me back to this hell hole. Drinking the tea quickly I knew I must make a fast escape or else my imprisonment would never end. I had previously vowed never to enter that cottage again. I was indeed back there but I mustn't allow it to be my tomb.

Within the cottage the fire and two candles cast little light. Outside though, on this late spring evening, the twilight had only just set in. The shadows of the farm buildings merged with those of the trees. The backdrop of the hills beyond silhouetted against the sky. I crept rapidly to the window, surveyed the scene hoping to spot the whereabouts of my demons. They were together as if in midst of discussion over by the barn. They probably were trying to devise a means by which to secure it to incarcerate me.

I opened the door a crack and slithered out of it, made a right to the side of the house and then shot across the rear yard

*Chapter 6: Some Friendly Help*

to the nearest clump of trees my feet like a mouse barely touching the ground. They had not been aroused. Now more slowly but cautiously so as not to make a sound I tip toed through the coppices and did not stop until reaching well beyond their lower pastures. I entered the neighbouring farmland owned by Mr. Patrick Morgan. I knew his house to be still some distance from me. It was now time to run. I ran with all my might, forgetting the pains in my head, forgetting the agony throughout my body as a result of my abduction. Jumping over rocky outcrops, leaping over fences and jumping over ditches I forced my way along the hillside pastures towards Patrick's home.

Mr. Patrick Morgan had also been kind to me in the past. He had a small holding similar in size to that of the Taylors. It was about one mile and a half from theirs.

With his house now in sight I picked up my pace. Patrick was in the field in front of his cottage knelt down picking potatoes. The lights in the cottage were burning and he was soon to go in for the night.

He was a sturdy young man in his twenties .Thick set with strong arms and powerful muscles. At least six feet tall he was a local hero at Hurling. With long thick brown hair and youthful but sun damaged complexion, he would be able to defend me if need be.

I didn't reduce my pace until I was by his side. I sensed he knew that Mr. Morgan had sent me off to Newry that morning. It was probably the talk of the village. When Mr. Morgan had despatched me off with Paddy on the cart there had been a few people around.

I quickly recited my story of my journey to Newry, the docks and my violent capture. I said of the terrible threat the family had made to crucify me if I were to go to the police or to try to run away again. He seemed undaunted by all of this.

Within minutes of my arrival I heard great treads thudding across the field coming fast towards us. The grasses separated as the figures brushed through. Heavy breaths of angry men were heading our way. The two figures stopped abruptly ten feet in front of me and Patrick Morgan. The three participants raised themselves up into challenging postures.

Pat made a move towards me as if to grab my arms and pull me back and away from Patrick. Patrick stood resolutely firm and strong. His head held high as if to confront any attack from his assailant. With shock at the obstacle being presented to him Pat shuddered to a stop. He took one step back and looked around to Shamus.

Patrick knowingly and emphatically said "You don't frighten me like you do the boy. I'll pulverize you if you take one step forward. If you set hands on this lad again you will be the one who is crucified; you along with your bitch of a mother as well. And as for that your witch of a grandmother too, I'll nail the four of you up for all to see and gloat upon."

"Come on Pat", said Shamus sheepishly. "He's not worth messing with he'll bring us lots of trouble."

Patrick spat on the ground in the direction of Pat. I clung close by him assured now of his protection. Pat turned around to Shamus thumped him maliciously in the chest and pushed by him and away in the direction of their home. Shamus followed shortly behind without ushering a word. For the next nine months I would have a childhood. I decided to be a KING and learn to stand on my own two feet.

# 7

# A Belated Childhood

Pat and Shamus sauntered off tails between their legs. Pat gave the odd thump on the arm to Shamus, I felt somewhat sad for Shamus, and he'd had to put up with his elder brother his whole life and was still not rid of him. He had not been wholly bad to me compared to his family members. Pat gave the occasional glance behind his back as if to check Patrick was not hounding after them. They ploughed into the long grasses, this time passing through at a snail's pace. From there they disappeared into the darkened woods bordering the fields and thence out of my life.

Patrick Morgan stood firm unflinching until the pair had vanished. He needed to be sure that his message to that family had been absorbed as completely as it needed to be.

Patrick picked me up and gave me a reassuring hug.

"Boy", he said "I will look after you, you can help me on my farm and need fear no more from those scum. All the people in the village revile and hate them; they will not be well received from now. Their evil reputation bounds as far as Newry."

Patrick and I went inside his cottage; he put some ointment bound by clean rags on my wounds. We had some warm tea, potato cakes and finished up with some home brew. That night I didn't sleep in the school toilet, or in a barn. I had a small metal bed with sackcloth and straw mattress. I was warm, and I went to sleep with food in my belly and a feeling of sanctuary in my mind.

The one-room cottage was quite large; I would say at least thirty feet by eighteen. It had the usual chimney in stone going high into the pitch of the thatched roof. The hearth was home to a large kettle, but no big pot, just a series of metal pans with handles. He had a large and ornate metal bed with tall bedstead; my smaller and simpler style metal bed was at the opposite end of the room. Inside the entrance door to the cottage sat a big wooden table with two stout rounded backed chairs. The dresser was in the middle of the long rear wall of the cottage and housed pickling jars, tin plates and mugs, vessels for the home brew and an assortment of personal items including clay pipes and razor. A rickety makeshift wooden cupboard housed his clothes. His Sunday best was neatly arranged on a metal hanger and the few other daily vestments were attentively displayed on a multitude of pegs. His two pairs of boots were clean and free from holes and were kept by his bed. The clay floor had straw to carpet it and was kept clean with no chickens or other wildlife running to and fro.

Next day Patrick took me into the village and bought me a pair of strong boots, a pair of long trousers, two shirts and a woollen cardigan. He had taken me into the front room of the shop selling food which also traded in some clothes and other goods. I had passed by the premises many times before but had never entered it and thence had not glimpsed the variety of its contents. The proprietors, the O'Connell's, sat me down on a box inside the door of their shop and gave both Patrick and me a very hearty greeting. They had seen me many times before passing by on my errands to the village. As had been the case with so many of their other neighbours they had been too afraid to approach the Taylors and especially Pat who they knew always carried a pistol. They fitted me out grand. Patrick told them of my exploits over the past week or so. They listened attentively. Excitedly they heard of how he had seen off the brothers and cursed their family for good. He believed they would be sorely received in future. John Byrnes would stay with him as long as he needed to and would help him on his farm. Mr. and Mrs. O'Connell made sure Patrick only paid for the boots. They said it was the least they could do for me and it would ease their conscience to some extent and that of some others too.

We returned to his farm. I washed in a bowl of warm water poured from a jug on the dresser and put on my new clothes.

His farm was well arranged. Two neat fields grew a variety of crops which supported us throughout the year. The inevitable proliferation of potatoes filled the vegetable plots to the rear and to the front of the cottage. He didn't have any pigs in a pigsty close to the house; instead he maintained some goats and a small herd of cows on the lower pastures a short distance to the south. Turnips and swedes supplemented our diet. The baker in the village provided our bread; twice weekly I would be sent to collect enough for a few days.

His first task was to teach me how to look after myself, how to wash regularly, keep my hair clean and tidy, to look after my clothes to make them last longer. He soon bought me a second pair of trousers and a smart jacket with a grey shirt which he said I was to keep for Sunday best to go to church. The O'Connell's he told me had donated my jacket; it had grown too small for their youngest son.

I knew little of what it was like to keep a tidy home. I had been used to the deprivation of the Taylors, so cleanliness and order were innocuous to me. The first weeks needed a lot of instruction about basic hygiene and cleanliness indoors. I was all too keen to learn. I knew all about organizing the fire and keeping it burning throughout the day and evening especially in colder periods; but as for changing the straw on the floor and making sure the cooking utensils and vessels were clean I knew nothing. As for personal hygiene and looking after one's clothes and boots this was all new to me.

He showed me how to make up the home brew fermenting potatoes. Cultivating the vegetables and other crops I was taught finer details of how to get best yields; he showed me how to properly tend the animals to make them healthy and productive. I soon learned how he managed to look after himself so well. His life was clean and organized. People respected him. I was so lucky he had rescued me from the brothers.

That late spring and summer was warm and dry up on the hills above the village. Patrick took great delight in teaching me all he knew about farming. It was as if I were a son he would never have. He showed me the techniques he used in hurling. He used rough stones up on the pasture to demonstrate and get me to try too. Jokingly he told me about Cu Chulainn and his ability to throw stones from one mountain to the next.

He told me the tragic story of the Spanish noble woman who had come to the Cooley Mountains with her new Irish husband from her prosperous life in Spain. He had taken her up the mountain. She had been shown all the lands around which she now owned; all the land her eyes could see was hers'. She was so mortified she dropped dead on the mountainside and there lies the grave of her seven foot tall body. Her husband died in grief and there the two remain together on the mountain to this day.

We rose early each day, had breakfast then would be prepared for whatever tasks were due to be done. We both took great pleasure in what we did. It was a kind of freedom with no others interfering in what we had to do. We were our own bosses. Roaming on the lower pastures of the hills or tending the crops near the house it was all tough work but it gave great contentment. As summer turned into autumn we made stores in his barn for ourselves and for the livestock. Patrick was very organized. It was without doubt my first experience of the joy of a happy childhood. I was fast approaching my tenth birthday.

*Chapter 7: A Belated Childhood*

During those long dark winter nights we drank the home brew and Patrick would recite tales of Gaelic Deities. We sang Irish folk songs and he would often teach me lyrics then accompany me with the harmonica. The fire would be burning red and we would have plenty of food from our labours in the better weather. Patrick was for that brief period in time the father I never really had.

I helped him every day except Sundays. He insisted we go to Mass every Sunday morning. We would rise early, he would shave and brush his hair and dress as smart as anyone I had seen in Omeath. He made sure I was presentable too. I would wash and put on my new clothes. We walked to the village and from there on the long road past its western fringes in the direction of Newry through the pastures and there to the woods in which lay the church.

The grey stone tower of St. Andrew's Church stood tall above the simple rectangular stone nave. The large grave yard surrounding the church was sparsely occupied by the village's descendants.

It was here each Sunday we met up with Patrick's friends, Mr. and Mrs. Taylor, (no relation what so ever with the Taylors from the small holdings where I had suffered so much). Mr. and Mrs. Taylor lived in the centre of Omeath and I grew in time to call them the 'Omeath Taylors'.

The Omeath Taylors were old for people of that time. Both probably in their early fifties, this was at a time when one would be grateful to pass forty. The shooting of National Commander-in-Chief Michael Collins in August 1922 one year previously had been their call to settle in Omeath. They had had a thriving business in Dundalk for more than fifteen years. Their trading vessel based in the docks carried cargo between Liverpool and Dundalk and had given them a good income and lifestyle. There had been an escalation of violence in Ireland following end of The Great War this evolved into the Irish War of Independence. The Omeath Taylors had been hoping for some cessation to the troubles. Unfortunately

# An Irish Boy

for them with the coming of The Anglo-Irish Treaty January 1922 their hopes were to be dashed later that year.

*There ensued a conventional war between the new Irish Free State troops and the Anti-Treaty IRA centring on Dublin and on the major towns. On the 10th August when the Republican forces abandoned the City of Cork and the following day when their Chief of Staff Liam Lynch abandons Fermoy the Anti-Treaty IRA find they have lost the battle of urban centres. This is the end of the conventional war and the beginning of the more characteristic guerrilla type war waged by Anti-Treaty IRA.*

*On 16th August 1922 three hundred men of the Anti-Treaty IRA 4th Northern Division attacked Dundalk. They freed two hundred and forty Republican prisoners and ceased hundreds of rifles and in the process many are wounded and six killed. The town is re-taken the following day by Free State troops.*

*The shooting and subsequent death of Collins on 22nd August 1922 embittered feelings between the rival factions. Collins had been negotiating with the Anti-Treaty leaders for an end to fighting. His death meant a protracted period for the troubles.*

As a result of this Mr. and Mrs. Taylor had closed up their fine house in one of the major thoroughfares, in Dundalk's Crowe Street, and had sold their steam cargo boat, The Louthe, for as much as they could get given the desperate times. The previous year they had taken up the lease on one of the larger houses on Village Green in the centre of Omeath. They had ensconced themselves within the village community and become friends with amongst others Patrick Morgan. Meeting other parishioners mainly on Sundays this would form the mainstay of their social life outside the home. They were intensely religious.

I was now as far as I can believe past my tenth birthday. This year, from what I managed to work out many years later, was 1923.

## Chapter 7: A Belated Childhood

The winter had been very mild in Irish terms. For me the troubles were a distant backdrop, something villagers mentioned in passing on the street but no more. In hindsight this was strange given the close proximity of Omeath to both Newry and Dundalk. The life of the village went on much as normal. I'm sure that in towns and more strategic locations the continued conflict would have been more apparent. A mile and a half outside Omeath up on the hillside overlooking Carlingford Lough Patrick and me were having a great time. My helping him all about meant his workload was less. I was only too pleased to work hard and in return I had someone to look after me and a good home. I was having the best part of my formative years.

We went to church regularly and got to know the Omeath Taylors really well. Some Sundays we would join them after mass at their home in the village for tea and cakes. This was grand. They would tell us about the boat they had owned and all the different goods it had carried. They also described vividly their lovely home in Dundalk which lay closed up because of the troubles. They had no children and they had told us sadly of their sole child, who would have been their son and heir, who had died at birth and that Mrs. Taylor had there afterwards not been afforded the gift of another baby.

Spring became summer. The days became long. Mr. and Mrs. Taylor said to the priest that they thought it would be a good idea if John Byrnes were to be given up by Patrick Morgan and come to live with them as a proper family. **It would be the correct thing to do.**

One Sunday morning in late July, a warm, dry beautiful day, Patrick and I had walked down to the village and then onto the church in our usual procession. The trees were full of leaf and coloured in all shades of green. The lough was an emerald green and set a most illusory image against the backdrop of the Mourne Mountains and the deep blue sky. The hedgerows were full and bounded with berries. A light breeze set the leaves rustling to a delicate tune. The odd cockerel crowed and the farm animals murmured to themselves in faint recognition.

We arrived at the gate to the church yard. A flock of parishioners were assembled in front of the great doors of the church being delivered pleasantries by the priest prior to entering for the service. We were greeted by Mr. and Mrs. Taylor who shook our hands warmly. The priest offered his greeting in a somewhat more subdued manner. He spoke to Patrick and asked if he could have a word after the Mass.

Whatever transpired in their communication after the Mass I don't know and never found out to this day? All I know is that after we had had tea and cakes with the Omeath Taylors we went home. When we were settled down for the evening Patrick poured us both a large cup of home brew. He looked sadly at me and said "John my boy, The Priest, Mr. and Mrs. Taylor and myself feel it is in your best interests for you to go and live with them in the village".

I was beside myself. He was full of grief. The next day I packed my little bag and we walked back down to Omeath and to Village Green and to the next phase in my life.

# 8

# The Omeath Taylors

*The armed conflicts had overtaken Dublin and the major towns as well as, by mid-August 1922, the nearby town of Dundalk. Alas one month later the troubles arrived in Omeath where Free State troops were attacked on 3$^{rd}$ October 1922. Despite this and partly because the Anti-Treaty IRA 4$^{th}$ Northern Division who operated in the area were largely neutral for much of the period, the village was something of a backwater to the Civil War. The guerrilla engagements continued until 24$^{th}$ May 1923. The 14$^{th}$ May 1923 saw a meeting between Republican Government and IRA Army Executive. The 24$^{th}$ May new Anti-Treaty IRA Commander Frank Aiken orders Anti-Treaty fighters "to dump their arms" and return home. Eamon de Valera supports the order. Skirmishes would continue for much of that year and most of the following year 1924, but in no comparison with that of latter 1922 and 1923.*

The Omeath Taylors had settled in Omeath the previous year ostensibly to escape the troubles. Now as the violence diminished with the IRA setting down its weapons their sights were set on a family in their new home.

On the north eastern side of the village green their house stood at right angles to two similar properties. Arranged on two floors the building was a long rectangular block with a pitched roof in slate. Its stone walls were whitewashed, there was a main centrally positioned front door with an arrangement of windows five upstairs and three to the ground floor. I would find that it was far more substantial to homes I had lived in before. It had five rooms all of good proportion. To the front there was a narrow fringe of garden bordering the village green, this was defined by a low stone whitewashed wall with an opening for the gate but no barrier. There were some roses and some other shrubs I was unacquainted with that reminded me of the wild flowers that are dotted about the meadows. To the rear of the house was a small yard laid to grass. Near the rear door stood a well with its water pumped up by a metal hand pump seated on a metal framework, this was mounted on a substantial square shaped stone block which one stood upon whilst operating the pump. To the right hand side of the house stood a large stone stable in which was housed their horse and a small trap with two seats and a fold away canopy.

There was no need to knock at the front door; Mr. and Mrs. Taylor were already awaiting us positioned pensively outside in the front garden. Mrs. Taylor wore a crotchet bonnet in white supported by long cream ribbons, her hair was held up in a bun beneath this; upon her shoulders hung a delicate blue shawl tied at the neck. Her dress flowed down to the ground and was in a darker blue in a heavy tweed type materials plain in design. Mr. Taylor wore a bowler hat, a great coat over a tailored waistcoat and collared shirt, his heavy trousers fitted into tall boots. Despite their years they were a handsome couple. Their slightly wrinkled faces were quite pale and clear in complexion, not weather worried like most local people were. They had the aura of having experienced a very different life to that which I was used.

Their attire that morning was similar to that we were used to seeing them in for Sunday Mass so was not daunting to me. We were greeted warmly in front of the porch. Patrick extended his greetings and then said that he would look forward to seeing us all the following weekend at church. He shook hands with the couple and then he strode away as if in some type of urgency.

The Taylors and I went into the front door which led as was customary into a large multi-function room and we sat down to tea and potato cakes. We sat around a fine round table with a heavily embossed table cloth, six chairs with upright wooden backs surrounding it. The entrance/reception room was not furnished ostentatiously but it was certainly comfortable. A couple of armchairs stood either side a decorative metal fireplace; over this a wooden mantelpiece incorporated an oval mirror with bevelled edges. There were two ornamental chests with deeply carved panels with cushions on top beneath the windows. Heavily embroidered floor length curtains with rope edging framed the windows. There was a delicately detailed writing bureau opposite and a multitude of pictures, mainly religious, but with two portraits probably of themselves in earlier years. A beautiful picture of the Holy Family sat proudly above the writing bureau on this the longest wall. Candles lit the room, four were burning on sconces on either side the bureau, and a further six could be lit and were mounted on an ornamental ceiling light fitting.

I would stay with the Omeath Taylors for just over two and a half years. They were a kind and compassionate pair. I had a bedroom to myself, plenty of food and was provided with more than sufficient clothing. They were very keen that I should be confirmed. During that first week they had presented me back at the village school. Mr. Coleman and his wife were delighted to see me and to find out that I had escaped the clutches of the evil Taylors. I would gain much religious instruction from them, particularly in Catholic Catechism. Within a year I would be presented to the Bishop in Carlingford for Confirmation. Admittedly other aspects of tuition were all but non-existent. Parrot fashion proved the most reliable method to memorise the religious messages. I would not gain any real ability to read until my future beloved wife taught me years later.

The first afternoon and evening had passed quietly with each party settling into their new roles. Supper had been a simple affair sitting at table with a mixture of root vegetables and herrings with freshly baked bread. To me the novelty of a multitude of eating instruments I found a little confusing and a little unnecessary. After our meal the couple read books and I gazed into the fire for some time for want of something more exhilarating to do. I had been shown my room on arrival and early that evening I put myself to bed. The Omeath Taylors went to bed a little later at an early hour, ten o'clock, which was their routine, I was to find out. I lay awake for a few hours taking in the events which had so rapidly taken place. I already missed Patrick and I wondered how he was managing with his return to solitude after our fine time together. Hopefully he could tell me all next Sunday. I certainly looked forward to seeing him again.

After a long cosy night in my new bed with its soft feather mattress and linen sheets and woollen blanket I was called by a shrill cry from the Kitchen down below. Mrs. Taylor had been up early and cleaned the clothes that Patrick had given me. They were hung on the line in the back yard drying in the sunshine. I had put on the other clothes Patrick had equipped me with. I had some tea and porridge and some bread. Later that day the couple took me to be fitted for a suit they said should be kept for Sunday best and Mass.

Mid-week came and it was time to go back to school. Somewhere I'd only spent the odd day here and there before. Dressed in my long trousers, shirt, cardigan and boots I looked spick and span. Mrs. Taylor took my hand and we made our way to the village school. Entering the class room she took me to the front of the rows of children who were already seated and in good order. She handed me over to the charge of Mr. Coleman. I knew him well and I certainly knew some of the other children. He directed me to the second row from the front and indicated a position vacant for me to fill. Sitting down on the hard bench I turned to my right and there sat my soon to be great friend MacMannus. Although I'd only had very sporadic attendance at the school, I felt pleased to be back. I had enjoyed those few days spent there before. The master and most of the other children gave me a warm welcome. I'm sure most of them had known of my ordeals at the hands of the Taylors, Omeath is a very small village. Smiling faces greeted me as I sat down beside MacMannus. He turned and gave me an affectionate slap around the head. Mr. Coleman glanced around the room and was assured his request for silence. Mrs. Taylor thanked him and bid him farewell.

*An Irish Boy*

# 9

# MacMannus

MacMannus was a boy slightly older than me. Quite plump and full of mischief, his clothes were more like I had been used to whilst at the earlier Taylors. He lived with his family, mother, father, three brothers and two sisters on a farm just beyond the extremities of Omeath in the direction of Carlingford. His brothers and father would pick oysters and muscles at three or four in the morning in Carlingford Lough. These would be weighed and put on the train to Belfast for shipment to England. They would also cut sea weed which was sold to farmers and used as manure. These hours of working meant his attendance at the school was if anything erratic. We would become great friends for over a year until he went away to work on the schooner ships that carried coal along the coast from Newry and Belfast to Cardiff. He would have been in his mid-thirteenth year I suppose when we met.

MacMannus and I soon became great pals. Within a week or so of my return to school I had been invited to his family's farm.

It had been a glorious early summer day. The sunlight had beamed through the small windows of the school room throughout the morning throwing strong beams of light upon the desks and their occupants. Particles of dust were reflected in the light rays mimicking thousands of insects cascading into a grey green abyss. The rays tickling the necks of some of the smallest youngsters had sent several fast asleep. Our kindly Mr. Coleman had overlooked their slumbers and had somewhat more quietly continued the proceedings. As the bell rang out loud to signal end of morning tuition all the children were only too pleased to fall out into the play area between the school house and the Head Master's House for the lunch break.

Three quarters of an hour later, after much fun and joy in the games of the play-ground, the afternoon session began.

MacMannus had gibed me all through lunch break to loosen up and to come over to his place to meet some of his friends after school. I had agreed reluctantly. I knew I was expected near to five fifteen back at the Taylors' for Tea. They were always keen to maintain a routine when it came to meal times. They were so good to me I tried my utmost not to upset them in any way.

The three hours of afternoon lessons trudged on. I had agreed to go with MacMannus straight after the bell had rang. The religious litany had continued unabated during which I had much difficulty containing my thoughts as to what his friends would be like and whether or not it was a good idea to stray so far out of that side of the village. In the back of my mind there was always the threat of encountering a member of that reviled Taylor family when they were trading in the village or on their movements on the eastern fringes of Omeath. To date I had been lucky and had only had the odd glimpse of one or other of the brothers driving their horse and cart along the edges of the village green from the safety behind the curtained windows of my new home. My hope was that I would never come into direct contact with them again. But their proximity was near and the village very small.

Mr. Coleman put down his book upon a small pile on his desk at the front of the class. Donning his neat dark brown hat he gestured for us all to rise. Uttering a short biblical verse, the bell rang out loud and clear. He waved his hands towards us indicating it was permissible to go.

MacMannus grabbed me by the scruff of my neck to my great shock and pulled me towards the door to the yard and then away down the lane and in the direction of the village centre. In my mind I had agreed with myself to fall in with MacMannus and go to his family's farm. I offered no resistance and fell into a run on my own steam. We two youngsters ran on through the centre of Omeath, fast past my new home and ignoring my new family who would be waiting therein preparing for our meal. We pursued soon out onto the main village street, Main Street, and as it narrowed the part pavemented road turned into the semi-made-up road; we were into the eastern outskirts of the village.

I gulped and a shudder went down my spine as I was retracing the path back towards the place of my evil incarceration. Where exactly was his family's farm. The road rose up against the banks of the lough and began to meander in ways I remembered only too vividly.

"MacMannus, I think I really need to go home for Tea", I pleaded.

"Shut up and come on; don't be a nelly", he replied.

Before I'd summoned up bravado to make a reply he suddenly grabbed me by the neck again and with a friendly punch in the ribs pulled me towards a small gap in the hedgerow, about nine feet wide to the lough side of Main Street. This marked an extremely small entrance to an unmade approach to what turned out to be the MacMannus Farm. I had never noticed this entrance before even though I had passed it so many times on my painful journeys into the village and beyond. The right hand turning to the Taylor's lane was ahead and agonizingly close, around a slight turn in the road and less than a couple of hundred yards.

The unmade approach was lined with dense foliage and led to a mishmash of shapes forming the farm's heart; it measured but two hundred feet or less from the main road. Emerging from the dark approach the huddle of buildings was in a clearing the backdrop of which was unobstructed by trees or other foliage. The farm lay on high ground upon the banks of Carlingford Lough. To the left of the collage of stone, metal and wood I could make out a steep access to the waters many feet below below and to a crude jetty with some small craft moored. The vista beyond of the Mourne Mountains rising up from the light blue waters with the farm buildings in the foreground on this promontory took my breath away. It was as if it had been planted there upon the high rocks not for sustenance of a family but truly for its aesthetic beauty.

I was absorbed emotionally by my surroundings and my fears about the proximity to the Taylor's home was diffused like a poison evaporating fast from one's body.

The ramshackle mixture of five or six buildings was unlike those I'd seen before. A traditional two storey thatched farm house was flanked by semi-derelict stone buildings with galvanized metal sheet roofing. They looked somewhat industrial. The farm house had conventional door with one window either side; then two windows above all facing a messy yard. The thatched roof appeared in good repair; there were two tall chimneys one at either side of the house. Closely aligned to the house and adjacent buildings were the other sheds and stores. These were greater in height than the farm house. Of their purpose I'm not sure; possibly they bore a relation to the family's work on the lough.

MacManus's pace had fallen to a steady stroll. We passed into the messy yard aiming for a double door, partly ajar, within a high opening in a tall shed to the right of the farm house. We passed beyond the door then through a dark space of which I recall nothing because of the gloom. MacMannus was pushing me on his hand on my back forcing me forward. Passing through a galvanized metal door we entered a dimly lit straw filled room. Its purpose was probably stabling for horses or other animals during the winter months, but it abutted the sizable building we'd passed through which probably was for some industrial use. The darkness of the first building led into the soft and glowing intimacy of the stable with its bales stacked high.

There sat upon bales of straw was a beautiful young woman, his girlfriend and two other fellows. Sat on a pretty barley twist legged table there was a wooden box gramophone with a big round metal horn above. His girlfriend, Rosie Quinn, had come back to the village from Belfast. Her dark auburn hair hung down upon her shoulders in abundant curls. She appeared tall and shapely and wore a lively and very modern short length dress. A pale green silk scarf adorned her neck. Her facial complexion was fair and delicate as porcelain. She had with her a record "Sweet Georgia Brown".

MacMannus and Rosie wound the gramophone up and it started to play. To my surprise they began some simple dance steps. When the music stopped they wound up the gramophone again and again and the other fellows joined in so I started to copy their steps. It was great fun. At first I felt silly, but soon I knew I had rhythm and could move to the music. It was to be a new love of my life.

After an hour or so we collapsed onto the straw on the floor exhausted. But we had had a fabulous time. I had to leave because I was already late for tea, but I was sure this was the start of something great and very different.

Some months followed and the evenings drew in and the weather deteriorated as winter approached. I went often back to the farm and met up with my new friends dancing and listening to music. Rosie had some other records as well, "Bye-Bye Black Bird" and the "Charleston" and "Black Bottom". We realized this music was immoral and threatening to older folks but that made it more exciting. I made sure that I did not stay out too late as I didn't want to upset the Taylors who had been so kind and thoughtful to me.

On my first visit to MacMannus Farm and the first time I was late for tea at the Taylors I had apprehensively stalked back to their house knowing that Tea Time was a couple of hours past. Instead of reprimanding me for this Mrs. Taylor simply said that she was pleased that I had met some friends in the village and to bring them home to Tea on some occasion. She added quietly that it would have been nice if I had let them know on the way through that day that I'd be a little late for Tea. She had said this very knowingly and knew it would instil respect in me for her; I would also tell them in the future if I'd be late so she would have an idea where I would be. On occasion I'd not do them the courtesy of this and would be out very late and test the boundaries.

# 10

# Dancing Nights

After church on Sundays Patrick would join us as before for tea and cakes. He would stay and chat with us for most of the afternoon. His mood was always jovial and content. The Taylors, as I, liked him very much. He seemed content with his lot. Maybe he liked to live by himself. He could keep the house as tidy as he liked. He urged me to 'toe the line' and not do anything to upset the Taylors. I was not sure what he meant.

Five or so mile away from Omeath on the lower slopes above Carlingford was Moneymore Hall. This held dances on Sunday nights to the great disapproval of the neighbouring priests.

One Sunday afternoon after Patrick had gone home after tea and cakes with the Taylors and me; I sneaked out of the back door and made my way to the MacMannus farm. MacMannus had pinched a bike from one of his brothers. We quietly pushed the bike away down the track from the farm and onto Main Street. Safely away around the corner and out of sight we attempted to both board the bike. He'd had some lessons, so we proceeded to ride towards Carlingford. The partly made up road was a bit rough going. I sat on the crossbar and he sat on the seat and peddled. It was huge fun. We zigzagged along the road for a mile up and down the mounds. All of a sudden on a steep downward decline the bike sped out of control; at great momentum it veered around a bend and off the road into a ditch. My hands had been trapped between the handlebars and the brakes. We were both thrown off and into the ditch. We were both scratched and I had some rips in my clothes.

That evening we did not get to the dance. Instead we went back to our respective homes and to severe dressing downs. My family, the Omeath Taylors, wanted me home in the evenings and in bed, lights out by ten o'clock. This was fair enough, but to have dirtied and damaged my new clothes and to have sidled off out of the back door without a word, this was being deceptive. To add to this they were always concerned for my safety, they feared I may be abducted again by the Taylors, or even worse be attacked or killed by them. The law had never punished that family for all its misdoings.

From then onwards most Sundays I got together with MacMannus in the late afternoons after Tea. If we were not heading for a dance we would go up onto the hills and get sticks under the boulders and send them rolling down the slopes making farmers fear for their sheep. The curfew gradually became laxer and the attitude of my new family was that the boy had had such a hard time he deserved some fun and latitude. It severely tested them when I started staying out really late; and very much so when the occasional complaint came from one of the hill farmers whose animals had been interfered with. I was approaching early adulthood, in those days you were a man at fourteen years or there about.

One such Sunday MacManus's girlfriend Rosie decided to walk with us to the village hall in Moneymore. Patrick had not joined our party for cakes and tea after church on this particular day. When Mr. and Mrs. Taylor and I arrived home I feigned a stomach ache and went up to my room. Putting back on my best Sunday suit I slipped out of the back door as I often did. Meeting up with MacMannus and Rosie we made our way from his parent's

## Chapter 10: Dancing Nights

farm, along the long road starting with Main Street Omeath and ending in Dundalk Road and the village of Moneymore. The hall was away from the village past the commons set upon a lower slope of The Cooley Mountains. We had chosen the roadway route for the outward journey so as not to get our clothes in a mess before the dance. It must have been a good three miles possibly four. By the time we got there Rosie was already feeling her shoes pinching her toes. To our great delight the man on the door realized we had no money but let us in anyway.

Even in those days the hall was of some age. Low and squat perched on a shallow bank it had the hills and thence the mountains rising up behind. The corrugated iron roof had just a slight pitch, it sat on timber walls with metal framed windows with small panes of glass; these split up by three doors each with a glazed upper section and triple wooden panels beneath. Within it was housed a single hall with an annex supplying cooking and tea making facilities. The hall had a parquet floor. The walls were made of match boarding with a wooden dado all painted in faded cream with dark green skirting, window and door frames. The floor was varnished but had seen many a good dance as there was much wear all over apart from the edges. Simple wooden trestle tables lay along the long walls and smaller round tables and fold-up director's chairs surrounded the dance floor.

There were seven musicians at one end of the hall seated upon a platform barely nine inches raised above the rest. One carried an accordion, two had small guitars, one had a miniature drum, and one played the violin and finally two carried recorders. There would be a variety of singers offering their contribution to the proceedings. Throughout the evening different combinations of musicians would form to perform Irish traditional tunes, dance music and recite stories. Each performance followed closely after the previous. There were a couple of intermissions during which some contemporary dance music would be played on gramophone.

Traditionally the men and the women were at opposite sides of the room. Each man would try to sort a partner for whichever dance he could. Some individuals of a more shy nature remained against the walls but we three danced all evening together. We had discreet amounts of the home brew which was also on offer. Some of the grown-ups seemed only too pleased to ply us free of charge with this. Many had flagons of the stuff conspicuously displayed about their chairs and on their tables. Clay pipes abounded and the air was full of the rich smell of tobacco and the sour scents of the beverages. Even so we were more interested in the dancing. We danced the night away. We seemed the centre and focus of attention. Rosie kicked high her legs and her skirt wove magical shapes to the music. Her beautiful auburn curly locks of hair mesmerized the onlookers as they flowed through the upper reaches of the smoke on the dance floor. MacMannus and I flowed to and throw displaying the skill in our steps that ensued from hours of practice at the farm

By the end of the evening our feet were raw and we were exhausted. We were some of the last to leave. For a shorter route home we went cross country. Rosie's feet were so bad we carried her in turn up hill and down the three miles back home. Leaving MacMannus and Rosie at the farm I walked merrily back on through Omeath to my bed. Mr. and Mrs. Taylor had gone to bed long before I got home. The following morning I would be reprimanded for staying out late. I had had quite a talking to when I'd ripped my clothes falling off the bike, this time I was prepared for maybe a hiding. As it happened I didn't get a hiding but just a severe telling-off. It was certainly not going to be the last!!

Despite the mud on my clothes Mrs. Taylor set to cleaning them whilst I was at school as she had done repairing the rips a few weeks previously.

The Taylors knew I was good friends with MacMannus. I believe they felt that after all I'd been through they could not be

*Chapter 10: Dancing Nights*

too hard on me. The whole year saw many such dancing nights, although poor Rosie never joined us again. It must have been too much for her.

Patrick continued to see us on Sundays but less frequently came back to the house for tea. Schooling continued but MacManus's attendance as the following year progressed became erratic then virtually non-existent. Later that year he departed for good for his new carrier on-board the schooner ships.

The Taylors were bricks. This period of two and a half years or there about was the most stable of my childhood. The time after MacManus's departure I calmed down a bit, still going to the occasional dance, it was not quite the same as when we had gone together. Instead of threatening the flocks of sheep and cattle rolling stones I contented myself to go for long mountain walks taking in the scenery, meeting a friend or other children in my travels and chewing over matters with friendly farmers tending their herds.

I was also in my thirteenth year and feeling quite grown up. It was late spring 1926. Mr. and Mrs. Taylor had taught me a few worldly wise things. They instilled in me some basic maths, how to count; how to know right from wrong and most importantly how to read people and not be taken in by words, and flannel. They were business people who new unfortunately that I was not to be. They were also tiring of village life and were thinking of moving back to their home in Dundalk. Things in the country appeared much more settled now. For how long no one was to know.

Over a period of a couple of months it was decided that I was old enough to go out into the world. I would make my own destiny and the Taylors would return to their previous lives in Dundalk. I would still be the son the Taylors had never born. I would always feel a bond with them as well as deepest gratitude. They knew I needed to make my own destiny and it would not be in the business world of theirs. Patrick had disagreed with our deliberations. He

*An Irish Boy*

would have liked me to return and resume helping him on the farm when the Taylors left. Over the next period he stopped attending church regularly and stopped visiting us for Sunday afternoon tea.

# 11

# Early Adulthood

One Tuesday on a warm July morning my cloth bag packed, myself washed, dressed in long trousers and clean shirt, boots polished, well breakfasted, Mr. and Mrs. Taylor walked me the short distance to the ferry. They had given me a bag full of change to use until I had money of my own. They urged me to return should I have any doubts and need any help. They had given me a letter of reference which advised of my good character and contained their contact details should a would-be employer or indeed I need them.

    What a huge change had occurred between ten and a half years and thirteen, or there about. I now looked like a young man; although short in stature I was strongly built and upright, not a boy any more. I had thick curly black hair and a ruddy complexion from all the outdoor labours. I could even pass for – fourteen?

With a big hug from Mrs. Taylor and a firm handshake from Mr. Taylor I turned to face the short stretch of water between Omeath and Warrenpoint. Two ferries were moored at the end of the jetty. Both were fairly sizeable boats of wooden construction and each about twenty five feet long. The first was full of passenger arriving from the north on a summer's day trip and had just tied up; the second had eight or ten people settling themselves down onto the wooden bench seats in anticipation of the trip. I handed my bag

*An Irish Boy*

to a boy who was assisting embarkation then climbed into the craft sitting myself down at the front to see the view.

Many years before on my first journey to Omeath I remembered having fond memories of my mother singing whilst working at the small hotel in Warrenpoint. When I had travelled to Omeath that first time in the train with Mrs. Taylor the sight of the town had rekindled these memories and every subsequent journey to Newry my eyes had wandered over the waters to that town. Now after all these long years I would be heading back to that faint memory of my infancy. One of the few I retained.

Three flags were at full mast on each boat. The master of the ferry boat engaged the Bolinder steam motor and the boy threw off the tie ropes. We lurched away from the jetty and made our way across the strong current that flowed from the lough into the narrow water. The crossing took just twenty minutes but what a captivating experience. The familiar dramatic scenery on this particularly vivid summer's day bobbing about on the lough I had viewed daily but this time I viewed it amid the turbulent waters. The black Mourne Mountains silhouetted against the crisp blue sky with the odd fluffy cloud; the deep blue waters of the lough a textured carpet before the white terraces ahead of the Warrenpoint promenade.

There was a large stone jetty with brick service buildings at Warrenpoint protruding well into the lough. Substantial docks lay to the west of the jetty. These incorporated a couple of large inlets and a number of smaller jetties. These were not as large as those I knew well in Newry but still had plenty of vessels moored up and a couple of very big cargo ships and lots of small fishing and holiday craft. The promenade ran alongside the water front. It was wide and had grass verges to seaward side. Imposing Victorian white rendered guest houses with good proportioned bay windows and steep pitched roofs lined the promenade for some distance. A huge windmill stood high behind the end of the promenade. We tied up alongside the end of the jetty. I jumped off the boat and ran up the

## Chapter 11: Early Adulthood

wide pathway. My heart pumping I would make my way to the market.

The market in Warrenpoint was held every week and once a month in the summer there was a fair with lots of stalls and amusements. In those days a section of the fair was set aside for individuals to sell their labours. All manner of trades would form into a circle, servants, labourers, farmhands and the like and offer them for work. Potential employers would choose their new employees. Mr. Malocos hired me in this fashion.

Mr. Malocos was a tall, upright quite slim build man. He wore a thin black moustache short dark hair and was well dressed in a tailored grey suit, collar and tie and smart black shoes. He spoke with a strange accent I'd heard nothing like before. He had a kindly manner and I warmed to him immediately and knew he would make a good employer and possibly a friend.

The Malocos family had come to Northern Ireland after the Great War. Many Italian families had moved to Britain and some to the province at that time. Some had set up restaurants in the larger towns and cities, others became shopkeepers and the Malocos opened an ice cream shop. Their shop was situated in Church Street. This was a good site for the summer being near the Public Park and the fair. During the summer many tourists would come to the town many staying in the numerous guest houses. Also lots of day trippers would come to enjoy the scenery.

The shop was small but had accommodation above; two large rooms above the shop and one room in the attic. The kitchen and a general living room were behind the shop on the ground floor. The large shop window was a problem in the high summer so had to be screened to keep temperature inside down.

Mr. Malocos had been walking around the circle of men looking them up and down. He wanted a clean, enthusiastic person he could train to help his family. Many of the men arranged therein were labourers and farm workers. These would be favoured more for their strength rather than their appearance or cleanliness. The domestic staff would be smart and well turned out and needed to have a somewhat subservient aura. I was a young lad, clean and well-dressed but probably not to overzealous in appearance.

Unlike many of the other young lads in the circle who were just out for that day touting for odd jobs, I needed a permanent post and hopefully a place to stay.

After some deliberation Mr. Malocos came up to me and asked where I was from and what I was doing there. I told him I was from the Free State across the lough and I was of age to leave home and find work and a life for myself. He said I looked very young but I insisted I was fourteen years of age and a good worker. I showed him the letter of introduction the Taylors had given me. He seemed very impressed and immediately said I could come to help them in their shop and that there was a room for me to stay.

I stayed with his family for three months. His wife was a similar age to him, I would guess mid-twenties. She was pretty with long dark straight hair and olive complexion. The nature of her work had made her a little portly. She wore pretty dresses in bright colours covered most of the time by hefty white aprons held together with great straps. The couple had two very small girls in very early years. They were in the early stages of walking and I realized they were twins. This was partly why they needed help with the work in the shop as Mrs. Malocos spent much time minding her children.

They gave me the loft room which was fine and airy. It had a small window overlooking Church Street. There was a good firm bed and all was clean and tidy. I helped prepare the ice cream with Mrs. Malocos in the kitchen behind the shop. They equipped me with a smart white shirt and dark trousers to wear when working. I started by selling ice creams from a basket on the front of a bicycle which I would peddle around the streets and park and square and along the promenade. When the weather got hot this was not possible as all the produce would melt so I helped sell in the shop. When demand was high in July and August and most summer weekends I would assist churning the cream, mixing this with the sugar and whilst whipping into conical shapes adding infusions of fruit purée and sometimes nuts. This was much fun and rewarded by taking many samples to taste.

I enjoyed my time with them, they were good people. Years later I would return with my wife to visit them. Sadly as the autumn set in I was not needed to sell ice cream; so I had to go in search of another job. I stayed with the family and they kindly looked after me and I was well fed until I moved to my new position. They could not keep me on all through the long winter months. Business for them was almost non-existent let alone supporting another fellow. They said to me they were very sorry they had to let me go but if I was still around in Warrenpoint in the spring they would be sure to be able to take me back on. Thanking them and slightly reassured by the thought of re-joining them the next year I was less daunted by my next post.

After spending three months with the lovely Italian family wearing nice clothes, doing a good clean job with accommodation included and with lots of great ice cream to eat all through the very warm dry summer I was not keen to go back to farming. Nevertheless in that part of the world there are not a great many alternatives. Come the early part of October I had to take a job working for a farmer with a dairy and a dairy herd.

About half way along Charlotte Street, then on the fringes of the town, set amid a terrace of small Victorian cottages was a dairy. Arranged on two floors the house had a street frontage with cream rendered walls and sash windows painted dark green. It donned a rough sign painted in faded brown lettering on a board simply saying 'DAIRY'. The adjacent cottage in the terrace also belonged to the Dairy but was not connected internally to it. The Dairy's front door was within in an arched alley to the right hand side of the structure. The arch formed an opening through to a small yard behind the terrace. It was probably built in that manner to facilitate a horse and cart accessing the land to the rear of the terrace. The yard was surrounded by a four feet high lime washed stone wall with two cross bar gates, it was a mud bath. It led onto a slightly larger plot again surrounded by stone walls, these unpainted, with a further gate at the rear of the parcel of land leading onto an adjoining field of one to one and a half acres in size and then open countryside beyond. The field was dotted with trees, some of them fruit trees. Small vegetable plots took up some of the ground; these were barbed wire fenced to protect the potatoes and other root vegetables from the cows. This parcel of land and buildings belonged to a Mr. Monagham. He was a mean and fat old man who lived alone as his family had left him years before. I had become acquainted with this old bugger through the Malocos family. He had supplied them with some of the foodstuffs for their shop. I had to regularly fetch the churned cream which had been prepared at the dairy. I was not keen on him when I first set eyes on him but with my regular visits throughout the summer some of the sharp edges were bashed off our relationship.

Mr. Monagham lived in the cottage next door to the dairy in Charlotte Street. It was in complete disarray. Despite being within the confines of the town the cottage was as grim as an isolated hillside farm cottage. Hygiene did not exist. He used only the ground floor rooms. The upper floor had been empty since his family had left. Water poured into the upper floor when it rained. Mr. Monaghan had an assemblage of furniture in the three rooms he used. The kitchen had a small unblacked Victorian range within the chimney breast, a large table with two high backed wooden chairs, a dresser equipped with an assortment of utensils, storage jars, and a wash stand with bowl and tall jug. The front room housed his bed, a huge metal contraption drowned with all manner of sack cloth and ragged linen, all permeated with snuff spilling. The middle room was to be mine. It had a small metal bed with feather mattress and some old sheets and rough blankets and very little else.

Set behind the cottage and Dairy with the arched opening, which was virtually unused and full of debris which camouflaged a broken down milk cart, separated by about ten feet of the yard was a dilapidated corrugated iron shed which was the storage for the dairy. The cows would be milked in the smaller of the two yards one at a time by him. The others cows being assembled in the outer yard. The milk was stored in large churns, some to be bottled and delivered locally, part to be churned into cream and part to be made into butter. Being an old man with only help from myself he only provided supplies for a small part of the community. There were a couple of other similar operations in the town both a little greater in scale.

During the summer the cows would roam in the field adjoining coming in for milking first thing in the morning but then returning to graze the rest of the time. Now autumn had set in it would be my most important job each night to get them into the larger yard and safely close them in for the night.

I had most reluctantly taken this job but having been back to the fair several times with no one offering me work and having received much assistance from the Malocos family I chanced on this opening but was convinced it would be for the shortest possible time.

I moved into the middle ground floor room I made myself as comfortable as I could. Despite working three months for the Italian family I had spent the little money earned going to dances. Being in a small town rather than a village there were all manner of things going on especially during the summer months. The pubs often had dancing evenings and there were organized events at the hall, as well as the regular fairs. I would go out most weekends and sometimes during the week too. To Mr. Monaghan's disgust the meagre wages he gave me would all go on my trips to the fair and dancing. I was not the drunkard that lots of the other lads of my age were; I was just really keen on dancing.

As soon as I could I would round up those cows and herd them into the yard. I had to make sure I got the right end of the last cow as I guided it in and shut the gate to make sure my dancing cloths were not covered in 'skitter'. Failing this I would not be going out that night.

Little was I to know I was to stay with the old man through the winter and into the spring. We would often row about trivial things. Mr. Monaghan would pick holes in most things I did. From daybreak the first words would be how long I'd slept in, that half the day was gone and that I'd been out all night at the Whistledown Hotel or some other party place dancing. When I went to the field to fetch vegetables I was always away too long, got the wrong size potatoes or brought too many and there would be none left for the winter for us and for the animals. I'd been lazy bringing in the cows too late and had been dreaming. When I made the milk rounds he would complain that I was so slow the milk would be off before the customers got it. There was always something wrong. In the evenings after the cows were sorted we had little to do with each other. I would take some food from the pot on the range and take it to my room. If I was not going out I would read magazines picked up on my delivery rounds about film stars or the great bands in America. I would be living in my own fantasy world for a few hours.

The winter became spring. I was still with Mr. Monaghan. Now he had me to make deliveries I'd often take supplies of cream to the Malocos shop. It was good to see them and to take a few minutes to talk to human beings. They often gave me some of my favourite ice cream which had the flavour of the raspberries and black berries picked in the late autumn. They asked of Mr. Monaghan and were always interested in his latest moans and grumps. One such April day Mr. Malocos asked if I would like to return to help them for the spring and summer. I was delighted at the thought of leaving the old man and that dirty cottage and messy cows covered in skitter. I accepted his offer at once.

Returning after my deliveries I took great pleasure in quitting Mr. Monaghan and his cows there and then. I packed my bag immediately and let him get on with his pettiness.

He only paid me four shillings and six pence on top of the bed and board a month so I would not miss his money. He had just paid me a week late for the previous month so I had nothing to expect to come.

"You'll be wanting your old job back come next October" he scowled as I parted company with him on not too unpleasant terms. How he would manage during the summer and beyond I knew not and didn't care. Admittedly the cows remained at pasture during these months, just coming in for milking. I was back to the Malocos.

I rushed along the road to Church Street and the shop I was so fond of. Yes I would have another summer of fun helping make ice cream in the morning, sometimes selling from my bike in the afternoon and many evenings out on the town at the various dances. The fair would be great once a month and Mr. Malocos would fill me full of notions of Italy and other foreign parts with his long stories recited whilst we worked. So everything was as before, and indeed come October everything was as before and I went cap in hand back to Mr. Monaghan's. He duly greeted me with his sardonic adulation.

This continuum was to last in total eight more years. In later life I would realize this was my adolescence, my formative years, and my youth. I would look back on this time with much affection. I would meet other friends during these times at dances and fairs and at the market, whilst out selling ice creams or delivering milk or conducting my daily business. Some would be local, others from further afield on their day trips or on holiday from Newry, Belfast or beyond. More of this later. For myself as is the case with most adolescents, hormones rage and temperaments run hot and cold. There is always the urge to visit pastures new and meet fresh faces. There is always an underlying dissatisfaction with one's lot.

I was now five feet eight inches tall which is not really very tall. On the other hand I had grown up a strong lad; the farm labouring as well as the dancing had given me strength and resilience. I could work hard and I could defend myself against the best of them. My early life had made me only too sure of the need to be able to do that. On the other hand I could be hot headed; I could have 'a bit of a Paddy'. This would be a benefit and also a handicap later in life.

# 12

# Kicking The Bucket

It happened on an early evening in late October 1935. I had returned one week previously, as was the norm by now, to the dairy and to Mr. Monaghan's. I was irritated at having to leave the Malocos and my comfortable bed and good food. The thought of another winter in that damp, dirty cottage with that temperamental, now very old man, was grim. The bright summer evenings had faded into the long dark autumnal nights.

I was about to go fetch the herd into the farm yard. The fat old man came into the yard and told me to go out into the field and bring in a large bucket full of potatoes for the animals food store. I hadn't at that moment put on my best suit but was still in my working trousers and shirt. He was now an even more temperamental old fellow and I was dearly miffed that he had not asked me to do this earlier. He had a habit of doing this in order to spoil my evenings. He was probably jealous of my youth and popularity with the girls. Making sure I picked up a bucket which had holes in I ran out into the field to one of the barbed wire fenced off sections of land where the vegetables were grown. Filling the bucket to the brim with the freshly dug potatoes I returned to the yard dragging the weighty supplies back to him.

By now I was hot and bothered and tired after digging up the vegetables. He looked at the potatoes and the bucket and said in a vicious manner foaming at the mouth "you've used a good milking bucket to put those old potatoes in boy".

I told him that the bucket had a hole in but he insisted that it was a good bucket. Now very annoyed and getting late for the dance I picked up the bucket and turned it over emptying the produce onto the mud and skitter in the farm yard. Picking it up empty and with the hole very near his face I said to him "you silly old man can't you see the hole in the bucket?"

"F– ye boy" he replied and spluttered a few coughs and then turned and went into the back door and to the kitchen with no other gesticulation. He had gained his usual satisfaction at my expense.

That night I didn't go to the dance. Instead I washed shaved, assembled my cloths and a few magazines into the cloth bag that served as a suitcase. After a reasonable night's sleep I raised early dressed and gathered my few possessions together. Taking a passing glimpse of my home of many a year I passed through the kitchen door into the yard beyond. Feeling still great anger at the old man's stupidity and after such a cacophony of similar events welling up through the years I went into the farm yard armed with a hatchet I smashed all Mr. Monaghan's buckets making great holes all over them. None of them would be used again for milking. All through this the old man didn't stir.

All the money I had in the World to my name was three old pennies. This was largely my fault as I was only too keen to spend all my income on my dancing nights. The cows were stirring in the field beyond the outer yard. A thick mist hung over the fields beyond and heavy dew was upon the grass. The small fruit trees abutting the yard had flakes of chilled mist cascading down from their limbs floating to the floor and dissolving upon the dew. The delicacy of the scene mellowed my thoughts of escape and diminished my anger of the night before. Falteringly I made my passage through the arch of the dairy and then I walked out onto Charlotte Street, did a left into Meeting Street and then forward to

*Chapter 12: Kicking The Bucket*

the railway station. Few people were about at that early hour and there was an intense stillness causing a tingling at the back of my neck. I walked at keen pace towards the railway station. I needed to disconnect from Warren Point as abruptly as possible less I be retained here for the unforeseeable future.

I boarded the solemn puffing giant that was stationed patiently on the far platform. It was the first train bound that morning for Newry. I sat down on the comfortable strongly upholstered bench seat the only person in my carriage of dark stained wood panelling at that quiet hour. I reminisced about the train journey I had made all those years before when the evil Mrs. Taylor had changed my life in such a ghastly way. I now felt deep trepidation concerning this short journey and how it may impact on my future. Smoke bellowed out of the chimney and a loud whistle shrieked out shattering the calm of the dawn. The carriage lunged forward and the train picked up momentum rattling and shuddering over the cold iron points of the tracks. Looking out as the train pulled out of the terminus I gazed through the window, now splattered with delicate tracts of rain, at the shipyards leading away from the promenade and the neat centre of Warren Point. These were almost deserted of craft with the exception of a large vessel which was under construction in one of the greater yards. It sat alone strong and resolute a leviathan in the centre of a basin the low tide ebbing at its bow. Propped up by stanchions, it was a sixty footer most likely, standing tall and proud above the mud. I wondered what ever I would do now. I had been at Warrenpoint just over nine years, a mostly happy period despite the temperamental old man. I had arrived there a boy and was leaving now a man. The year was 1935 and I was now a grown-up approaching my twenty third year, as far as I was aware.

*An Irish Boy*

# 13

# Joining The Army

The train travelled swiftly along the track depositing me twenty minutes later at, what the old locals called, 'The Warren Point Terminus'. I stretched my arms and legs in an attempt to instil enthusiasm into this quagmire I'd got myself into. Walking slowly along the platform as it curved towards the mainline platform I had serious second thoughts about my next move. I made my way along St. Mary's Street and then to Hill Street and very familiar territory, then onto St. Margaret's Square. Many times I had seen The Royal Ulster Rifles parading up and down the town in order to attract recruits. Dressed in their smart brown uniforms with their caps bearing the black and green badges denoting them as riflemen they were a disciplined lot. The Sergeant would march ahead commanding his platoon as they ensued through the thoroughfares; he wore a big red sash to denote his rank. These sights were captivating to the younger lads who stopped and starred or ran alongside the processions.

This day PT was being practised in the square. The thoroughfare thronged with activity. On the edge of the pavement a trestle table had been erected with some posters and information. The Sergeant stood in front and was talking authoritatively to a small group of twenty or twenty five scruffy young men who seemed energised by what he was saying. I waited in line for twenty minutes as he expounded the merits of joining the respective regiments in particular The Royal Ulster Rifles. I knew that they took men from The Free State as well as Ulster; in fact I had been told that half the fighters were actually from the south.

Eventually his speech finished and he spoke directly to me picking me out from the crowd asking which regiment I would like to join. Looking at the posters again I had already decided to join The Royal Ulster Rifles. He handed me two shilling pieces, one for signing up the other to go and buy tea and a bun. I saluted him in a half-hearted way and signed a docket which had been lying on the trestle table. He returned my gesture and beamed enthusiastically at me. Next, feeling somewhat hungry after my early start, I went to Ma Mercer Café around the corner from the square. From my many hours spent on visits to Newry I knew that was where the soldiers gathered. I had a mug of tea and some fried soda bread; it was really good and I knew I had made the right decision. The cafe was full of servicemen chatting to each other consuming their meals. The atmosphere was very buoyant with great comradery. Several men asked if I had signed up. When I told them I'd done just that they patted me on the shoulders and congratulated me. Leaving the cafe feeling very ebullient in mood I then walked up to the gates of the depot some distance from the town square. From the guard hut next to the gates a guard came out and asked my intensions and I said to him I had joined up. He gave me a friendly acknowledgement and returned to the hut. A few minutes later two guards appeared from within the gates and escorted me to an empty barrack room amid a maze of buildings and there I waited for three days.

Later on the first day in the barrack room a corporal approached me and produced a bible. Reading a passage from the Old Testament he got me to swear an oath to the King.

The following morning after a disturbingly quiet night alone in the barrack room the corporal returned and instructed me to go

## Chapter 13: Joining The Army

to pick up my kit from the stores. I was handed a neat bundle of items- the uniform, knife fork spoon and enamel mug. All items of kit and equipment were numbered. Returning to the barrack room I tried the kit on and found several items too big. These had to be replaced.

At that time recruitment was brisk and within three days there were thirty one new recruits plus myself in the barrack room. This was the quantity required to make up a Platoon, (32 men). My Platoon was called 'Laval'. I had joined the army; the date 7th October 1935; my army number 7012768. We were soon to be sent to Armagh for training.

On my third day at barracks I went down to breakfast in the Mess Hall but forgot my berry. The Sergeant Major called me over and I attempted as good a salute as possible. In response he screamed at me full in the face with an animalistic cry. His red and rounded cheeks were almost bursting with intense fervour. I could just make out the jist that if I did that again I would be charged and sent to the guard house. This was something I'd been told about and wanted to avoid at all cost.

I felt very red faced and humiliated as I sat down at the table with my new chums. I had become acquainted with a dozen or so fellows that I seemed to get on well with from among the new arrivals from the past days. They were all a bit subdued by the dressing down I'd received. One or two gave me discreet but sympathetic glances. The breakfasts were little better than those I'd been used to at the old man Monaghan's establishment. Porridge and soda bread with hot but stewed tea and this was on a first come first served basis.

After breakfast there was to come the drill experience. Assembled in front of the makeshift scattering of sheds that made up the barracks we were very green new recruits. After doing a few right and left turns where some were turning right whilst others were turning left we made a discordant group of men. We

105

were assembled in a circle and told to raise our right/left hands respectively the result showed the obvious problem. Next we were paraded in a line single file to the barbers and given very severe short back and sides.

After tea that evening they said there would be some supper in the hall. We were given our own mugs which if broken we would have to pay for. When we got to the hall all the other soldiers had already got to the bread and there was none left for me. Next night at 7pm the same happened so on the third night I went before 7pm and dived in with the rest as the coco came and got some. The coco had no milk or sugar, just thick brown liquid. It was better than the stewed breakfast tea.

Most of the recruits were from poor backgrounds. The religious rivalry was very strong in the barracks rooms. For those drawn from outlying country districts in particular it was a first time for such a mixture of Protestants and Catholics. For many it was a first experience of proper clothes and regular food.

Within days we would be marched to Newry Railway Station and then be transported to Armagh where we would be based for training at Gough Barracks.

After an hour or so aboard the train we arrived at a smart Georgian style limestone clad railway station. Assembled at the front of the building we were set to march in as orderly fashion as was possible along a steep and major thoroughfare towards the south east of the town, Barrack Hill. To north side of the road emerged a substantial light toned brick building with decorative stone dressing. It had formal portico protruding sections dividing the structure into several bays. In front of the lengthy façade lay a wide yard. It was a grand vision for us mainly natives of the countryside.

We were marched through the courtyard to a smaller assembly point beyond the main block. Passing by the stables housing the officer's horses we were assembled in front of some less daunting

*Chapter 13: Joining The Army*

buildings two floors in height with brick walls under pitched rooves. Beyond these we could see we were on the fringes of the town which followed on to open fields. We were assigned our barracks and duly fed in the Mess Hall.

Next morning after breakfast the training started in front of the main building in the large yard. There was much marching up and down for hours at a time with occasional ten minute rests. The sergeant would be shouting lift up your feet they will fall down on their own. It was a harsh regime and took all the energy and enthusiasm out of us very quickly. After the first week we got our own rifles to drill with. When we got them they were filled with grease and took a lot of cleaning. The number of my rifle was 701.

On my first night out with my mate he said lets go over to Park Way. There were some girls there the older soldiers said they were prostitutes. My pals name was John Hanna. When we got to the edge of the park quite a few girls were milling around and it was quite dark. What we weren't told by the older men was the sergeant was watching and this area was out of bounds. When we saw him hovering around behind some foliage in the distance we ran like hounds. We went off across the top field and cleaned our boots in the grass to disguise the evidence as to where we'd been, and then walked past the depot down the hill. At the bottom of the hill was the sergeant. He stopped us and said had we been in Park Way; he looked at our boots and let us go on our way. If we had been caught we would have got seven days confined to barracks answering the bugle calls.

If one were charged and tasked to answer the bugle call you might be cleaning your boots when the bugle call was sounded; you had to run to the guard house and attend to whatever job you were given. It would be sounded from 5pm to 9.30pm each evening according to the length of your sentence. I was glad I was never caught; I never went to Park Way again all the time at that depot.

Our sergeant was quite mad, or at least to every sense and purpose appeared so. This was probably from his experience in the war between Italy and Abyssinia.

He would stand in front of each recruit individually and pointing or prodding with a long bayonet stick into their chests shout disjointed ranting phrases. Every morning we had to parade outside our barrack room and show our knife, fork and spoon and enamel mug. If you didn't have them on parade you were put on charge.

On my first pay day we had to approach the Colour Sergeant Officer seated at a table on the parade ground with the pay clerk on his side and salute before being given our money. My first pay was five shillings. The clerk would call your name, the officer would do the paying and the sergeant would write your name in the ledger then you would sign for it. If you didn't salute properly you would have to do it again and again before you got your money. After getting the money the sergeant of my squad said he wanted two pence for whitewash to paint the coal bucket white. The coal and the coal bucket were painted white and you grasped the coal with a knife. The other officers had other different requests for money for items such as broken glasses. You paid for the glass that was broken and the one that was put back. You then paid for cleaning items such as Blanko Boot Polish and Brasso; out of five shillings there was not a lot left.

After six weeks of doing our recruit training we got ten shillings; we received fourteen shillings a week after joining our Battalion.

On my first Sunday church parade we went to Armagh Cathedral about three miles away. In those days we wore long Putties at the bottom of our trousers. After marching about a mile I realized I'd tied the left one too tight but could not ask to stop so had to wait until we got inside the cathedral before I could kneel down to loosen it.

## Chapter 13: Joining The Army

When we went into church we took our rifle with us, (without ammunition), which seemed to me to be like going into battle. When we marched back we were in lines of four which was the way the British army marched in those days. I often wondered why they didn't let us take to church our 'walking-out Canes' which had rounded silver tip at one end.

Every Wednesday one job was to take buckets of coal from the coal dump up to the married quarters. This would take several hours until their tubs were full. After this our next job was to march down to the bath houses and wash in whatever water was available, hot or cold. After this we would have to march around the parade ground single file in one long line and look for matches whether there were any or not. The sergeant would shout look to your left or look to your right. Even if there were no matches the motions would have to be gone through.

Every Saturday morning we would have to go across to the floor of the gym between 10-12 am to scrub it until you could eat off it.

The PT vests had to be washed by the soldiers, but all the underwear which was woollen, shorts and other vest, were sent to laundry.

After cleaning the equipment there was very little of the weekend left. Lights went out at 10pm even on Saturdays. The bugle would call with different tunes.

One would have two of everything, one to be worn and one for inspection. The inspection would take place after the laundry had been delivered back. The beds would be lined up with string so that there would be nothing out of place. There was a diagram on the wall to show how the kit should be left for inspection. The bed's coyer mattress was made up of three cushions and was very hard. The pillow was another coyer cushion. The base was two metal door-like sections, one pushed under the other. The blankets were folded into particular shapes. The sheets were folded into small rectangles and the edges turned in. They even counted the folds on the sheets. There should be six folds. All cleaning items were marked in pencil and placed on the bed. Your name was on the top of the locker. Mess tin and lasses folded in the shape of an anchor were shown. Whilst being inspected you would stand strictly to attention; if the sergeant did not pass you it would have to be done again. The Duty Officer would have sergeant in charge take various notes he was preparing for anyone who had let him down. I never had any problems with regards to this.

On the day of my first sports occasion we were called out onto the barracks square and the 32 number of our squad were now the senior squad as we had been in training some considerable time. We were issued with hockey sticks and small posts to be used as goals. After some practice matches 11 were chosen, included me, to play against Enniskillen the following week. During the match I let in a goal, I went to kick it and the ball went under my foot, so we lost the match.

I also played against Enniskillen Camp in football as inside right and we won two/one. Your name was then put on the board.

This was coming up to six months of being in the British Army.

One Friday we were dressed in PT kit and assembled in the Mal in the town and all timed for a three mile run. This was three and half times around a field surrounded with trees. I did quite well in this. I was beginning to realize my aptitude for sports.

Not long after this my training at Gough Barracks was finished. My last job at the depot was coming up. The last week very little had to be done apart from marching up and down and cleaning equipment before handing it back to the stores ready for the new recruits.

# 14

# Passage to Liverpool and the End of Training

On a Thursday afternoon in spring 1936 we were filed past the Medical Officer for examination. Then we had tea and were assembled ready to be marched down the hill to Armagh Railway Station to board the train to Belfast docks and from there to embark upon the ship bound for Birkenhead, Liverpool. This was the first time I had been in Belfast, it was night time and the lights were on but it looked very grim with the Harland and Wolff Ship Yard towering above the rail yards in thick fog. The boat was a normal passenger vessel not a troop ship. We were given one sandwich and a mug of cocoa. The boat got into Liverpool at about 6am as it was timed to do so; the crossing was about 9 hours. After we got to Liverpool we were assembled on deck for disembarkation and given a sausage sandwich and a mug of tea.

On the crossing I had been sick. I'd never been further on water than the boat crossing from Omeath to Warren Point. We were kept in large rooms below deck and not allowed to move from there like heard of sheep. On arrival the first glimpse of Liverpool was grey and foreboding; with the massive edifices lined up along the Mersey and the enormous docks full of vessels stretching for miles, all steaming and engulfed in fog.

We were told we were to join the No.2 Battalion of the Regiment in Gravesend. (The No.1 Battalion was stationed in Hong Kong).

We were herded on the key side for two hours or more standing waiting for the train to Gravesend. I remember thinking to myself whatever had I let myself in for. Some of the soldiers with money bought themselves out; three or four of them, it cost £100.00 before training, £200.00 after being trained. One was signed up for 7 years, plus 5 years after the 7 years remaining as a reserve, so I couldn't get out of it.

Soldiers bound for other regiments had been assembled on the crowded key as well. When the troop train arrived separate parts were for different regiments. The train would be divided on its journey so each section would go directly to regiment, so there were no train changes to make on the journey to Gravesend.

The steam train was brown with its windows operating up and down. The carriages were divided into small compartments with 8 seats in each. The seats were quite soft; there were toilets, but apart from going to the toilet you were not allowed to go anywhere else. With all our equipment and belongings it was like being in a sardine can. The train did not move from the key for a further 8 or 9 hours after which we travelled through the night. The men within my compartment were numbed by the experience. We tried to make small talk now and again but there was not much enthusiasm to do so. Sadly my friend John Hanna was in a different part of the train so we could not alleviate the atmosphere with our bantam. Apart from being fatigued by the long wait standing on the key, being incarcerated without sign of movement for so long led a couple of fellows to feel claustrophobic and want to leave the carriage. They tried to force their way towards the door or window but were pulled back down to their seats by understanding comrades. When the train eventually moved from the key the epic journey with its four long stops for the separation of various sections of carriage felt immeasurable.

## Chapter 14: Passage to Liverpool and the End of Training

When we arrived at Gravesend in early morning light the band of the battalion met us at the station. They were a sight to behold to we travel weary soles. The thirty or so smartly assembled musicians formed four lines. They were dressed in immaculate white tunics bound with thick black belts; shinny boots and straight black trousers; neat buries were on their heads donned with tall plumes. The music was loud and brash with strong momentum. An officer fronted the procession carrying a long ceremonial staff, he was followed by a tall heavily built soldier hammering on a huge drum, and he was ahead of many trumpet and bugle musicians.

We followed formed into an orderly troop behind the ensemble somehow forgetting our weariness caught up with the rhythm of the music and the colour of the moment. We were forwarded thus ways up to The Royal Ulster Barracks, or Milton Barracks. This was about three miles away. The barracks were used as temporary accommodation for troops awaiting deployment overseas. The Milton Rifle range was a mile or so away. Inside the large entrance gates the barracks was formed of low level buildings in grey brickwork spread over a substantial area with little uniformity. It had been used during the First World War as a military hospital.

When we got to the barrack gates the band stopped playing and we stood at attention ready to be inspected by the Regimental Sergeant Major, (RSM). As he was coming through the main central gate he was shouting "number 4, number 4 in the last rank"; it was me and I was chewing gum. He said "spit it out, spit it out". He walked over and asked me my name. I had to say "Rifleman Byrne sir 7012768"; he said "I shall never forget that name".

We were marched through to the square within the gates. We were directed to the stores and were given an enamel plate and mug and went to have breakfast, now much anticipated but sadly just some beans and tea. After that we had to reassemble before the RSM to be marched up and down to see how we fitted and could perform, to see which companies we could be split up between.

There were Signals, D Company, B Company and C Company. In each there were 70 men or more. I was sent to C Company.

He marched us up and down then sectioned off with his arm groups of people. It was good luck for once that I went to C Company as the sergeant major of C was quite a good chap compared with the other animals.

After the allocation had been carried out the RSM said to the sergeant from the depot that had come over with us "is there anyone here who plays football?" Unknown to me the RSM was in charge of the football team. The sergeant said "Rifleman Byrne is not bad at football sir". So the RSM called me out in front of him along with a recruit called McCullock. The RSM said after 1pm you will go down to the stores and get a pair of football boots and I will see you at the Guardroom. I had been made aware whilst at Armagh that the Royals Ulster Riffles were very keen on sports particularly football, hockey, running and shooting.

It took us some time to find a pair that were not too hard and were the right size. So wearing PT shorts and football boots we waited for him outside the entrance to the Guard Room. The other soldiers were left to clean equipment and do other chores. It would prove to be a sort of privilege to play football. The rest of the battalion then assembled and were all told to run to the football field.

The RSM was there and was acting as referee. He trained the team although he was one of the shortest RSM in the army. He was renowned to be one of the smartest. He had a Batman to do his cleaning and help him dress. He would stand for one hour in front of the mirror before parading each morning to check his appearance.

I performed well on this trial with the team. It helped that I enjoyed sports and after years of physical work on the land then in my duller life with Mr. Monahan I certainly was fit. The RSM commended me after the trial match and advised me I would join

## Chapter 14: Passage to Liverpool and the End of Training

the team and represent Battalion. Thereafter I would get on well with the RSM as I had done well with the trial within the team. When I got back to my mates in the company they thought I must have been good to have had a trial with the battalion team. So I was in the team and was to gain lots of benefits from this. While the battalion were at Gravesend I always kept my place in the team. I was always either Inside or Outside Right. Being involved in sport got me off a lot of fatigues, (general duties).

That evening, with luck we had some free time after our meal. In the barracks I met up with John Hanna, we had been separated much of the day. He congratulated me on my performance in the trial which he amongst others had closely been watching from the side-lines. He said that it was good luck for me to join the team and that I would be spared lots of the drudgery of the chores he had already experienced.

If I was not playing for my battalion I would be playing for my platoon. I also played Hockey and ran for my company as well.

I was to enjoy my soldiering life at battalion as we seemed to have much more time to ourselves than had been our experience whilst training at Gough Barracks in Armagh.

I wondered why some of the men at battalion had civilian suits; I asked an older soldier who told me that a man from Burtons in Gravesend came once a month with a variety of suits in various colours and collected six pence weekly.

When off duty one did not have to salute or be on orders. Before leaving the camp you were inspected in the guard's room to see that your suit was presentable. When on charge all privileges were lost including that of going out in civilian clothes. If a soldier could not afford these suits one could buy a formal dress suit for the battalion for £7.00 –side hat, button jacket, and black trousers. These would be put under the mattress to iron; cloths were not ironed but were generally creased under the mattress.

*An Irish Boy*

In between the brick huts forming our barracks there were deep channels to take heavy rainwater away. Several people fell in these when they had had a few pints. There was a Scottish guy who used to cry when happy every time he got drunk.

Doctor Barnardo had a home just outside the barracks. Children used to play in a neighbouring field. On one occasion Alec James of Arsenal came down to referee. The children were 10 or 11 years. Other notable footballers would come down to train the boys from the home.

"I was soon to take part in a sporting tournament in the Army Cup at Aldershot. We did very well to get up to the final. We had to play the Fourth Battalion of the Tank Core. We did not know but all the cream of all the tank cores were assembled into the Tank Core Team. A couple of days before we played them we had to go on a route march. Most of the chaps feet were blistered and cut so you can imagine going to the final meant they beat us 6 to 3; our back gave away two penalties, I scored one goal. I think we could have beaten them if everyone had not had sore feet".

"I had the privilege of meeting Prince Albert, Duke of York, (later to be George VI), at the match at Aldershot. Most of the British Army in the area was watching. The Duke shook each player's hand after the game as both teams filed past his party. Strange as it seems I have served no fewer than three monarchs. The stadium was immaculate and had very large stands. It was maintained by old soldiers waiting for their time of service to come to an end. This was the only time my battalion had lost the football and the boxing in one day. It was unusual to get into both finals. We were known as 'Let the stickers past'. Our band used to play "look at the soldiers, look at the men". I thought they were the worst band in the British Army. We called them a band of robbers".

"On my first long march in battalion we had to carry a lot of cloths in a rucksack and a ground sheet. This first long route march was nearly 50 miles. On route we slept in circular tents in fields

## Chapter 14: Passage to Liverpool and the End of Training

overnight. In the morning we all showered in one big shower, some 60 men; after breakfast all had to stand on duty to be inspected to see if we had shaved adequately. Then we were all marched across the field to see if there were any match sticks, so that the field would be left clean for the farmer".

"When we got to our various destinations we had to unload the horse drawn carts containing little round tents, similar to Indian tepees. These tents each would sleep 8 or 9 men. We would sleep with our feet pointing to the central pole of the tent. The smell of feet was bad following the long march. We left the camp at 9am and got to the next camp overnight stop at dusk. Some days were spent on manoeuvre in the form of war games. One poor chap was on a Court Marshal charge so was taken out on manoeuvres with us; they put a pack of sand on his back and made him run up and down a hill. We were on manoeuvres for four weeks. The morning we assembled to go back to Gravesend one chap of B Company had a blank cartridge left in his rifle which went off and he lost an eye".

"We all marched behind the band at Devises in Wiltshire then we got on the train which would take us back to Gravesend. We arrived later that afternoon and were met at the station by the band which once again played as we marched back to barracks. When we got back to barracks the sergeant major ordered that all those needing haircuts should get one and get equipment ready for inspection by the CO's at the end of the week".

"My first battalion guard duty arrived and for it everything had to be perfect. So I borrowed different parts of equipment from friends and my friends helped me clean it all. When the guard was arranged there would always be an odd number of men, a seventh man. This person would be the tidiest man and would stand duty up to 12am outside the guard's room to run messages for the CO. The CO had to be saluted every time he came out of his room. The position fell to me; I actually did not have to run any messages that day. The other guards would go to the guard's room and do various duties for 24 hours. Being awarded the stick was a good advantage as you could get off duty at 12am".

"On one occasion it was a close shave deciding who got the stick and it was decided by whose studs on the soles of their shoes were most shiny. I only did one guard duty. All members take turn so to get around all the soldiers takes a lot of duties".

"If some other service was needed, like spud bashing; a sergeant would come into the barracks and say "is there anyone in here that can play the piano, or has anyone got a white handkerchief". When someone said yes they would be sent to the cook house to peel potatoes or some other task. When men became aware of this he would come in and ask for volunteers, if none came forward he would say "you and you are volunteers" and they would have to agree".

"It was not long after our last ALL Ranks Dance that we had to get our new kit bag from the stores. Everything was packed into it; it had your name printed on it and which barracks you were to be sent to. My battalions' next destination was Catterick Camp in Yorkshire. As we left Gravesend all the towns people seemed to be waving us good bye. It was so typical of the army that just as you were getting used to a place you had to go somewhere else".

"It seemed to me to take a long time for the train to get to Catterick. It must be routine that troop trains have frequent long stops in their journeys all the time. We were given some tea and hard biscuits with bully beef which were so hard you seemed to need a sledge hammer to crack they were bloody hard. The journey seemed very long and cold with the scenery of the north of England appearing grim with its factories and slag heaps and all the men wearing cloth caps. On arrival the camp looked grey and foreboding with its mass of barracks in all directions. My first impression was that it was cold and bloody awful".

"Each regiment had its own section; then there were sections for the regiment's horses, the horses were used to pull the gun carriages. The horses also pulled carts for the cooks who cooked in urns on the back of these. The carts could stock up as they journeyed along the roads. The train came within a mile of the camp".

"Catterick was the second biggest garrison for the British Army in the UK. The nearest town was Darlington, a place I never went to. On arrival there seemed to be barracks everywhere".

"The Union Jack Club was a place for soldiers to go outside the camp to have a pleasant plate of rice and read papers. I went there twice a week usually with my friend John Hanna and a couple of other chaps with whom we developed a rapport. We all like a laugh, (good crack).We would make light of the rigours and discipline which surrounded our daily lives".

"Each company had a different schedule of works but the usual soldiering and marching went on. If we were doing PT other companies would be doing drills. After PT you no sooner got the water on in the shower then you we being called for parade. We used to say "bull-shit bugle brains" excuse my expression".

"You had to shine your boots dipping your handkerchief into the polish and moisten from your mouth. God knows what time was spent on such cleaning. The older soldiers had been doing it so long they would burn their boots and belts and sand paper them until you could see your face in them. It could take months to get yours to their standard. They would say that when you can shave looking in them like a mirror then all was well".

"On one occasion coming back from Union Jack Club I went into the guard's room to give my name in to find that the guard on duty had been unable to march up and down and had been put on charge. The road was so slippery I could hardly stand. The brains of the army are in their feet all they do is pound the ground all day long. I would never want my sons to sample that sort of life; this regimentality should have been done away with in Victoria's time".

*An Irish Boy*

# 15

# My First Leave in the Army

*That year had been a momentous one. January 20th 1936 had seen the Coronation of Edward VIII following the death of his Father George V. The Constitutional Crisis had emerged only months into his reign because of his relationship with Wallis Simpson, a divorcee who he proposed to marry upon the divorce of her current second husband. He abdicated on 11th December of the same year and was succeeded by his younger brother George VI, (formerly Prince Albert, Duke of York), as King after the shortest reign of any British Monarch 326 days. The Coronation of George VI was to take place 12th May 1937 some six months later.*

My term at Catterick was 7 months; now approaching December quite a lot of soldiers were told they were to join the First Battalion in Hong Kong. We were sent on leave for ten days prior to being sent abroad. This was the case for me and John Hanna.

John had talked of Belfast virtually every night that we had gone to The Union Jack Club. He was eager to return there and see friends and family. He more or less insisted that I join him on the long journey. He knew I had no family and just a few friends at Warren Point. I had related many episode of my tragic early life to

*An Irish Boy*

him and he was, as were my other chums very disturbed. They knew of the existence of such people and desperate poverty; even though they were from very underprivileged backgrounds generally, none seemed to have experienced the extremities of my own childhood predicament.

I agreed and decided to go and stay with my pal John Hanna in Belfast. It was so nice to be in civi Street for a week. During my time on leave King Edward VIII abdicated and the following June married Mrs. Simpson in France having succeeded in her second divorce; we heard the news on the wireless. On leave my pal showed me some landmarks of Belfast. On a couple of evenings we went to the pictures. John Hanna's father was not a well man and I was to hear that he had passed away shortly after our departure.

This was the first leave for me since I had joined the army. Even so I was not physically tired. We travelled in a civilian train back to Liverpool. This was busy with troops and general public but nowhere near as compressed as the last troop train we'd travelled in. It also hastened us to the port not delaying for the many dissections the troop train had endured. We arrived in Belfast aboard a regular passenger vessel, this time we were on deck so I was allowed to see the scenery. I was amazed to see on my approach along the shoreline how green Ireland was. I was told this was because of the mist and frequent light rain. Belfast being on a huge bay was a draw for masses of shipping of all descriptions. The ship yards built massive liners and overhauled all types of vessels. Lots of associated industries were there like factories making ropes and nautical products and ware houses storing goods of all description used to fit out the military and domestic vessels and stock them whilst in port.

The girls would walk to work en-mass with shawls over their heads being called by the sirens of the mills; the men likewise with their shabby overalls and cloth caps. The roads were filled with trolley buses and trams and many horse drawn carts and carriages.

## Chapter 15: My First Leave in the Army

The year was 1936, it was December, and thus cold and dark much of the time.

The brick and slate buildings were grimy, decrepit and dirty from smoky chimneys. Rows of two up two down cramp terraced houses fed up and away from the port in all directions, these housing the thousands of workers employed in the shipping industries and related trades. There were many shops of all description and public houses all about. John had a friend who had a butcher's shop who also played football. He played for Belfast Celtic Club; later he was to play for West Bromwich Albion and after for England his name Jackie Vernon. Next to his shop was Quinn's Stores which was a single storey building as was the neighbouring Gallagher's Stores which sold general merchandise. Most of the surrounding houses similarly blended into the brown haze.

John Hanna's house was also two up two down and was just over a mile out of the hubbub of the central docks area. His brother unlike himself was still at home and was a mill worker in his twenty's. Their father also lived in the house and both made me very welcome. There were two bedrooms upstairs, the front one facing the road slightly larger than the rear; down stairs were a Parlour, Kitchen and Scullery. The front door led straight in from the narrow pavement outside to the Parlour. Three plumped up armchairs sat around the room. These bore patches from much use over the years and much staining. A small caste iron fire place with metal shelf affixed sat as a centre piece. The rug on the floor was well worn and slightly sticky and brown in colour where the pattern had met the floor boards. The kitchen had a range within the chimney-breast. There were table and three chairs which had seen better days. Holy pictures donning the walls centred on the obligatory crucifix. There were candles in jars lit all day in front of a figure of Christ on the mantle above the range. There was the usual bucket under a wooden fixed seat in the small brick extension in the rear yard.

After months in army barracks accommodation John Hanna's family home filled me with warmth and emotion; it had reminiscences of my life outside the army and bore close resemblance to places I had lived in. John's brother and father met me outside the front door and gave me hugs and strong handshakes. We went through to the kitchen, crashed onto the wooden chairs and relaxed recuperating after the rigours of the long journey. Sat affront of the fire burning in the range we took our wet coats off and warmed ourselves after the damp and cold Belfast December scene. John Hanna's father went into the kitchen to make tea. John said that he would be lodging at a mate's three doors along the road so that I could stay at his family's home. I tried to persuade him that I should stay along the road, but he insisted not. The friend John was to lodge with was later shot by the Black and Tans. I don't know his name.

Johns' house was actually in Falls Road. Protestants never ventured into the area.

Catholics would never venture into Shank hill Road. Falls Road was very poor. People could be seen looking out from behind the small windows at any event in the street.

"John often told me about the troubles in Belfast. His brother some years later was to work at the Post Office. Tragically he was shot dead one morning coming out of the building. So you can see what it is like now, *(the 1980's)*, but it was far worse then. I have always believed that Ireland is ruled by the gun as well as by religion. On another visit to Belfast during the Second World War I was in Falls Road about to visit John Hanna; I was approached by two B. Specials who asked me where I was going. When I told them I was going to see a friend in the road they told me to get out of Falls Road or take the uniform off".

Our week together was great fun. John's father and brother liked a drink. Each night we'd have some home brew then go out and about in the Falls Road frequenting various establishments. We would always have a hearty meal before leaving. There was always much meat on the table, mince, chops and some chicken as well as my favourite potato cake with bread. We met up with his many friends; he was a very popular person. The boozy nights saw a lot of drinking. Within the small public bars usually in the front of the establishments, we would join a ring of soles sat many carrying violins, recorders, with occasional piano accordion. We'd join in the old folk songs we knew and improvise in those we didn't. The cacophonous atmosphere was ever more shrouded in the thick smoke from the fires and the prolific smoking of pipes. On each opening of the street door the clouds of moist air flowed out onto the pavement as did eventually ourselves. I don't remember much about the daylight hours during that week.

Bidding a sad farewell to John's family and to several friends come to say their dues, we made our trek back on foot, the mile or so, to the docks, then onto the ferry to Birkenhead, Liverpool and thence onto the long train journey back to Catterick Barracks. All the way we were accompanied by many fellow soldiers returning from leave heading back to their respective barracks and then onto unknown destinations.

*An Irish Boy*

# 16

# About to Journey Abroad

Christmas came and went almost unnoticed on the camp. Some obligatory simple services were held on mass on the parade grounds in very unpleasant temperatures and occasional drizzle. With officers leading protocol there was little sincere religious content for the respective faiths. New Year's Eve saw some heavy drinking in The Union Jack Club. John Hanna and I and a few palls had even erupted into some tunes from the home country. No one seemed to mind. There were a great many fellow countrymen all about. The whole camp at Catterick was subdued and not seasonally elated. 1937 had arrived and what was in store for us no one knew.

About ten days after my return from Ireland I received my first inoculations. It was a terrible experience. Five days later I had the second ones. We believed there was enough in the syringe to kill a horse. We were excused duty for 48 hours. Most of us had a huge blister form. The MO came around to inspect how the jabs had taken. About a week later we were handed our equipment from the stores and given our 'K.D.' Khaki Drill, which was a set of light clothes to be worn in hot climates. To wear on your head was a 'Toby', to keep heat off, and we were issued with short putties with green tops to be worn after we had reached Suez in Egypt."

Once again we were paraded on the barrack square ready to board the train to Southampton. This was to be another long journey, especially as before eight soldiers to a compartment. There were no civilians on the train; it would become packed with different regiments of the British Army. The train travelled throughout the day making several very long stops where additional sections were added containing troops from the various regiment. At each stop we lowered the top sections of glass to our compartment down and they filled our mess tins through the window with tea. When the train reached Southampton each regiment took its turn to march to the troop ship. The ship was called 'Dilwara'. The train had stopped upon the key side as had been the case in Liverpool. The massive body of water surrounding the key was populated by dozens of huge ships anchored to massive concrete structures. There were hundreds of smaller vessels afloat within the harbour. The metropolis of Southampton seemed to surround the whole estuary. Now dusk on this early January evening the mist was encircling the water's edge and the sky was becoming heavy with dark grey clouds. A gentle flickering of lights glistened all around the estuary from the suburban hinterland. The water was cold but calm.

The Dilwara was a troop ship. Standing high above the key in grey and white it probably contained eight decks. A mass of cranes towered above the top decks. Compared to some of the other ships in harbour it was not vast. The two major decks had a throng of troops already aboard, many of these were leaning over the rails taking in the scene. Some were cheering, some singing, others motionless, probably perplexed.

We in due course were marched to the entrance at a lower deck of the ship. We were boarded and allotted accommodation we were given food then allowed out on top deck. A large crowd was on the key side shouting greetings and waving their handkerchiefs; at least several hundred were spread behind the barriers to the key. It seemed like hours before the pulses from the engines began to slowly energise the giant. Now in virtual darkness apart from the floodlights of the port and the dim lights on the decks, the ship

## Chapter 16: About to Journey Abroad

edged away from Southampton Docks. The ship gave three great bellows like fog horns and the triumphal band played God Save the King as the ship pulled away into the night. Almost all the soldiers including myself stayed on deck for quite a while. John Hanna and I had once again been in separate compartments during that long train journey. It was good to get together with friends that evening on this new adventure and talk about the expectations of this great trip and enthuse as to what sights we may see and share expectations.

Many stayed late on deck watching the lights of Southampton disappear into the mist circling the estuary. The massive form of the Isle of White appeared to block the way out to sea, its silhouette against the night sky spreading east and west. The ship entered deeper waters and took a westerly course monitoring the perimeter of the island until, gaining momentum thrust towards the blackness that was night in the English Channel. Now nothing could be viewed apart from the many lights on the decks, masts and funnel. The bell rang and we had supper of bully beef hash and cocoa, it was about midnight.

During the whole of the next day our progress was swift. The crossing of the Channel towards Britany peninsula, usually noted for its rough fifteen meter waves had passed without evidence in the darkness of the night and most had slumbered after the fatigues of the previous day. The French coast was twenty to thirty miles away and given the time of year and the sultriness of the skies it might as well have been mid Atlantic.

We had been assembled for PT on deck. To our great pleasure we discovered that PT was to be the only formal activity during the time on board on what was we found to be a six week voyage. Dispersing after the rigours of the exercise the troops milled around the decks occupying themselves with games. There was a game we used to occupy ourselves with called Potato Picking. There were two teams of six, a bucket of six potatoes; one would lower a potato down and another would pick it up; the team to be first to pick up the six would go into the next round. My team of six including John Hanna won the competition and we were issued vouchers for food. Apart from such activities many played card games and others read the odd magazine or book they had brought from barracks. Some wrote to loved ones. John wrote to his folks back in Belfast. I had no one to whom I felt I could write to pass on my experiences.

Venturing south into deeper waters we were amid the Bay of Biscay. The strange calm encountered on our progress disintegrated. Skies blackened and the surf on the waves foamed emanating into ever increasing torrents of water surging about the ship's bow, then onto its upper decks; the bow seeming to pass below the upper reaches of the waves. The Dilwara was certainly not a huge ship. In later life in the early 1990's I was to encounter duplicate sea conditions on a massive twelve deck modern ferry. The similarity of riding up and down in a virtual elevator cannot be disputed. The effect on both ships was identical. For many of the troops and certainly for me, with little experience of strong seas, we were pulverized by the action of the waves. Men on deck clung desperately to any fixture that might harbour some safety. All were regurgitating but trying to control their convulsions. With much panic we were projected through doorways and down stairways to internal areas of comparative safety. Seated on the floor of the lower decks many were uncontrollably vomiting. This was to last two days and nights.

Now totally wasted of stamina many confined to beds with sickness we entered calmer seas to the west of the Iberian Peninsula. The next two days we fared much better travelling south then passing through the Straits of Gibraltar. From here we entered the Mediterranean Sea then to stop over for supplies in port at Gibraltar. For much of the journey there had been no sight of land so entering this sheltered haven with its giant form towering above

## Chapter 16: About to Journey Abroad

and its huge fleet of ships moored about it was a very welcome and reassuring sight.

We were not to disembark here and later we were instructed that we had docked in Gibraltar to take on some supplies but also have some minor repairs to the hull performed following the tempestuous passage. Small teams of engineers were boarded at intervals for the couple of days we were there. Various tasks of work were undertaken mostly out of sight of us troops.

There was a great sense of satisfaction being moored amid multitudinous British naval vessels of all sizes in safe haven surrounded by the waterfront of quintessentially English architecture. Nestled under the gaze of the great pointed rock we waited in this very continental climate so different to that which we had departed five days previous. Many various nationalities were carrying on their business on the jetties and promenade. There were lots of soldiers similar to us in traditional military uniform; then others from the Far East and Asia in smaller numbers in a variety of dress; then obviously native southern Europeans with rich olive complexions, merchants or local resident one presumed. The variety of different nationalities was something that took most of us aghast.

The third day all ancillary people disembarked; gangways were dispatched and the engines engaged in reverse to take us from our position between the adjacent and somewhat loftier ships. Temperatures had been very pleasant fourteen to eighteen degrees on our time in Gibraltar in those late January days; much more pleasing than those which we were used to. Some of my mates including John and myself took advantage and sun bathed on top deck. The accompanying officers did not protest this. Our few days there were very pleasing after the journey and previous training regimes.

Taking its position in a channel between anchored lines of vessels with their bows proudly standing above ours, engines expanded their thrust and we coasted through the multitudinous fleet and out past the vast harbour limits into the deep blue Mediterranean waters. The skies a light blue with the sea much richer turquoise in colour and relatively becalmed.

We would follow a path north of Algiers, Tunis and then Tripoli; past Port Said, through the Suez Canal our destination for re-equipping would be Suez. Our course would be deep water so despite proximity to North African Coast we would have no sight of land for the best part of a week. For much of the time the waves would be shallow. The skies remained clear with just some fare weather cloud interrupting a perfect journey. A great assortment of large military and merchant ships, ferries and other craft donned the seaways and bustled across our path throughout the journey.

For us men in new environment it was a most pleasing time aboard. With the daily PT activity being our only rigour most of the time was spent resting in between the not so enthralling meal breaks.

Towards the fourth day of the voyage many of us in the calm afternoon sun were again lying on deck soaking up the rays, reading the odd scrap if literature that might be available or playing a game of cards or just dosing in the heat. Many were bright red from too much sun and starting to peel. This was very true of red headed John and me from cold Northern Ireland. We began to suffer from the effects of the sun and had to spend increasing time down below. The Dilwara's momentum slowed and the engine seized their monotonous droning noise.

Some ten miles off in the distant haze began to emerge a thin line on the horizon, a light greyish yellow ochre strip of colour travelling into infinity. Our small ship almost bobbing about on the light waves came closer and closer, this line beguiling us towards itself. Two hours past during which the coast of Egypt came ever closer and clearer, the shimmering sands appearing to spill into the turquoise sea. Some more hours passed; the sands now only a few miles from our path were merging with a vast metropolis larger than anything I'd seen before, Port Said. For over an hour we ferried passed the huge conurbation its low lying buildings gradually getting denser in proximity and larger in stature. Some fourteen mile we travelled along its shore.

There were two punctuations in this maritime city. These were where the Mediterranean is met by the Suez Canal. It was to the most westerly waterway we were heading into.

As the waterway narrowed we were closer to great buildings lining the water's edge. White edifices some three or four storeys in height with terraces on each floor. A giant light house guarded the approach. Huge commercial buildings continued the vista; domed civic structures in white stone with arched terraces on all levels were dotted about. Wide avenues of formal houses stretched inland. A mass of dockyard structures proliferated for miles ahead along the canal. A myriad of tiny craft circled around the anchored ships. Around us too as we progressed further into the wide waterway small boats surrounded us. Men came alongside with their cargo of fruit, baskets of fish and trinkets trying to get us to buy them and haul them onto our decks by ropes and nets. Young boys dived into the water to retrieve money we had thrown to them for goods. Sea gulls hovered overhead occasionally swooping to get a prize catch. We delighted at all of this; all was so colourful and new to us.

Two hours later the metropolis was thinning and the buildings began merging with the sands. On the eastern bank the architecture had disappeared some time before but now the easterly canal waterway merged with ours to form the canal proper. The Egyptian sand lined the banks dotted with palm trees and the occasional small mud brick settlement. The vast desert landscape was dispersed with agricultural fields of luscious crops and tall reeds which fed into the water's edge. The Suez Canal was now much narrower than at its mouth the traffic for larger vessels was one way with two passing points in its entire length. Both of these were man-made lakes.

It was at the second of these, a small inland sea made up of a series of large lakes, Great Bitter Lake, that we made way for an Italian troop ship. We assumed they were returning from the war in Abyssinia. Dressed in our newly issued fresh and bright Khaki Drill we all wave to them in reciprocation of their greetings. They looked very brown and sun wearied. Their uniforms were soiled with dust. We had rumour of them using gas upon the tribesmen. Behind our friendly accord we bore some degree of disgust for what we believed had laid at their hands. Their ship passed northward into the distance and we resumed our travels. The one hundred and two miles to Suez would take more than eighteen hours.

Travelling through the night we had experienced the sun setting over the desert in a huge fireball with its rays burning spider's webs through the sand before disappearing leaving blackness all about. Staying late up on deck with some friends our eyes gradually became accustomed to the darkness. Moonlight glistened on the waters ahead and a cascade of stars filled the skies above. An eerie silence was all about with the rumble of the ships engines being the only disturbance accept the crisp action of the waters below and the occasional call of a jackal or shriek of a bird of prey.

Many men had fallen asleep on deck and quite late at that. So it was a shock of bright light that scorched our eyes even for those within the vessel when we woke the following morning. Although it was an early hour the sun was high in the sky and heat was quite intense despite our Khaki Drill. I went over to John and a couple of other mates and we decided to go two decks up to the top main deck. Emerging into more intense daylight we viewed the canal had again widened. To the east lay a peninsula of flat sand with no buildings just desert. To the west in contrast we were alongside a huge port. Beyond the port was another vast metropolis extending for miles combining with the desert. Further ahead were more docks and many anchored vessels of all sizes. This body of water, the canal estuary, merged with the sea; dark blues flowed into emerald blue and then were absorbed into the light blue sky.

We stayed in position on deck watching the vista as The Dilwara manoeuvred into the first great docks. Like in Port Said the water front presented some formidable architecture. A great white mosque with minarets and a large domed roof bore a prominent position amid major commercial or public buildings. Further along the promenade were hotels and domestic dwellings consisting of metal balconies on two or more levels. At street level many shop front and cafes had decorative protective awnings to shield the sun from those taking coffee or to protect their wares. The prolific populous busied about their lives with great intensity. Exotic young women carried baskets upon their heads with their fine linen head scarfs and galabeya blowing around them. The male traders dressed in heavier galabeya and white shirts, some with trousers under. Most wore taboosh head dress. Many Egyptians could be seen to have preference for European dress. Smoking of pipes and the Hubble-bubble abounded.

We were retained in Suez; again a large maritime city. Were remained on board as we had in Gibraltar; this time only for twenty four hours. No repairs were needed to the ship. Substantial cranes lifted supplies directly onto the vessel from the adjacent quayside. Small boats bustled around beneath us with locals offering their trinkets and fruit.

The oriental odours even reached the ship and as we remained stationary we felt incongruous to this romantic mythological land. It was with some regret that we'd not been able to go ashore and immerse ourselves in this rich culture.

The following day at eight o'clock in the morning shortly after breakfast the engines once again engaged. Retreating from the key out into the centre of the dock we awaited final clearance to embark on our next phase in the journey to Singapore.

A dull rumbling from below decks signalled the slow departure from the endless docks and flotilla of vessels. Centred in the wide waterway the canal estuary emanated into The Red Sea; speed accelerated to a modest ten knots. A warm fresh breeze flowed through the decks. The Red Sea seemed to absorb us and the land east and west again faded into a thin grey-yellow ochre line thinning then disappearing completely. We were in an inland sea but its size meant that the shores were not visible to us. We might as well have been again in a huge ocean. There were now more craft accompanying ours through these waters as there was not the limitation of single file convoys as had been the case through the canal.

We would pass near Sudan, Ethiopia, and then Yemen before leaving the Gulf of Aden merging with Arabian Sea then the Indian Ocean. Some ten days or so later we entered the Malacca Strait eventually via the Singapore Strait arriving at Singapore. Of all these we generally had little or no knowledge. Our experience was of the adorable climate and bejewelled waters surrounding our humble craft.

We were to stay in Singapore for one week. During the time in the idyllic climate we played a hockey match and drew 00. We were joined before leaving by more troops for the voyage to Hong Kong. We were now accompanied on board by Indian cooks!

# 17

# Brief Notes on My Experiences in Hong Kong, Shanghai, India and Afghanistan

Brief Notes of My Experiences in Hong Kong, Shanghai and India and Afghanistan:

**Hong Kong**
"After our six week voyage we arrived in Hong Kong. The Battalion Band with bugles bellowing led us from the port up to the barracks. Hong Kong was known in those days as the Island of a Million Candles. Seeing it for the first time you could understand why".

"The food was good and the Chinese did all the cooking and cleaning for the battalion. Every battalion had these services. Hong Kong was the best place I was ever to be stationed at. Once a month we would go to the firing range. We would start at 100 yards and go back to up to 600 yards from the targets. All the different places you fired from were marked. If you didn't hold your rifle tight your shoulder would get quite sore. What I liked about Hong Kong the most were the picture houses. They were the best I had seen and showed all the latest films from United States".

"One morning on parade the sergeant major said to us to gather around, "I want to have a few words with you new soldiers about VD. I'm telling you once and for all that if anyone is caught with VD you will have all your privileges taken away. If any men were thought to have been trying things they would be called into the nearest room, drop their trousers and checked to see if infected. There was a lot of VD amongst the soldiers throughout the colony. In the shower one day I saw for the first time a soldier who had been infected".

"I went to the dance halls many times with a group of mates including John Hanna, we were to think of our time there as the best of our lives so far. When you arrived you purchased tickets, usually ten, and these you gave to the girls, one ticket per dance. This is how they earned their commission. Outside the dance halls were prostitutes. To me each dance did not seem very long. The soldiers paid these girls much money and the men were in and out of the hospital all the time. Thank God I never had VD or syphilis. Some men would regularly get infected so they would be sent to another part of the billets and were called Outcasts. They didn't seem to care. Some times when stationed in Kalong on the other side of Hong Kong you would have to take the ferry to go out at night. There was the risk of not getting back by midnight so you'd have to run for the ferry. On one occasion talking to a soldier he got me to go to a brothel with him. Inside all the girls were lined up for you to choose. I had not seen such a sight in my life so I left him and got out as quickly as I could. He said I was yellow; but I preferred to be yellow than have VD. I never went into any more whore houses in the rest of my days abroad".

"Shortly after arriving in Hong Kong a typhoon storm hit. All were confined to our barrack rooms until the No.7 signal was given. We were told it could last for days. It seemed to go over quite quickly; but we discovered that a supply of bully beef was kept in a box in each room for such emergencies".

"My first big parade was St. Patrick's Day. There was much marching and all were issued with shamrocks to be worn on the march- first occasion for me to parade with a shamrock".

"Nearby our battalion was the Welsh Regiment. On the occasion of their special parade their mascot was a goat. The night before the parade some lads got the goat and painted it green all over. The commander of the Welsh Regiment was up in arms and we were all confined to barracks for the day. No one found out who did it".

"There was much sport in the army; hockey and football leagues with the other regimental teams and also Chinese teams. In our first season we won the league by five points, we were very proud. I found it very exciting playing football and hockey for my company. Two notable Chinese players were Ling and Lance; they were very talented and many of the English clubs would have liked them to play for them".

"One day a mate called Jackson and I went to a shop that hired out bicycles by the day. We did 37 miles on these uncomfortable bikes with hard saddles. Jackson had done the ride many times before so he knew what to expect going up and down the hills eventually coming to a peak where the view was breathe taking. The view was all around the harbour with all its ships and the Chinese Sampans".

"One occasion we were issued with shovels, and then we boarded Lorries with Chinese drivers. We were taken into the country and set to dig trenches. They told us to be aware of scorpions. Some men found several scorpions and saved them in jars to take back to catch spiders. Some of them were in fighting matches. On return we cleaned the shovels and had tea, day over. We spent weeks digging these trenches".

"The buildings even then were quite tall, five or six floors. Land being limited they were built up the hillsides. The streets were filled with thousands of people. Walking through the streets was like cutting through bread. They were lined with stalls selling everything you could think of. The women carried long canes on their shoulders with two wicker baskets on them. Around each billet there were sewing girls who were available each day to sew on buttons and make all types of repairs. Some of the boys used to come around to clean our equipment with Blanco; so we used to pay them for our sewing and cleaning".

## Shanghai

During The Great War Japan had taken over as the country with the largest number of foreign residents in Shanghai. In 1914 they had sided with Britain and France in the war and conquered all German possessions in China. By the 1930s Japan was becoming the most powerful national group in Shanghai accounting for 80% of all expat foreigners in China.

In 1931, supposed "protection of Japanese colonists from Chinese aggression" was pretext for the Shanghai Incident when Japanese troops invaded Shanghai. From then until the Second Sino-Japanese War, (1937-1945) the Japanese had taken over enforcement of law and order with their Japanese Consular Police and Japanese Municipal Police from the previous control of the largely British controlled Shanghai Municipal Police.

In 1932 there were over one million Chinese living within the International Settlement another 400,000 fleeing into the area after the Second Sino-Japanese War breaking out. For the next five years the International Settlement and French Concession was surrounded by Japanese occupiers and Chinese revolutionaries.

"Soon afterwards we packed our kit bags ready for the next move to Shanghai, and the British part of the International Settlement. Here there were various nations, each had their own

*Chapter 17: Brief Notes of My Experiences in Hong Kong, Shanghai, India and Afghanistan*

role during the conflict in the war between the Chinese and the Japanese.

Our role was to protect British property in the area".

"My battalion were not there long before we suffered six men killed in a mortar bomb explosion in a bar they were drinking in. Some days later five more were killed in another mortar bomb explosion. The Japs would fire these mortars where they thought the Chinese lines were. Our lines were usually close to the Chinese lines".

"One day I was on look out and I spotted a group of Japanese soldiers coming up a side street. I called to the corporal in charge and we formed a line across the road to face them with fixed bayonets. They came to within fifty yards of us then retreated".

"Another morning British and Chinese officers wearing casual clothes attempted to locate Japanese positions so we could target our bombs on them".

"Shanghai was in ruins when we arrived. It had been a wealthy settlement up until that time with large houses, office buildings, wide streets with many cars and rickshaws. In the centre of the roads were posts supporting crows' nests for the police to stand in to direct the traffic. We would use these ourselves as lookout posts. From them we could see the Chinese practicing with their bayonets. The officers were billeted in hotels not totally wrecked in the fighting and would come to inspect us each morning. The Chinese were allowed up to the barbed wire on the edge of the settlement. When we were not on duty at the boarder or patrolling the perimeter we had to guard the railway and stop the Chinese from entering the settlement. We had to watch to check Chinese were not crossing the border from Canton".

"I was on duty on the perimeter on an occasion when a large Mercedes drove towards me. The German gentleman and his driver were allowed to go into the British sector as he was on business. He stopped and we chatted. He gave me some black tea. This was the way they had tea in Germany. We chatted for fifteen minutes. He asked if I was going to be there tomorrow. The following day he came back and we chatted again, this time about the British Army, the quality of my rifle, then general things. Next he asked me what I thought of Adolph Hitler. I said "I think he's mad". He was very angry and got back into the car. He drove off and I never saw him again. He was probably trying to set up fifth columnists".

"Shanghai was a separate colony from Hong Kong and the Japanese wanted to over run it. This is why the United States, the Italians and the British with the Canadians had the International Settlement there. All the banks were grouped in the city centre. There was a large population, it was very modern and progressive and was very clean despite the conflict which had caused parts of the city to fall into ruin".

"The Union Jack Club was the largest of the five clubs in the World. It was very well equipped and was run by the Church of England for the soldiers. It was housed in a large modern building with a marble hallway. Good food was served by attractive women and we were made very welcome".

"Not long after this the Japanese withdrew all their troops and stopped their bombing raids. My battalion was withdrawn and relieved by the Buff Regiment. They had strange headdresses which looked like sack of potatoes; we used to laugh at them. We used to say "stand by the Buffs, let the stickers pass". We went back to Hong Kong after this. It was very good to be back there!"

"Unfortunately it was not long after this we had to move on to Singapore. It was here that we had our first glimpse of the big guns which were being installed in the harbour there. They were sixteen inch I believe and were so big that no enemy ship would be able to enter the harbour if they were ever to try. They were situated in reinforced concrete look outs and were an impressive sight. Obviously in hind sight I realise they were all pointing out to sea so eventually when the Japanese invaded they approached from the land behind".

"We had much time on the firing ranges whilst in Singapore then we returned to Hong Kong".

"The Chinese seemed to spend all day searching for passengers for their rickshaws. These had two wheels similar to cycle wheels and were the equivalent of taking a taxi. Even so I never travelled in one preferring to walk".

"Before leaving Hong Kong to go to India two soldiers in my company requested permission to marry Chinese girls; they were refused this as the company were about to leave for India".

**India- 1938**
"The battalion spent most of one week packing everything into boxes ready for the trip. When packed everything was loaded onto Lorries, nothing was left, no rubbish for the incoming men and no match sticks."

"We were all marched to the football field to be inspected by the Commanding Officer, then onwards to the troop ship. We were assembled and had a long wait before being boarded. Moral was low and most were in bad moods. We were all disappointed to leave Hong Kong, for me the country I liked most of all my travels abroad. The ship had many other units from other regiments on board."

"The ship left Hong Kong bound for Bombay and throughout the passage the weather was very hot. It was the first time I wore my Topie to keep the sun off my head."

"Most troops did PT each day for half an hour. At night it was so hot I slept on deck, it was too warm below."

"One day we glimpsed a whale passing beside the ship. It was such a lovely sight I often reflect on those trapped and killed by hunters tragically in Alaska."

"During the journey the Commanding Officer gave lectures on what to expect and what things would be like in India."

"The food was not very good, I didn't like the look of the Indian cooks, and they seemed to always wear dirty clothes. We got used to it, but most of the lads thought the same as me."

"On one occasion Rifleman Quirk was being given his meal next second he put the cooks face in it. All the cooks were up in arms over this. For this he was marched to the deck below the following day presented to the Commanding Officer. His sentence was to clean all the toilets on the ship- a huge task for receiving a lousy meal! Looking back the food always seemed half cooked making you wonder why you joined up."

"There was one officer who played football; when it was his turn to inspect the cooks he called them to stand to attention and said they were a bloody disgrace. Nothing much improved even after this."

"Going through the Indian Ocean you see many different kinds of fish. They seemed to follow the ship for the food. Any left-over food was always thrown overboard. They were so plentiful that eventually you forgot they were there."

"First sight of India in the distance there was much excitement as the troops were pleased to get off the ship. We arrived in Bombay, modern day Mumbai on the west coast of India. We were wearing the tropical uniform suitable for the climate in the region. All the troops joined their own regiment. My regiment boarded a train and were transported to a place called Rawalpindi. The journey took four days. Rawalpindi is in modern day Pakistan south of Islamabad and near the notorious North West Frontier."

"The journey was terrible. Imagine the flies and the heat, the smell was bad. God we all said lets go back to Hong Kong. I never liked India; whilst there all I ever saw was dust, with crippled people all around no matter where you looked."

## Chapter 17: Brief Notes of My Experiences in Hong Kong, Shanghai, India and Afghanistan

"The journey from the station to the barracks was four miles. We were marched to the football field to be inspected by our Commanding Officer. After this each company were settled into their respective barrack rooms."

"The barracks had long verandas to each room. In each platoon room there was an Indian person sitting on a platform pushing squares of netting which were used to keep the rooms cool. These were throughout Rawalpindi. When you were sitting cleaning your equipment they would often fall asleep, so you would shout "Panko Walla get weaving", they would reply "Sab, Sab". I don't know what they were paid, sometimes we would give them a few Rupees, but they were always begging. Outside each room were slabs of concrete onto which tap water ran; there were no basins to catch the water so imagine the waste when all the battalion were shaving there. One day a week we would clean away all the stagnant water from around the barracks. This was to avoid the mosquitoes breading, (in seven day cycles)."

"In the barrack rooms above each bed were mosquito nets; these were let down before going to sleep and were very successful at keeping out the insects so you could sleep better."

"We were soon to discover that there were many castes in Indian society. Different people would only do certain jobs. The lowest caste would clean the toilets, another would do the cooking, and so forth, and some would not go near the cook house because of the smell of animal fats."

"Outside the barracks were Tonga, a type of horse driven vehicle. If you wanted to go into Rawalpindi it would cost you four rupees."

"Our days started at 5AM and finished at about 3PM. You needed to be back in barracks because the heat of the sun. On a route march the sun would be scorching down on you by this time in the day. We would put our heads under the taps to try to cool down; our tropical clothes were soaked in sweat. If we were not route marching we would do rifle drill outside barracks. We were issued with five rounds of dummy ammunition, five sections in a clip all marked red. The marking showed they were not live rounds. The sergeant would issue the order to load and fire."

"One occasion B. Company were sat cross legged the other side of the barracks. They were being lectured by a Corporal. It was explained that we were to aim at a target sitting on the veranda opposite and engage five rounds of rapid fire. For some reason I took aim at the head of a person sat on the veranda as instructed but moved my aim to a white marking above his head. God must have been with me that day because upon firing I took a large piece out of the wall above him."

"After the shot was fired I was in terrible shock to think I could have killed someone not of my own fault. The Corporal and I were summoned to see the Captain; he wanted to know what had caused this to happen. We both received severe reprimand and the Corporal almost lost his stripes, but in the end didn't. After this everyone throughout battalion inspected their own ammunition to check they were dummy cartridges. We were soon sent to proper firing ranges each company for a week."

"Not long after arriving in India the War Ministry sent to all the British Army home and abroad an extra six pence a day if they were a first class shot; an extra three pence a day if you passed your second class examinations. I never achieved this, all I managed was a third class pass but this gave me a foot on the ladder. They said to me that if I spent more time on studies and less on sport I would be tops. But all my likes and interests were sporting."

"We were on guard in Rawalpindi for some months at the Ordinance Barracks. These were set fifty yards apart from one another. Throughout the night you could hear the hyenas howling continuously. We were on top of high walls in lookout posts guarding over the valuable stores. Periodically the night officer would come around and you would shout out "who goes there".

*Chapter 17: Brief Notes of My Experiences in Hong Kong,*
*Shanghai, India and Afghanistan*

He would then step forward to be recognised and would ask what we were guarding. Sometimes he would try to creep up on us to catch us off guard; if he managed to do this you were for the high jump. When back at barracks you would be put on charge and in this way many soldiers were caught out."

"One occasion 'D' Company were on duty; one of the lads heard a noise and shouted "who goes there"; receiving no reply he fired one round. Severely startled, the officer who had crept up attempting a surprise shouted "orderly officer". The soldier was quite right to fire. If the officer had successfully surprised him, the soldier would have been on court martial."

"Whilst on guard duty you had to keep your equipment at ready all the time. You would have two hours on and then rest for four hours; but you would have to lie down to rest with your equipment on. When resting you could have tea and small cakes; these were sold outside each barracks by Char Walla. Most soldiers would pay the Char Walla for these at the end of each week when they got paid. Their name was often a source of amusement. They would often come into the barracks in the evenings and keep the tea warm on charcoal."

"Coming back from the firing range one day a friend asked if I could bring him back his tea as he was about to go onto the firing range. Returning with his cheese and bread some buzzards flying above swooped on the food and took the lot. I had not noticed these birds before despite their numbers. We decided in future to cover the food with paper to disguise it as they were very daring birds."

"In 1937 the British Army had been issued with new guns Fargo Slave known as the V.B. Gun. It was very light to carry; its legs would fold up under the mussel then it could be carried over your shoulder. The magazine held 32 rounds and it was very easy to keep clean and could be dismantled quickly."

"I was given the no. 1 in my section and carried the new V.B. Gun. I had to keep it clean and carry it whilst on the range. Because of this I did not have to carry a rifle or bayonet. Instead of this I was issued with a revolver which I would wear whilst on guard duty. It was very good not having to carry a rifle on parade or on route march. I was a good shot with the rifle and with any small gun. I went on a course using various different weapons. After the course I was given a badge which I sewed onto my tunic."

"The battalion went on regular cross country runs in competition with other regiments, 11 in total. Our battalion was often represented by a rifleman named Hamilton. He was built like an ox. He was the best runner I ever witnessed in the army and he won over all the competition. He was given a job looking after the stores for 'B' Company. He had as many shields and cups as there were clothes and equipment in the stores. In the evenings when not looking after the stores he would be running around the football field. Many took bets on how great a distance he would win the next cross country run by."

"There were lots of sporting events. The platoons were made up of 32 men; in all there were over a thousand men. Each person in each platoon had a number; mine was no. 13. Not an unlucky number. My platoon won top prizes in football, hockey, running, shooting and drill. We were very pleased and had our group photographs taken with the senior officers.

Unlike in Hong Kong where the facilities were very good in our spare time we would often go to the cinema here in Rawalpindi, the theatres were very poor with just bare planks to sit on. The films were very old and crackly and were shown three nights a week. It was mainly people from the garrison at the cinema. On one occasion we returned from the cinema to find that one platoon had had all its blankets stolen whilst the soldiers were away. If the rifles had not been locked away they would have been stolen as well. The rifles were protected in each barrack room by two long iron bars with four chained clamps; the orderly of the day was responsible for them and retained the key."

## Chapter 17: Brief Notes of My Experiences in Hong Kong, Shanghai, India and Afghanistan

"One day the sergeant major appointed me and a man called McQuay to look after the officer's rest rooms. They had had their morning tea or drinks and the Indians had brought their food. Our jobs were to light the fires and clean the rooms. The officers came twice a day so after they had gone we helped ourselves to tea," Buck Shee" meaning something for nothing."

"We were on this duty for two months; which was really a good thing as it got you off guard duty. Furthermore if you were on guard duty in the evening you would need to shave for the duty as well as in the morning; so we did not have to do this."

"We all agreed that in the army there was quite a lot of bullshit which ought to have been done away with long ago."

"Time came that we had to learn mountain warfare. We were assembled and our equipment loaded onto mules led by Indians. They would come at about four in the morning. I had to attend to the V.B. Gun and tie it down before the inspection on parade.

One morning, unable to sleep I got up twenty minutes before the bugle sounded, picked up a fire bucket and beat it loudly waking all. They said I was mad."

"Periodically we were sent to a beautiful place for a reprieve for two week breaks.

Bari was on the side of a mountain and we went there by train. It was cool and we all liked it there. It was a break from the plains and the heat. We all relaxed and had no duties of any kind. We could walk around all day or lie in the sun and enjoy ourselves."

"We returned to Rawalpindi after one such break and had a few weeks with the normal drills. There was much work on the rifle range. I enjoyed shooting practice very much. Then packing once more we were to be dispatched to relieve the South Wales Regiment on the boarders of Afghanistan."

"All our private personal effects such as photos were packed into boxes. I had quite a few including trophies from competitions. A list of what was to be taken was posted on the notice boards.

Anything outside these items was stored away. The officer's things were also stored. It took a week to complete packing. Two soldiers were left in charge of our stores whilst we were away. Each company were told what to expect soldiering in that part of the world. I shall not forget my time there!"

## Afghanistan 1939

"The battalion left Rawalpindi and it took us three days to reach Kabul and our encampment. Our march to the camp seemed endless. On arrival the vast camp was a sea of tent. These tent each concealed large holes in the ground. The tribesmen in these parts would fire at the tents so you would need to be below ground like moles to avoid being shot at night."

"The camp was situated in a valley with large mountainous terrain all around. On top of the mountains either side were lookout encampments. The troops in these were changed every three days from each company. Mules would transport the guns and food up the mountains to the lookout camps. The change would be done before 11am. During the change over the mountain artillery would stand by their guns ready to fire all along the tops of the mountains should the tribesmen start to appear and threaten fire."

"On some occasions it seemed like the whole garrison would travel out up to seven miles to take up new positions. They would use soldiers to collect large stones to construct fortified positions. It was like the worst we had heard of the conditions in French Foreign Legion. On these troop movements we would be on the lookout as soon as we left the garrison. The tribesmen would start firing almost immediately. God knows where they were hiding. They could survive for days with no supplies, not moving and then start firing totally undetected. They would sit for days just waiting for the chance to kill. One could never be off guard, a previous company from the Scottish Regiment were ambushed coming back

## Chapter 17: Brief Notes of My Experiences in Hong Kong, Shanghai, India and Afghanistan

from a duty and lost twelve men. My battalion whilst there lost one man and two received arm wounds."

"My task was to be the runner for my captain. All the time on the mountain I would be sent to deliver messages to various platoons of my company."

"On one such reconnaissance we were returning and were almost ambushed in a similar way by the tribesmen surrounding us from above. It was fortunate these tribesmen did not have machine guns or else we would have been wiped out. After this close shave all company in battalion were issued with Picket Screens. A runner would be last man to follow down from the mountain. He would carry a picket screen coloured yellow. He would have to be a very fast runner. When all other troops were clear of the top of the mountain the runner would show the yellow side of the screen as a sign to the artillery to start firing at the mountain tops. This would give cover to the troops on their decent as the tribesmen would need to stay down and avoid our fire. I was chosen to be one such runner because I was fast."

"The Pathans were the tribal people who minded there goats in the mountains. Living nomadic lives in tents, they would always carry rifles."

"Similar procedure guarded the twice weekly convoy of supplies. After guarding the convoys through the narrow valleys on arrival at the garrison great speed was needed to unload and get everyone and everything under the protection of the tents. After fall of darkness the Pathans would start their onslaught of sniping. This would intensify to a peek of constant battering. This would continue throughout the night. The men would need to stay down in the hollows under the tents listening to the bullets pierce through the canvass at regular interval. You just lay low until daylight came. No one got killed or injured but on one night a mule was wounded in its side."

"When daylight broke the mountain artillery would fire for half an hour at the mountain peaks."

151

"When I was not on patrol with the company I would be one of eight men to be positioned in a lookout point. These positions were surrounded by barbed wire with lots of tin cans hung on this to make sure once you were inside you would hear the Pathans trying to get in. Some years earlier the sentries had fallen asleep and the Pathans had killed all eight."

"One night's duty was coming to an end and a soldier heard something on the perimeter of the lookout post. He fired his hand gun repeatedly and I sent a volley out of the V.B. Gun. When we thought all clear we found that a donkey was chewing grass outside the post. Sometimes the Pathans used such things as a distraction. The Pathans would know you were on duty when we had lit our camp fires. The donkey was very lucky this time and despite the 32 rounds of ammo fired in seconds and back up magazine at the ready he survived unhurt."

"We were on patrol one day and came under heavy fire from the mountain tops. The Pathans were nowhere to be seen but the fire continued unabated. Being in charge of the V.B. Gun the corporal ordered me to run a circle to the rear of the firing positions and try to flush them out. There were some large rock outcrops to the top of the ridge so I went above these and fired lots of rounds at the rocks. The men stopped firing and fled; but they disappeared so quickly they were like ghosts. There was no sign of them. We all assumed that they must have tunnels to hide in. But there was no sign of such tunnels."

"The corporal in charge got a medal after this incident. Apparently he was the last person to get to the top. Personally I believe I should have received the medal as I had risked all and had gone in first and cleared the threat. But it is the same throughout the British Army that medals always go to the wrong people. It was certainly true of the last war."

"The journey back to garrison after these events was also momentous. The mountains and valleys are very dusty and barren.

But on occasions the heavens open up and torrential rains fall. On the journey back this happened. Mountain streams turn to fast flowing rivers with boulders being swept along in the mud. There were thunder strikes and heavy rain fall."

"A group of men from my company were the last to cross a raging river. We tried to get across on some large boulders but were swept off into the water. We were carried away down the river but luck would have it that we were thrown up onto a ridge. We were not badly injured although we could have been crushed by the boulders or drowned. My stomach was full of yellow sand and I was covered with blood."

"We were duly rescued and back at garrison were taken to hospital. To purge the sand we were all given castor oil for two days. Eventually when out of hospital we were sent before the commanding officers. He said we had been mad to try to cross the river when it had been so high. We explained that we had not wanted our guns to get into the hands of the tribesmen, especially the V.B. Gun. Coming out from his office we had another lecture from the Regimental Sergeant Major. On reflection he never left the camp the whole time we were in the North West Frontier."

"In modern times one can appreciate the difficulties the Russians encounter in the same terrain. The tribesmen were the same we had encountered but their enemy now the Russians; the armaments of course more advanced in nature but the outcome the same."

"The food we were given whilst in the North West Frontier was terrible. You felt you were going mad with hunger. There was so much bully beef buried in the ground it must have come from the First World War. Along with this all you had were what we called 'dog biscuits'."

"The latrine tents were set apart from the dormitory tents. The routine was that before using the toilet you were to test with your bayonet that no tribesmen were hiding in them this was particularly the case at night. It was not unheard of for a soldier to be attacked at night when going into a latrine tent. Whilst in the tent you were to be attentive so that a tribesman would not try to stab you in vulnerable areas if you became off guard."

"For bathing we washed in streams as you can imagine there were a lot of cold bodies. Whilst washing in the streams we were guarded by other soldiers."

"Our mail whilst based here was dropped by an airplane from above and would land scattered on the ground. We would have to run around to pick it up."

"Soldiers were also made very aware of the dangers of becoming separated from your units or being abducted in some other way. If a soldier was captured by the tribe's people death would be inevitable but instant death would be preferred to what the tribe's women would do to you. It was practice that a soldier's stomach would be opened up and filled with stones then to be left to a slow painful death."

"Eight months later, (should have been six but was extended), we were out on the ranges firing when news came to us that Britain had gone to war against Germany. Germany had invaded Poland on 1st September 1939 and Britain and France were to declare war upon Germany two days later. This news did not seem to affect us very much, probably because Europe was so far away. It was to be much later that the Japanese were to enter the war. As luck would have it this meant we would go to fight in Europe rather than stay in India. If we had stayed in India we would have ended up in Burma. I have to thank God for this because we now know how cruel the Japanese were to the British soldiers captured in the Far East."

"The Battalion stayed on for one more month then news came that we were going back to Rawalpindi. Our place in the North West Frontier was to be taken up by Royal Devon Regiment. We were all pleased to get away from the bloody place. We were marched

*Chapter 17: Brief Notes of My Experiences in Hong Kong, Shanghai, India and Afghanistan*

to one of the outposts this time guarded by another brigade. It was nice not to be guarding others for a change."

"We arrived at the station and were given two hard boiled eggs, some bread and some tea. We all knew what the journey would be like, so slow you could get off and have a Jimmy Riddle and still catch the train. When back in Rawalpindi we got our blankets and supplies from the stores and spent the next day cleaning our equipment and guns."

"My first duty was guarding Gandhi by the side of the railway station.

He was dressed in a scruffy, off white loin cloth like blanket. Sitting cross legged on the porch of the station he looked old and weary. He had two goats by his side. We believe he was going back to Bombay. He looked to us to be an amusing figure. Little did we know the impact he was to have on his country's future and on his part reshaping the new order which our own nation was to be thrown into."

"The battalion was to leave Rawalpindi for a three day journey by train to arrive in Bombay. The train covered the 1450 miles incredibly fast, it was the fastest express train in India. It was great to be leaving that barren violent land. Briefly at Battalion HQ in Bombay disarray was all around. Some remaining members of the regiment were on cooking duty. There was great confusion when the train arrived in Bombay; the previous regiments had left without packing all their stuff. We might as well have been going to Timbuktu for all we knew of our destinations; "walls have ears!" The sergeant majors for various divisions were running around shouting orders, it was like a mad house. We had to pack boxes of kit left over from the previous regiment as well as our own and get everything to the docks to be loaded onto boats."

"We were told to get everything packed for a long sea journey. No one knew our destination apart from senior officers. Some of our regiment were sent on ahead in an advanced party. Tragically

155

we heard that their ship had been sunk by a German submarine in the Indian Ocean. No one was saved."

"It took a long time to pack all the equipment. The heavy equipment was moved to the railway station and guarded. All the metal beds had to be stacked on top of one another in the barracks which meant that the last night in India we had no beds to sleep in. This was to be my last experience of India."

# 18

# The Journey Back to a very different Europe

"A great mixture of troops boarded the troop ship. Talking with them no one knew the destination. We were instructed to look out for submarines and to keep watch for fire. If not on duty you just relaxed. I slept on the floor on the top deck and never got used to sleeping in a hammock."

"We were at sea for three days when a fire broke out. Much metalwork on lower decks and on the bottom of the ship was burnt and mangled. All our battalion kit was lost in the fire. Salt water destroyed much of our personal effects, photos, presents and the like; our battalion 'Walking out dress' was also destroyed. The extent and the cause of the fire were kept from us." We all presumed that we had taken a hit from a submarine.

"To make things worse the defeat of France by Germany brought control of the French Navy into enemy hands. So we were now in conflict with the French fleet."

"The time on the high seas seemed long. Our next port of call was Durban in South Africa."

Docking in Durban we were told not to venture too far because the bugle would call us back to the ship. John Hanna and I would not worry too much about that. We had seen so much violence and suffering and gone through so many tragic experiences we decided to go off on reconnaissance mission.

Durban was a great experience after our time on board ship and prior to that the dreadful events and conditions in India. John and I walked out into the city and looked at the colonial buildings with quintessentially British architecture. There were several lovely hotels to one of which we were attracted. Looking at the prices on the menu board in the entrance porch we were wondering if we could afford a good meal. Next thing we knew the manager came out and approached us. To our surprise he said he would like to buy us a meal. We had a delicious meal served on a table with table cloth and pleasant cutlery and china. It was a wonderful treat; the manager said we were the first white soldiers he had seen since the Great War. We were amazed at the relaxed atmosphere; people dressed in light and attractive colonial dress many were on the dance floor dancing. I was in my army boots; as my walking out dress had been lost in the fire on board ship. Nevertheless we joined in and as always I loved the dancing and always seem to have the desire to get on the dance floor. During the meal we heard the bugle call; but we decided to ignore it.

We had a wonderful time, the first since Hong Kong; we thanked the manager and left. Walking down the street we saw a patrol of Red Caps, (Army Police). They caught up with us and in an irritated way said they had been looking for us. They told us that our ship had already sailed. They took us to the dock for us only to find that forty three of my company had also missed the ship and were assembled on the dock.

We were to have three lovely days to come. We were to be taken on board an Orient Lines vessel to catch up with the troop ship. We were on deck for quite some time before it departed. The passenger ship was luxurious compared to our holed troop ship. We were told by the Captain that because we were at war what we had done could be considered desertion. We could have been shot.

We were all given seven days CB confined to barracks. Being on a passenger vessel this was not the penalty it might have seemed. My job was to clean the Dining Room and to cut the bread. This was certainly OK except it only lasted three days. The liner caught up with the troop ship and we were transferred to it to join the rest of the troops. We were all very sorry it had to end that way.

Inspecting us on deck the Commanding Officer seeing our unshaven state said we were a disgrace to the British Army. To his dismay because the Captain of the Orient Lines vessel had already given us seven days confined to barracks, despite only having been on the liner for three days, he could not give us another penalty and could not charge us again. We were marched away to shave but all forty three of us had to use the same razor. It was like trying to cut grass with a knife.

"I shall never forget my short time in Durban. The people there believe they have the best climate in the World, and I would agree."

"We knew we were journeying around the Cape of Good Hope so our next port to pick up supplies would be Cape Town."

Docking in Cape Town all the soldiers were taken off the ship and marched around the dock whilst fresh provisions were loaded. We had to keep in formation and certainly not allowed to go off to explore the city. This was our punishment for the exploits in Durban. There would be no more stops from here to Scotland. It would be very long journey indeed in excess of thirty days. The journey north through the warm Southern Atlantic into the scorching equatorial waters was increasingly unbearable. The heat of the sun allied to too much time captive below was a strain on most. Then as we progressed into the North Atlantic our passage became increasingly cooler. We would arrive in Scotland towards the end of December of 1939. Now at war with Germany we were at risk of attack by air and sea as had been the experience of our regiment's advance party in the Indian Ocean. The contrast between our journey en-route to

Hong Kong three years earlier and this conveyance back to Europe in turmoil was incredulous.

*On 1st September 1939 Germany invaded Poland under false pretences that Poles had carried out acts of sabotage against German targets near the border. Two days later on 3rd September after a British ultimatum to Germany to cease military operations was ignored, Britain and France followed by the independent dominions of Australia, Canada, New Zealand and South Africa declared war on Germany. This had little military support for Poland. The Western Allies also began a naval blockade of Germany, which aimed to damage the country's economy and war effort; but Germany had responded by ordering U-Boat warfare against Allied merchant and warships which escalated into the Battle of the Atlantic.*

*On 17th September the Soviets had signed a cease-fire with Japan and invaded Poland. By 27th September the Polish army was defeated and Warsaw surrendered; Poland was divided between Germany and Soviet Union. On 6th October Hitler made peace overtures to Britain and France which Chamberlain rejected on 12th October saying "Past experience has shown that no reliance can be placed upon the promises of the present German Government". Hitler now ordered an immediate offensive against France but bad weather postponed this until spring 1940.*

The Soviet Union forced the Baltic countries to allow Soviet troops to be stationed in their countries in a "mutual assistance" pact and when Finland refused the Soviets invaded in November 1940.

Our brief memories of beautiful Durban faded as the troop ship manoeuvred into the grey waters of the Glasgow docks. It was to be late on this wintery day that we disembarked along the jetty onto the concrete mooring. Two or more hours lined up in

## Chapter 18: The Journey Back to a very different Europe

the penetrating sleet led us into a demoralised dejected state. When nightfall came there began movement from the front ranks.

A short march away we boarded a long train designated for troop carrying. Into each six seat compartment we crowded in with all our paraphernalia taking up much space. The journey from Glasgow through the night to Oxford seemed interminable. There were frequent stops for no apparent reason lasting for many minutes. Occasionally other transport would pass filled with troops on other movements. We passed endless darkened stations empty of people. All the time the wind whistled fiercely by and drizzle covered the steamed up windows. In the compartments the heat was quite unpleasant. We all felt short of food and water. It was a huge relief when the train slowed in Oxford Station.

Assembled in front of the station now on a bright day with clear sky out of the cramped train we breathed easily and began to feel pleased to be back in 'Blighty'. We would be marched three miles to a small village on the fringes of the suburbs of Oxford. On arrival there we were promptly dismissed having been given advice as to our billeting. Then we made haste to the huge mess tent to get relief and a well-earned breakfast with much tea.

*An Irish Boy*

# 19

# Back in 'Blighty'

Our encampment in Oxford was entirely under canvas. We were to remain billeted in tents the whole time we were in Oxford.

We were to find out that many things were changing. We had always believed the British Army was years behind the times. We were still using the same rifles as in the Great War. We had been given lectures on German Rearmament for years previously. The uniforms we arrived in looked terrible especially when we saw the new battle dress the soldiers in the UK were already issued with.

The old style drill formation of four deep was changed to three deep. This is still the formation today. Groups of soldiers were taken to learn to drive the three ton trucks that were to service the army. I personally had to learn to use the Anti-Tank Gun. We had to carry this on route march. The gun was four feet long and I don't think it would have been very good. I never had the situation to fire it at a tank, but trained with it on the firing range, firing at a target. The battalion seemed to embrace all the new machinery well. Soon we had all our own Lorries and motor bikes.

My friend John went in R.A.M.C. (Royal Army Medical Core). He was there for quite a while before re-joining battalion.

It was a few weeks before any of us were allowed out of the camp. Obviously the impetus was on getting the outdated army ready for a war which had already begun. Following intensive training with the new equipment and procedures we were sent to Newbury where we would be based for some time.

## Newbury

"The food was much better in Newbury. There were lots of dances. We were issued with gas masks which had to be worn all the time whilst on duty. When off to dances we were supposed to take the gas masks along with us; but I took my dancing shoes along in the box instead."

"Time came for us to have our first leave. With bad luck I was in the second batch which was a shame because I was only given four days. I was to go back to Ireland for the leave which meant only two day in Ireland. Myself and a few other lads got our doctors to give us doctors reports which were sent back to our Commanding Officer in our battalion. The doctor's report gave me four extra days leave. On arrival back in Newbury I was put in the Guard Room then sent in front of the Commanding Officer. I was accused of being absent without leave. I explained that my doctor had sent a doctor's note giving me more leave. He asked the R.S.M. to get the note. When he saw it the charge was dropped. Others who had been on leave with me but had not sent doctors notes were given fourteen days confined to barracks."

"The barracks at Newbury were in converted old race horse stables. The stables were near the race course. It was not long before I saw my first flat course race horse. He was in stables nearby our barracks. His name was Gainsborough and the groom who was walking him said he was twenty one years old. His name was above the door to his stable. Being an old horse the groom said his legs and feet were quite sore so he made sure he had plenty of straw for more comfort. He looked a very proud horse; I gave him a pat on the head which he seemed to enjoy."

"It was at Newbury that I went on a course and learnt to ride motor bikes along with four others from my company. It was great getting away from the same routine of the army. The course lasted two weeks."

"Unlike previous manoeuvres we were transported to and fro by lorries instead of marching. These exercises tended to last two weeks."

"On return journey from one such manoeuvre a motor bike rider hit a pot hole, was thrown off his bike and killed instantly."

"Returning from a cross country run one evening I was told to report to the Commanding Officer. I wondered what I had done wrong. Reporting to R.S.M. he said "Rifleman 7012768 you will be the Batman to Captain McBride". He was new to the company. I said that I did not know what was involved and did not think I could do the job. His reply was to say- "stop talking and report to the officer." Leaving the office I thought why should I be given a job I knew nothing about. It was typical of the army; you had to do what you were told. I went to see some men who were Batmen for other officers and they filled me in on some of the things that might be expected of me."

"Reporting to Captain McBride he seemed a very amiable man not as old as some of his peers. He said he had asked the RSM to recommend someone who would be reliable, I had been recommended and he seemed pleased with my attitude. I said I had never looked after an officer before."

"One of my first duties was to serve at the officer's dinner table. This I didn't like, it was like being in prison. This happened twice a week. After the meal one had to clear the table and wash crockery and glasses "

"I took his washing to a nearby house to be cleaned and got it back a few days later. I would pay for this and he would reimburse me once a month. For looking after the Captain I received ten shillings a week. This enabled me to start saving up some money."

"Once he asked me to go to the shop to get some crumpets for tea. I looked in the window but didn't know what crumpets were

165

so went back and said they were all gone. He said he had seen a big plate in the shop but had to go without them that time."

"He used to ride a motorbike out on manoeuvres coming back he preferred to use the jeep; finding out that I rode motor bikes he would get me to ride it back for him."

"He would send me to deliver maps to other officers in other battalions when out on manoeuvres."

"Sadly he was posted to a different part of the country and he could not take me."

"After he left it was back to routine of drilling and saluting. We used to make fun of this by saluting the dustbins and the toilets. If you were caught taking the Mickey you were sent around the parade ground saluting the billet."

## Salisbury Plains Garrison

"We were not at Newbury long before being moved to the Head Quarters of British Army at Salisbury Plains. On arrival there we were given seven days leave. I spent most of this time in Newry and a couple of days at Warren Point. All the evenings were spent going to dances."

"We were all awarded the North West Service Medal for our period in India and the North West Frontier. I have never rated medals highly; producing them on parade several times a year. They would never make up for a death, lost limbs or other injuries. It would be better to receive more by way of monetary payment."

"In the garrison on Salisbury Plains the huts were wooden and old. We would huddle around a small round fire in the middle of each hut burning all the cardboard and wood we could find to try to keep warm. Outside each hut we had to dig long trenches into which we had to jump during air raid by Germans fighter planes to try to avoid their machine gun fire. Some nights coming back from the NAFFI some soldiers ended up falling into these."

## Chapter 19: Back in 'Blighty'

"In a football match against D. Company we beat them four/one, I didn't score that time. There were lots of matches each week with many other companies as well. There was also basketball, hockey and cross country; I enjoyed it all."

"We were told all of us were to join the Airborne Gliders. We were issued with red berets which were quite smart but had the habit of falling off your head when you were running. We went to see the small gliders, called Hospers, at Netheraven. These were mainly made of three ply wood. Within a couple of weeks most members of battalion had experienced their first flight."

"These Hospers were quite small holding six men plus the pilot. They were towed by large planes to get them airborne. They would fly around the airfield going up and down on their manoeuvres. This often made the men sick. There were lots of planes taking off and landing all the time."

"One such flight I was to ride in the back of the Wellington Bomber and tell the pilot when the glider was airborne. At the back of the bomber there were twin guns used to shoot at enemy fighter planes. They had neat thumb pieces which I felt I wanted to hold and pretend that I was in the sky being challenged by fighter pilots, rather than in an airplane towing a glider. When I said to the pilot the glider is dispatched he said to me "the bloody thing was airborne twenty minutes ago". I had been so interested pretending to play with the twin guns that I had been oblivious to the pilot releasing the glider."

"The pilot was a good sort and he said to come up to the cockpit and sit in the front for the flight. We flew for two hours and must have covered many miles. We flew over Swindon Station and he said that he would love to drop a string of bombs on it. He said when he got back he was sure to be told off for spending so much time in the air. I never saw him again each of the many times I went back to the aerodrome. I always reflect on those two hours in the cockpit looking down at the countryside below oblivious to the war going on."

"Our course lasted three weeks and we got lots of time flying; the pilots became well practiced. The one thing we didn't like was the landings; we never knew whether we would get down in one piece."

"My worst experience in the glider happened when a group of six of us were ordered to go to Belfast for the weekend on a trial flight. We left Netheraven Airdrome and the pilot towed us in a good flight position and flew steadily for half an hour. But gradually visibility diminished and the flight became more erratic. Suddenly he announced that he would have to unhook the glider because his visibility in the fog was too bad and he could not see a bloody thing. He said that we would be over the sea in ten minutes and it was the last chance to hook off."

"We were well into Wales by this time and now unhooked the glider pilot was trying to find a safe place to land. He told us to get down as low as we could. The glider pilot was coping very well despite the poor visibility."

"Now a severe thunderstorm began. The pilot was trying to aim for some fields avoiding some patches of woodland. There was also a large river he needed to come in short of. He did a mighty good job bringing the glider down and to a stop. Nevertheless it was badly damaged with a broken wing and many other breaks. When the glider came to a stop it was on the banks of the river but not in the water. The river was to the tops of its banks and flowing fast. If we had landed in the water we would have been swept away. We didn't know where we were or whether to send for the police or the army. We walked a long way and when they found us we were like drowned rats. One man received injuries to his leg and got cuts on his arms. But the rest of us escaped relatively unscathed. We eventually were met by civilian police and taken to the nearest police station and given hot tea. The following day lorries came to collect us to take us back to Salisbury Barracks."

"This apparently had been the first time the gliders had attempted to fly over the sea carrying men. Previously the weight had been made up with sand on these experimental flights. One can say that we were the first live guinea pigs for these experimental gliders.

It was not long after these early gliders that bigger, stronger gliders were produced which could carry jeeps, big guns and also the light personal carriers along with soldiers."

"Coming back one afternoon following another route march, the Sergeant Major told me I was to be Batman once again. This time I was pleased to be given the job of looking after this officer. It got me out of guard duty and had other benefits. This officer whose name slips my mind was connected with the Foreign Office. After two weeks I had to join him to assist him whilst he was on a course. It appeared to involve various languages which I knew he was able to speak several. During my time in the army you got to know officers who could speak several languages or have many and varied specialities."

"My duties for him were similar to those for the previous officer. I had to organise collection and cleaning of his clothes. I had to serve at meal times mainly in the evening. These mess duties I got used to and had the great advantage that after you were finished the rest of the evening was yours. If there was a dance locally I would be there. I did this job for three months and whilst doing so gained extra money."

"Coming back from a route march I looked at the Company Notice Board and read a notice recruiting men to join the Paratroop Regiment. I went to the Company Sergeant Major who told me to come to his office the following morning. Next morning attending his office he told me I was too valuable to go off to join the Paratroops. He wanted me to stay with the company."

"The Battalion had a football match with the Oxford and Buckingham Regiment, we beat them four/two; I got one of the goals."

"I followed boxing all my time. I went to garrison boxing match regularly. One match Battalion was fighting Oxford and Buckingham Regiments. Rules in the army were different from Civilian Street. The officers stood outside the ring doing there marking and shouting stop red you are holding and stop green you are holding. There were fights every week.

The best fighters of each weight were matched from each regiment. Our battalion had a prise fighter in the feather weight class. He never lost a single fight and won five cups and a shield, as well as a belt for the best boxer."

"After two more weeks the notice for recruitment into the Paratroops appeared once more, and reared its head. We all wondered why it had come back so soon. Perhaps the top brass had wondered why no one from The Royal Ulster Rifles had joined the Paratroops.

When I went to see the Captain of the Company for the second time he said that he was sorry that I wanted to leave but would not stand in my way leaving the company. The Captain had been with the company the whole time I had been with C. Company. So the bonds were strong."

"I stayed with the Company for one more week before leaving for the next phase in my army carrier. During that week I kept wondering whether I was doing the right thing moving to the Paratroops and leaving all my friends, John Hanna amongst them, behind."

**End of Part One**

*An Irish Boy*

*Mourne Mountain Pastures*

An Irish Boy

Carlingford Lough

Carlingford Lough and Newry River
(Mountains of Mourne on left and Cooley Mountains on right)

*An Irish Boy*

Above: Headmaster's Home, Omeath

Inset: Old School House today

Left: Omeath Old Railway Station

Omeath Jetty for boats to Warren Point

*An Irish Boy*

*John Byrne aged 23*

*Army Book (note date of birth 25/13/17!)*

# *An Irish Boy*
Part 2

*Chapter 1: Off To Join The Paratroop Regiment*

# 1

# Off To Join The Paratroop Regiment

*Following Winston Churchill's call to establish a corps of parachute troops on 22$^{nd}$ June 1940, parachute training commenced at RAF Ringway near Manchester. Number 2 Commando, the fledgling parachute unit was posted to Knutsford in Cheshire. On August 1941 the decision was made to form the 1$^{st}$ Parachute Brigade under Brigadier Richard Gale. This was to be located at Hardwick Camp near Chesterfield in Derbyshire. Hardwick Hall became the nucleus for parachute training and physical selection for airborne forces.*

*The magnificent house and grounds in 1941 were part of the Duke of Devonshire Chatsworth Estate. Army command leased 53 acres to establish a camp of red brick huts with training areas. The camp was located south west of the Hall with a Parachute Jump Tower on periphery. Assault courses and trapeze in-flight swing training structures were also next to the camp. When per-jump training was successfully completed, the recruits that passed out were required to speed march approximately 50 miles to join the parachute course at RAF Ringway. They further marched back to Ringway from the Tatton Park drop zone each time they completed a training descent.*

A tethered barrage balloon was installed at Hardwick on 1st November 1941 to provide refresher training for qualified parachutists and supplement descents made from the Jumping Tower.

Winston Churchill had been impressed by the success of German airborne operations during the Battle of France; he directed the War Office to investigate the possibility of creating a corps of 5,000 parachute troops. On 22 June 1940 No. 2 Commando was redeployed to parachute duties and on 21st November re-designated the 11th Special Air Service Battalion, (later the 1st Parachute Battalion), with both a parachute and glider wing, the men who took part in the first British airborne operation, Operation Colossus, on 10th February 1941. The success of the raid prompted The War Office to expand the airborne forces, setting up the Airborne Forces Depot and Battle School in Derbyshire in April 1942, and creating the Parachute Regiment as well as converting several infantry battalions into airborne battalions in August 1942. This resulted in the formation on the 1st Airborne Division with 1st Parachute Brigade and 1st Airlanding Brigade. Its commander Major-General Frederick Arthur Montague (Boy Browning) expressed his opinion that the fledgling force must not be sacrificed in "penny packets" and urged the formation of further brigades.

All the parachute forces had to undergo a twelve-day parachute training course at No. 1 Parachute Training School, RAF Ringway. Initial parachute jumps were from a converted barrage balloon and finished with five jumps from an aircraft. Anyone failing to complete a descent was returned to his old unit. Those who successfully completed the parachute course were presented with their maroon beret and parachute wings.

Airborne soldiers were expected to fight against superior numbers of the enemy armed with heavy weapons, including artillery and tanks. Training was as a result designed to encourage a spirit of self-discipline, self-reliance and aggressiveness. Emphasis

*Chapter 1: Off To Join The Paratroop Regiment*

*was given to physical fitness, marksmanship and fieldcraft. A large part of the training regime consisted of assault courses and route marching while military exercises included capturing and holding airborne bridgeheads, roads or rail bridges and coastal fortifications. At the end of most exercises the battalions would march back to their barracks. An ability to cover long distances at speed was also expected: airborne platoons were required to cover a distance of 50 miles (80 km) in twenty-four hours, and battalions 32 miles (51 km). This ability was demonstrated in April 1945 when 3rd Parachute Brigade advanced 15 miles (24 km) in twenty-four hours, which included eighteen hours of close-quarters fighting.*

"When I went to Battalion head Office I found there were six others from my company going to join the Paratroops Regiment. I was very pleased to find I was not the only one leaving to join the Paras. We were taken by lorry to the railway station. Our journey took us to Chesterfield with its church with the crooked spire. Getting on the train we realised there were many other soldiers embarking who were also going to join the Paras. We all got chatting. We arrived at our billet at Chesterfield, got some food and then were told our training would start tomorrow morning."

"Next morning we were lined up for breakfast and told that from now on everything we did from this time would be at the double. We would have to run to the Dining Room for all our meals. The first day was spent on ordinary army exercises running and jumping. There were about 1000 soldiers starting on the same course as myself. The first day went quite quickly and we all remarked how our legs and arms were quite sore and had taken a pounding. After that day our training was done either in the gymnasium or in one of the big hangers. The only part we did not like was falling on the coyer mats and landing on our bare shoulders. Swinging to and fro when they said jump you had to be ready to fall on the mat. All this done in our PE kit, just shorts and boots. This lasted three weeks."

"After the first week we were taken to the parachute. It was always hanging open ready for the first jump. The fall was 85 feet. When the chute was about 14 feet from the mat they would call out 'jump'. Those who jumped were ok; those who didn't knew all about it."

"In my second week we were told that it would be our first jump from balloon. When it came to my turn there were four of us together. We watched those before us. They were instructed by loud speaker, being told to keep their legs together and other commands, and whatever else they were doing wrong. My jump would be at 600 feet. When we approached 200 feet the four of us looked at each other and thought God what have we let ourselves in for. We were all very frightened but the instructors said there was nothing to it. When we were almost at drop height he said who would go first. I was number three. We were told to look up as we went through the hole or else we would get a bloody face. I did not know what to expect; my first shock when I went through the hole was my shoulders getting such a pull from my chute, this is known as a dead drop. When my parachute opened I felt just like a bird in the sky. I thought it was lovely watching everything around me. I could have stayed like that all day. When I landed and rolled to the ground I looked around and saw a soldier next to me lying on the ground his face covered in blood. We were told he had not looked up and had caught his nose."

"The next morning we went for our next jump. At least we knew what to expect. The soldier who had blood all over his face did not come with us."

"The next decent was much the same. After the initial apprehension going through the hole in the base of the balloon's basket, and after reassurance that you had not caught your nose on the edge of it, the euphoria of birdlike flight and the vast expanse of the sky around reminded me of the one occasion in the cockpit of the plane my pilot friend had allowed me during my time in the Gliders."

"We all said how our shoulders and arm pits felt sore. After the jump we were taken back to Company to have dinner. Those who were not on guard duty had the rest of the day off. I was not so lucky and was on guard duty. There were soldiers from other units on guard as well; when we were told to fall in it was just like Dads' Army we all did it in different ways. We must have been quite a sight. The sergeant really went off his rocker. In the end he told us 'shoulder arms', to do it in the way all battalion artillery units should do it."

"After the third week I had done four jumps. For this you get the 'Balloon Badge'. The day after being given the badge we were marched out and inspected. Those who had received the badge would leave that afternoon for Salisbury Plain to join the 1st Paras, (The 1st Parachute Brigade). There were a few who did not receive the badge including the soldier whose face had been covered in blood. These men were sent back to battalion. As we got ready to leave Chesterfield a new troop arrived to start the course. Once again I was on board a train about to experience a new type of soldiering. Within the Paras I would find many people who were ok but others I felt were not so nice."

"Our subsequent jumps were to be by plane, some five in all; we were route marched to the flight, but the bit I liked was the return by lorry, especially good if you had blisters on your feet."

"Coming back off cross country, after my shower I was told by the sergeant to get my kit packed then go to the Cook House and get my tea, then report to the Guard Room. I wondered what was going on. At the Guards Room I was told by the Sergeant Major that I would be looking after a Major who was going to Brigade HQ quite a way from the Salisbury garrison. When I met the Major, he said he had been told I was a good man to assist him as his Batman. He and I were going to get along really well."

"When we arrived at Brigade Head Quarters, I collected his things, made up his bed. He was in another room with two other officers. They were billeted in a large country house in a very quiet location. It housed Majors and two Captains. He was given a motor bike. When he found I could ride he seemed pleased; when out on duties he preferred to travel by jeep; I would return riding his bike just like my earlier appointment at Newbury to Captain McBride. I always felt it was my lucky break going to Brigade HQ."

"We did PE in the mornings; I didn't have to do any guard duty as this was done by Military Police. We played a lot of basket ball in the evenings against the officers. We all enjoyed this. Most of the soldiers and officers there had jumped, (done their drops). It was with the officer I got to see The Glen Miller Band. I felt he had the best band in the world; it was tragic when he died."

"The Brigade HQ next went to Harpenden. The town was quite nice; for me it had the best dance hall I had ever been in. All the best bands would be playing every Saturday night. I always got my late pass signed by the Major. Every night I went to the dance hall I danced with the same girl. She was very light on her feet. I really enjoyed those dances."

"The Major was to be away for a few days. He was a most amiable man and had said I could have the use of his motorbike whilst he was away. The Major regularly allowed me to use his bike. One evening I was out on the bike and decided to pass where the battalion were doing their training. Going through the camp I was stopped by a sergeant major who was the biggest bastard I had ever come across. He wanted to know why I was not wearing a helmet while on the bike. I told him that I was not with the battalion anymore and that the Major had sent me out to give the bike a spin to see how the new chain would behave. This sergeant major had arrived at the company I had been in just as I'd left. I was so pleased to get out in time. When in the dance hall he would not dance; he would observe all; if he spotted you with a top button undone you would be on charge. The Military Police would be standing just inside the doors; they would like to come in from the cold. If you saw him you would make sure your tunic was done up. The girl I was dancing with and all the other people in the hall thought he was terrible. We later heard that he had died in France. It was rumoured that some boys from his own company had got him. Nobody had a good word to say about him."

"To get my 'Wings' I had to complete a number of drops from a plane. The experience was such that no sooner was I on the plane then the green light came on and it was my turn to drop; next before realising it the parachute opened. I landed, had some tea, and had my second drop. I was pleased to get two of the drops over in one day. I felt very pleased with it all. Next we were taken to a very large hall where there were girls packing the parachutes. Here we were shown how to pack the parachutes. There were long tables with fans blowing along to straighten out all the creases. All the rigging lines were neatly packed. Over each table was a sign saying for each parachute depends one life be sure you do it OK."

"Within a few days I'd done the last drops and I felt I'd achieved something in my life. A couple of weeks later I received my 'Wings' to put on my tunic. I was soon to be on the move again. This time to Hereford; I was sorry to leave Harpenden; probably because of the dances and football there."

*An Irish Boy*

# 2

# Arrival in Hereford and Discovering My Beloved Grace, Winter 1942

The major had been driven by jeep so I was to ride his motorbike. A much preferred option to the crowded troop trains of other transfers. The roads had been busy with small convoys of dark green and brown canvass clad military vehicles often at a standstill. There were many platoons of troops marching on manoeuvre which we passed by giving good clearance. I felt great empathy with the troops marching on foot. Many supply vehicles were en route in various directions laden with all manner of goods. The late winter morning was cold but dry, but the skies were grey and heavy with the threat of a downpour. As we proceeded northwards towards the industrial Midlands soot seemed to cling to the air. From Harpenden through larger towns and through outskirts of Coventry there was massive upheaval. The roads though large were virtually clogged with traffic, people, horse riders and horse driven carts and even livestock.

Leaving these grey conurbations behind and passing nearby Stratford-upon-Avon our convoy was entering the Cotswolds. It was like a breath of fresh air leaving the smoke blackened Victorian power houses and experiencing vast open spaces with rolling hills and narrow roads lined with dry stone walling. The brows of the hills had pelmets of leafless trees. Tiny hamlets of cream coloured stoned cottages and barns dotted the valleys. Our passage was much swifter despite encountering the odd lorry or troops on manoeuvre. We could see that good natured farmers had held their sheep or cows back from the road not to deter our passage.

The architecture was changing rapidly with cottages dotted along the lanes of dark red brick many with tiled rooves and also many heavily timbered black and white cottages with steeply sloping thatch rooves. Travelling through the grand city of Worcester, with its prominent and very square cathedral and red brick merchants houses, we crossed the River Severn on the banks of which the city stood. We emerged into the soft undulating countryside now more wooded and agriculturally varied with many orchards and climbing frames.

Westward bound our narrow road weaved its way around the Malvern Hills over and into Herefordshire. Despite it being early evening and late winter the fading dusk gave out a clear and mellow white light over the vista free of the earlier mist and damp. A long distance ahead was visible the cathedral tower crowning a darkened mound amid a large flat valley circled by distant hills. The road narrowed further and the bends accentuated leading down into Ledbury. Turning right into the main street with large black and white buildings all around we passed The Feathers Hotel. Looking up at its lofty black and white façade with its leadlight windows emanating a golden glow from within I thought what a comforting and endearing place we were entering; somehow detached from the war raging around. Ahead a central market building on stilts perched adjacent to the market square with traders packing away their wares. We passed straight through the many carts, people and horses and headed out of the town past a long and very high railway viaduct. The road ran alongside this red brick structure for

## Chapter 2: Arrival in Hereford and Discovering My Beloved Grace, Winter 1942

a mile then plunged into tall hedgerow and became more and more meandering. Past several pretty black and white villages which straddled the road we past many hop yards with their bare wooden forms awaiting springs new growth.

It was now almost dark and at the brow of a long hill we sighted the silhouette of The City of Hereford in the middle of a marshy valley on a slight promontory. The fields surrounding the city seemed to be partly submerged under water with the thin straight line of the road making a bridge with which to approach. A few lights that had dared the blackout twinkled from high above as we drove towards the rise of Tupsley Pitch and then into the city. We passed through 'High Town' almost in darkness. This wide central market place had a wall of tall buildings surrounding it but in the blackness of night little was visible.

The rest of our short convoy went ahead to our base on a large camp to the north of the city, Credenhill. This was to be our billet, but the Major and I detached and had a brief respite from the journey staying a while in the city. Engaging in a drink at one of the friendly looking establishments of which there were quite a number this was a welcome end to the day's rigours. Our journey had been some seven to eight hours. There was an Odeon Cinema on a back thoroughfare. I noticed that a dance was advertised to be held there that very night.

The Major was driven onto the camp and I followed behind on his motorbike. In due course formalities were completed and we took procession of our respective billets. I performed all the required chores and finally when all was in order I obtained a pass courtesy of the Major and returned to the city and then to the Odeon.

I had decided to go to the dance that night despite being extremely fatigued from the journey. It was late when I got there so even though I stayed an hour and a half it was very late and extremely dark. With no lights on outside the building I had to walk along some strange alleyways, over a wide bridge then up a long hill probably about two miles back to the camp. I made my way grasping at foliage and stones along the walls to where I thought my billet was. I realised that I had lost my bearings so sat down on the side of the road for a while to have a rest. Eventually I found my way along a very narrow road to the billet. I was glad to get there after being out so late the first night in Hereford; it had been my own fault.

The Major I was looking after was to go to Scotland on a course for two weeks or so. I asked him what things needed packing for his kit and they were driven to the railway station. Whilst he was away I had quite a good time doing duties in the officers' mess. When not on duty my time was free to do what I wanted, I had plenty of time to enjoy myself. The camp at Credenhill was extremely large even encompassing railway and rail sidings. It covered they reckoned about 250 acres and included supplies and ordinance facilities and a 112 bed hospital. The mess facilities were also extremely good. I was privileged to be based there and to be the batman for the Major with all the benefits that gave.

During those two weeks the Major was to be away on his course I would often go out running on my own. The countryside surrounding the city was beautiful and unspoilt. The narrow and undulating back lanes were largely free of traffic; they were bordered by high very dense hedgerow which cocooned you whilst running along them. The weather was improving as spring drew near. The evenings also drew out giving longer days with quite mild weather for the time of year. The countryside was showing signs of coming to life. The intensity of the green reminded me of the boarder country in Ireland of my youth.

One Sunday I was on a run through a small village to the east of the city, the other side of the marshes called Lugwardine. It was four miles or so from Credenhill. Running along a narrow lane leading out of the village I rounded a bend with a steep bank

## Chapter 2: Arrival in Hereford and Discovering My Beloved Grace, Winter 1942

covered with early spring wild flowers; I saw a very pretty young girl sitting on a five bar gate by the side of the lane leading into a large field. She had long fair wavy hair, and a lovely complexion; she was reading a book about film stars.

I stopped and said "what is the time"; she told me. I saw the book she was reading was about films, so we just kept talking. Eventually I said to her "would you like to come to the pictures?" I said I would be outside the cinema waiting to see if she would come along. I thought what a lovely smile she gave me on our first meeting. I held her gently by the arm and I walked with her towards her home as far as the village post office. She lived a little further along the lane in an old house with central porch and windows either side. The narrow lane ran around a wide corner of its pretty garden. It was called 'Old Manor House'. Our eyes meet for a fleeting glance then I leave after setting eyes on Grace for the first time at Lugwardine at 12pm; by the time I got home it was 13.50- I felt I was yours.

So we said we would see one another at the dance on Saturday night. I was looking forward to the dance night; it could not come quickly enough for me. I was waiting outside the dance hall in my 'walking out' uniform. She came along with her mother and passed by me not recognising me. I heard her mother say to her "I thought you were meeting someone at the dance". She said he was not there. Then she turned around and I waved and our eyes met. I could tell she was impressed by how smartly dressed I was.

We were soon meeting regularly. We would go to the pictures twice in the afternoon then go on to the dance on the Saturday night. After taking her back home after the dance she would lend me her bicycle to go back to the camp. That was very nice of her. Some times we would meet in her lunch break. One lunch she brought her sister Iris; a very difficult girl to understand; we would have fish and chips together. They both worked in the bottling plant at Bulmer's Cider. Grace was soon recruited to the war effort in the Munitions Works to do the difficult and important job of inspecting ammunition on the production line. Very straining on her eyes and nothing could be allowed to be wrong or else there might be fatalities.

So going to Hereford was the best of places for me as I had met my future wife Grace. I can thank her for all the lovely ways she showed me about family life; her father and mother were very warm people; I thought the World of them. Our bond was growing very strong. We seemed to like the same things. In that brief period in our young lives we spent every hour possible together.

I was invited to dinner at The Old Manor House and Grace introduced me to all the family. While I was in Hereford we had a fantastic time together. Grace would come to meet me at the camp on her bike. On one occasion her chain broke so I paid for the repair, she was very pleased and had such a beautiful smile. All my mates on the base said that I would marry Grace. I told her all about myself so everything was above board; about my father, mother and sister and some of the tragedies of my childhood and then the escape to Warren Point from Omeath, then the years in the Far East and India and Afghanistan. She knew that life had not been kind to me. We felt that our feelings for each other more than made up for trauma of the past. All her family and all my mates at Credenhill knew we were very much in love. They said we made a lovely couple.

Coming back from training in the Black Mountains we were told that we were to leave Hereford and go to Carmarthen in Wales. I was very sad to leave Hereford and the wonderful girl I had just met and got on so well with. It was tragic also that the Major I had been looking after who had given me so many opportunities and privilege never returned from his two week course in Scotland.

We arrived in the new camp and were billeted in tents. I and another soldier were given all the menial jobs especially around the cook house. Twice a week we had to pump out the cess pit that was filled with the waste water from the cook house. The water was pumped onto the grass and smelled very bad. We were nicknamed 'The Dirty Rats'.

I was always waiting for the Post Corporal in anticipation of getting a letter from Grace. When my first letter from her arrived I read it over and over. That was the first letter I had ever received in my life. I was thrilled.

I had been in the camp for three weeks before receiving leave. I immediately returned to Hereford to meet Grace and to get married. The year was 1942 in the month of September.

Being a Catholic we first approached the Catholic priest to marry us. He insisted that Grace should change religion and take tuition in all the necessary teachings of the Catholic Faith. We had very little time as my leave was short. We next approached the local Church of England Vicar of the Village of Lugwardine. Similarly there were religious issues and also the case of bands being read for three weeks. So we opted for a simple marriage at the Registry Office in the City Hereford.

We decided to go to Blackpool for our honeymoon. We had a good time dancing at the Tower Ballroom, going to shows and staying at a good guest house. Bearing in mind food was rationed it was extremely good.

My leave finished I returned to Wales leaving my beloved wife with her family at The Old Manor House.

Returning to the pumping duties outside the Cook House I was saddened to hear the soldier I worked with had lost his fiancée. She had died in a car accident just prior to them getting married on his next leave.

The cook at the Officers Mess was given a 36 hour pass to return home to visit a sick relative. The other batmen asked me if I could be cook whilst he was away. I agreed and executed the breakfast. I managed to burn the porridge which most of the officers left and could not eat so much was thrown away. I cooked for them boiled eggs which were ok. Surprisingly not many returned to the mess for their evening meal. I was very pleased about this. They probably didn't want more burnt offerings.

More parachute drops followed and the troop numbers grew rapidly. It was apparent that preparations were afoot for an ensuing battle.

I was part of the 6th Airborne Division; I had previously been in the 6th Airborne Gliders. I was never to see them again. Luck was on my side; most of my fellow soldiers were sent to join 1st Airborne Division, I was sent to Divisional HQ. This is where all the top brass are. I knew of most of the Major Generals and ADCs. I was to be in 1st Parachute Battalion. 1st Airborne Division incorporated the 1st, 2nd and 3rd Parachute Brigades.

Coming back from manoeuvres one night we were told we had been given 36 hours leave. We were all delighted receiving leave; quickly had tea then left. We all knew that the leave meant we were about to be sent on an expedition.

*Chapter 3: North Africa*

# 3

# North Africa

It was now November 1942. The Italians before the war had controlled Libya; after hostilities broke out in 1940 they invaded Egypt which was defended by many British forces. Following numerous skirmishes many Italian prisoners were taken, (130,000). In response Germany sent the 'Africa Korps' led by General Erwin Rommel. For two years a brutal series of battles had pushed back and forth across Libya and Egypt. Eventually General Bernard Montgomery's British Eighth Army broke out and drove the Axis forces all the way from Egypt to Tunisia. In November 1942 Operation Torch brought in thousands of British and American forces. They landed across western North Africa and joined the attack, eventually helping force the surrender of all remaining Axis troops in Tunisia in May 1943 ending the campaign for North Africa.

In November 1942, the brigade now commanded by Brigadier Edwin Flavell, was detached from 1st Airborne Division, to take part in Operation Torch, the Allied landings in French North Africa. On the 11th November the first major British parachute landing was made by the 3rd Parachute Battalion, which without its 'A' company, flew from England via Gibraltar in a fleet of American piloted Douglas Dakotas. Their objective, the airfield at Bone, turned out to be deserted and was secured with no opposition. No.

6 Commando and a flight of RAF Spitfires reinforced the battalion later the same day. The following day the rest of the brigade who had travelled by sea arrived at Algiers. During the next airborne mission on 16th November, the 1st Parachute Battalion secured an important road junction near Souk el Arba; 90 miles (140 km) west of Tunis then the next day ambushed a German convoy and were involved in several small battles. The Commanding Officer (CO) Lieutenant Colonel James Hill was wounded attacking an Italian position and replaced by his second-in-command, Alastair Pearson.

On 29th November the 2nd Parachute Battalion, now commanded by John Frost, parachuted onto an airfield at Depienne, 30 miles (48 km) south of Tunis. The airfield was deserted so Frost marched the battalion 10 miles (16 km) to a second airfield at Oudna. Due to postponement of their advance, the First Army did not relieve the battalion as planned and instead it became trapped 50 miles (80km) behind German lines, where Frost was informed by radio that they had been written off. After ambushing an advancing German formation, the battalion were attacked by a second German unit and surrounded. On 1st December the Germans attacked with infantry, armour and artillery, almost wiping out 'C' Company and causing heavy casualties in the rest of the battalion. Frost ordered the battalion to disperse into company groups and head for Allied lines. On 3rd December the surviving 180 men reached the safety of Majaz al Bab. With no more opportunities for parachute operations, the brigade fought in the front line as normal infantry. In February they held the right flank of the Allied line at Bou Arada and on the night of 2/3rd February, the 1st Parachute Battalion, along with a French Foreign Legion unit, captured the Jebel Mansour heights and were then subjected to constant shelling and infantry attacks. After three days without relief, their ammunition almost expended, having suffered 200 casualties, they were forced to withdraw. This was followed by the brigade fighting two fierce engagements at Tamera and checking the German offensive of Operation Ochsenkopf. When the Allied advance began again after the winter rains, the brigade was assigned to the force tasked with capturing Bizerta on 17<sup>th</sup> March. The remaining Axis forces surrendered on 13<sup>th</sup> May 1943 bringing the Tunisian campaign to an end with a cost to the 1<sup>st</sup> Parachute Brigade of 1700 killed, wounded or missing. They nevertheless proved themselves in combat and have been nicknamed the Red Devils by the German forces they had fought against.

The plan for Allied invasion of Sicily, Operation HUSKY, was almost complete by the end of June 1943. 1<sup>st</sup> Airborne Division had now regrouped and its order of battle consisted of 1<sup>st</sup> Parachute Brigade, 2<sup>nd</sup> Parachute Brigade, 4<sup>th</sup> Parachute Brigade and 1<sup>st</sup> Airlanding Brigade. Brigade was to undertake airborne operation in advance of the leading elements of ground forces and secure the approaches immediately to the south of Catania.

1<sup>st</sup> Parachute Brigade launched its operation from Kairouan and the landings took place on the night of 13<sup>th</sup> July. The operation was cursed with misfortune. Anti-aircraft fire from the invasion fleet brought down a number of aircraft and caused others to return to base. In spite of this, the objectives of the Brigade were achieved although German airborne reinforcements resulted in a bloody battle for the Primosole Bridge. Wireless communications to the airborne base were not established, neither were some of the command links because so many of the wireless sets were missing or damaged. Also, because of the lack of communications, no call could be made to re-supply. As a result of this, it became standard procedure that re-supply would be made automatically unless cancelled by wireless. It also subsequently became standard procedure that no ground wireless set was allowed to be closed down until some form of communication had been established with the airborne base; and then only if agreed by the Chief Signal Officer that the net was unworkable or unnecessary.

Catania fell on 5th August and Sicily was cleared of enemy by 16th August. 1st Airborne Division was back in its airborne base in North Africa by 30th July to rest and to take in reinforcements sent out from England.

Following the Allied success in Sicily and the downfall of Mussolini the next phase of the campaign was launched. The invasion of the Italian mainland started on 3rd September 1943, with a landing by the Eighth Army on the peninsula of Calabria (Operation BAYTOWN) followed by a second landing by sea on 9th September involving 1st Airborne Division in the Gulf of Taranto (Operation SLAPSTICK). The US Fifth Army landed further to the north at Salerno also on 9th September.

As part of the general advance, 1st Airborne Division was involved in various minor ground operations along the Adriatic coast north as far as Foggia. In November 1943, the Division was replaced by 78th Infantry Division and withdrawn from the line to leave Taranto by sea for England. 2nd Parachute Brigade, however, remained in Italy under command of Fifteenth Army Group so that balanced forces remain in theatre. 2nd Parachute Brigade subsequently expanded into an independent brigade group.

The brigade returned to England in late 1943 and trained for operations in North-West Europe under the supervision of I Airborne Corps, commanded by Lieutenant-General Frederick Browning. Although they were not scheduled to take part in the Normandy Landings, Operation Wastage was a contingency plan drawn up whereby all the 1st Airborne Division would be parachuted in to support any of the five invasion beaches if delays were experienced.

"We travelled to North Africa and within days were getting to grips with German and Italian prisoner."

"Whilst away my daughter Rosemary was born; it was to be seven months before I would see her. Grace sent me many letters which I loved receiving. Some were up to two weeks late or more. I was told that I would receive money to replace my kit and all I had

*Chapter 3: North Africa*

lost on the journey back from Bombay. I sent it all to Grace to buy a pram for Rosemary."

"The fighting was very grim. There was lots of dust and grime; quite a few lads lost their lives; this I felt was a waste of life."

"Whilst we were around Tunis I had the experience of General Montgomery. I never had time for him or for his way of fighting. One thing in particular epitomised him was how he would engage soldiers to make him a path lined with stones and shells for him to walk along to go to the toilet. It reminded me of children playing by the seaside. I always believed General Alexander was by far the best officer to be in charge of the British Army. Monty was the blue-eyed boy to the top brass."

"We moved on from Africa to Sicily; the Paras do not stay long in one place; this is where we got the name of the Red Devils. At the bottom of our jump suits was a flap between our legs which looked like a tail; from this the Germans derived the name Red Devils."

"There were many Americans on Sicily along with the 1st Airborne all preparing for battle. Near me a major was standing reading his maps when a sniper shot him. This is when I found out how much the Americans got paid for their jumps. We were shocked to find they received £ 2.00 for a jump on top of their army pay whilst we only received two shillings."

"After Sicily most of the 21st Army went on to Italy; we went back to Africa. We returned by boat and were given a few days off. We were billeted at the Americans' base. Our first meal we could not believe. We had so much of everything; it was like another world. We had not seen food like that for a long time."

"After a few days at the camp 12 of us were sent by plane to pick up stores needed by the 1st Division, returning from this by boat we were to land in Algiers. Whilst on board it was Christmas Day. Sitting on deck our Christmas Dinner was half a tin of bully beef and some biscuits. I always remember this Christmas Day. On arrival the stores were loaded on deck and a long journey began. The boat left and there were quite a lot of black American soldiers on board; many were very big men. We discovered with much pleasure that our destination was Scotland."

"We were to stay only briefly in Scotland and soon after were sent for further training to Divisional HQ in Lincolnshire, England. The Divisional HQ was stationed in a small village called Fulbeck. It was in a very large mansion. To here each day came all the Generals and Top Brass. The planning for the Arnhem Campaign must have been done here as well as at the War Office."

"Major General Urquhart and General Hacket were there every day. These were to go on to deploy the Arnhem Campaign, 'Operation Market Garden'."

"Whilst at Fulbeck we had more jumps at Cranwell Airdrome a few miles away."

# 4

# First Leave in Seven Months

"A week after arrival in Lincoln I received my first leave in seven months. I was looking forward to seeing my daughter for the first time and my lovely wife Grace.

I had written to Grace to tell her about my leave, but as usual the letter was late arriving. When I walked through the door of the Old Manor House her face lit up."

The scene at Old Manor House was a warm respite from the travel and experiences of the last seven months. The house was a long low building of two floors with steep pitched rooves, just two rooms deep it was quite typical for that part of the country.; it was formed of a main two story central building with stable single story extension to the left with pitched roof and a small single story store room to the right containing a toilet with double toilet seat. There were three windows upstairs and downstairs a central front door with a porch with two windows to the left and three to the right. Originally of black and white timber construction the house had been pebble dashed at some stage giving it a more recent appearance although being probably at least two hundred years old; rumoured to be the oldest house in the village. The rear of the house had a single story wooden extension the whole length of the main house with a steep roof meeting with the roof of the second floor.

Substantial gardens surrounded the house which stood on a wide bend in the lane on a steep bank. Low cut hedges bordered the bank with very colourful flower gardens of about half an acre within which lay a multitude of planting. The stable lay alongside the lane to the front of which were seven steps up to a path in front of the building servicing the pointed front porch and front door. To the side and rear of the house were orchards of apple and pear trees, approximately another two and a half acres. There were large vegetable plots to feed the family as well as chickens for eggs and many pets. The whole of these orchards were shielded by high hedgerow from open fields which led up to hills beyond. The other side of the lane was the boundary of a large estate within parkland.

On the ground floor the front door opened into a large room with a type of mosaic floor. To the left of this room was a kitchen with a big bread oven. The other end of the entrance room led to a smaller room with a staircase leading up to the first floor. The top of the stairs opened into a bedroom and then a door to a further bedroom. A most strange thing was that there was a further room on that floor but with no door to access it. It was as if it had never been finished. To get into it you climbed up a ladder and through the window from outside. The family used it to store apples.

All Graces' family were nice; they treated me as one of their own. My mother and father in law I liked very much. There were eight children of which one had died at 18 months. Of the remaining seven children there were three sisters and four brothers. Three of the brothers- Ronald, Vincent and Denis were overseas two in the navy Ron in the army; Leslie was much younger and still lived at home. The sisters were Girlie (Alice by name) Iris and Grace. Iris had lost two husband tragically during the war and now was married to Bernard from Canonbury in London but spent much time during these war years in Hereford; Girlie lived locally with

## Chapter 4: First Leave in Seven Months

Horace who she had recently married; Grace lived with her parents at home along with Rosemary our first child.

Believe it or not despite the crowded conditions another family was housed in Old Manor House that had been evacuated from London. Imagine all these people housed in so few rooms. The house was the social hub of the village. Within its orchards and gardens, which were used to produce as much food as possible, these were also the setting for many a party or gathering around a big table with lot of friends from the village joining the family late into the evening. Much homemade Cider and Perry would be consumed. The family also had use of an allotment which supplemented their food requirements.

"Casting my eyes on Rosemary I picked her up and carried her around for quite a time. My darling Grace and I were so happy to see each other. We were to enjoy the seven days so much."

"My Mother-in-Law looked after Rosemary when we went out to the cinema. In the afternoon we would take the baby for long walks. We often talked about my childhood and that I had had no education. I said that if we had any more children I wanted them to have a good education. Grace was all for that. She had had a good education and she was to teach me a lot. If it were not for the war I am sure she would have been in an office or some type of secretarial post. Certainly her teachers had been very disappointed that she had not continued her studies further. I must say I am very proud of my children; what they have got as well as their very good jobs. All my married life I never had a lot of money with the type of work I did. Nevertheless Grace always dressed the children well and everyone said so. She did a lot of sewing and knitting and made some lovely dresses for Rosemary. She would always be making something."

"After my leave returning to Divisional HQ the number of parachute jumps increased so much so you knew something big was going on. Whilst at Divisional HQ I had a few games of football playing for Lincoln City. Quite a lot of servicemen played in the

*An Irish Boy*

British teams in the war years. Their Sergeant Majors would notify them the day before the match."

"On Sunday afternoons Lorries would take soldiers into town; I would go to the pictures most opportunities."

"It was in Lincoln that I bought my first present for Grace; it was a beautiful handbag for which I paid twelve pounds. Today twelve pounds is not a lot of money but then it was several weeks' money!"

"All in 1st Airborne were wondering when we would be sent across the Channel; perhaps to help 6th Airborne. Most days we would be doing much P.E. or training on the assault course. We would start very early but would get the evenings off."

"I was told by the Sergeant Major that I was to receive my first stripe. He had spoken to the Captain about me. Next morning I was marched before him and made up to Lance Corporal. The Captain told me I was not to walk out with the other ranks. After leaving his office I thought to myself that if the other ranks are good enough to fight for King and Country then why should I not walk out with them? I have always said the British Army has some stupid ways. I had the stripe for six weeks when I asked the Sergeant Major when I would receive the pay for the stripe. He replied 'three months'. I told him after the six weeks that I wanted to revert to the ranks. He brought me in front of the Captain and he gave me bloody hell. He said these were the rules of the army. I was not allowed to comment, but if I had done I would have said they were out of order. I was glad to be along with my mates. I believe that if you do the job you should get the pay for it."

"We were on manoeuvres for three weeks with all our equipment as well as the glider troops. Most of my section had stomach trouble caused by pilfering apples from a neighbouring farmer' trees. The farmer complained to the Major. We said to the farmer what he would have done if it were Germans eating them'."

## Chapter 4: First Leave in Seven Months

"There was one soldier in my platoon we named The Duck. If anything was missing you had a good idea who had taken it. One evening the farmer came and said that milk and bread had been taken; we said we knew nothing about it. We knew that The Duck had drank the milk and eaten the bread; we all had a piece of bread from him. It was best we were not there long because he would be taking eggs and all types of food. He was always up before the Captain or Commanding Officer. He was always being CB confined to barracks. We don't think he was aware of what he was doing half the time, but he was very likable, we all liked him just the same. He was on detention nearly every couple of months; perhaps this was what he felt could be his ticket out of the army."

"There was another soldier who managed to get himself discharged. He would draw a duck on the wall and try to feed it. I never saw him but we heard he had managed to get out of the army."

*An Irish Boy*

# 5

# The Battle of Arnhem

"Getting back from the manoeuvres we were instructed to get ready for inspection by Major General Urquhart. On parade he noticed my Indian Ribbon on my tunic. He asked how long had I been there and that he had also been there some time ago. I said I had been there before the war in Bombay and prior to that I had served in the North West Frontier."

"After parade we had the rest of the day off. I went that evening to the pictures in Lincoln. The middle of the following week we were told that no one was to leave the camp and go to the town. We had to be on stand by. Eventually time came for us to be assembled and a roll call when your name was called you had to answer your name. We were taken by Lorries to the aerodrome. When we got there we saw them loading onto the gliders heavy guns. We all said to each other this must be action; when all the heavy guns and machinery had been loaded onto the gliders we were given our boxes of ammunition to load ourselves then sent to collect our parachutes. My thoughts after getting my parachute were would I ever see my lovely wife Grace and my baby daughter Rosemary ever again? These thoughts were the only thoughts going through my head."

**September 1944**

In early September the brigade prepared for Operation Comet, during which the 1st Airborne Division's three brigades were to land in the Netherlands and capture three river crossings. The first of these was the bridge over the River Waal at Nijmegen, the second bridge over the River Maas at Grave and finally the bridge over the Rhine at Arnhem. The objective of the British 1st Parachute Brigade would be the bridge at Arnhem. Planning for Comet was well advanced when on 10th September 1944 the mission was cancelled. Instead, a new operation was proposed with the same objectives as Comet but to be carried out by three divisions of the First Allied Airborne Army, the British 1st and U.S. 82nd and 101st Airborne Divisions.

Landings by the 1st Allied Airborne Army's three divisions began in the Netherlands on 17th September 1944. Although the allocation of aircraft for each division was roughly similar, the 101st Airborne Division landing at Nijmegen would use only one lift. The 82nd Airborne Division at Grave required two lifts while the 1st Airborne Division at Arnhem would need three lifts. Whereas the two American divisions delivered at least three quarters of their infantry in their first lift, the 1st Airborne's similar drop used only half of its capacity for infantry and the remainder to deliver vehicles and artillery.

The 1st Airborne Division had the required airlift capacity to deliver all three parachute brigades with their glider-borne anti-tank weapons or two of the parachute brigades and the airlanding brigade on day one. Instead, the vast majority of the division's vehicles and heavy equipment, plus the 1st Parachute Brigade and divisional troops were to be on the first lift, with the rest to follow the next day. Following the first lift, the airlanding brigade would remain at the landing grounds to defend them for the following day's lifts, while the parachute brigade set out alone to capture the bridges and the ferry crossing on the River Rhine.

Planes carrying the brigade left England at around 09.45 and arrived over DZ'X' at 13.00. After an uneventful landing the brigade, once organized, set off for Arnhem. The 2nd Parachute

Battalion followed a southern route along the River Rhine, to the north 3rd Parachute Battalion took the Heelsum-Arnhem road through Oosterbeek, while the 1st Parachute Battalion initially remained in reserve at brigade HQ. The 2nd Battalion, with 'A' Company leading, came under sporadic fire from pockets of German troops. 'C' Company were directed to capture the Arnhem railway bridge, but it was blown up just as they arrived. Pushing ahead, 'A' Company came under fire from German armoured cars and discovered that the central span of the pontoon bridge was missing. Entering Arnhem as night fell; the leading battalion elements reached the main road bridge at 21.00. Having secured the northern end of the bridge, attempts to capture the southern end were repulsed and the battalion started to fortify the houses and dig in. Following behind, other units of the brigade started to arrive, including a troop of guns from 1st (Airlanding) Anti-Tank Battery, brigade headquarters without the brigadier, part of the 1st Airborne Reconnaissance Squadron, and detachments of Royal Engineers and Royal Army Service Corps men. In total about 500 men were now at the bridge.

A lucky break allowed 3rd Battalion to ambush the staff car carrying general major Friedrich Kussin, the German commandant of Arnhem, and kill him and his driver. Nevertheless, most of the battalion had been stopped by the Germans in Oosterbeek while 'C' Company had entered Arnhem but were halted on the road leading to the bridge. At 15.30 the 1st Parachute Battalion were released from the reserve and directed along the Ede-Arnhem road. Here they first encountered German armoured vehicles and a column of five tanks and fifteen half-tracks, which were engaged by the battalion. They continued fighting their way forward, and by morning had reached the outskirts of Arnhem. By this time around a quarter of the battalion had been killed, wounded or were missing. Before this, at nightfall, Brigadier Lathbury had contacted Lieutenant-Colonel Frost in command at the bridge and informed him the brigade would stay put during the night and attempt to reach him in the morning.

At dawn on the second day, the defenders on the bridge saw a small convoy of trucks approaching at some speed from the south, which at first they misidentified as the British XXX Corps. That they were enemy trucks did not become apparent until they were on the bridge whereupon the defenders opened fire and destroyed the convoy. Soon afterwards, German infantry and armour approached the bridge from the east. One tank reached the space under the bridge before it was destroyed by one of the six pounder anti-tank guns. At 09.00, thirty armoured cars, half-tracks and trucks from the 9th SS Panzer Division attempted to rush the bridge from the south. The first five armoured cars, using wrecks of the dawn convoy as cover and with the element of surprise, managed to cross unscathed. The rest of the force was engaged and twelve of their vehicles destroyed with the survivors returning to the southern bank. All day long, the force at the bridge came under fire from mortars and anti-aircraft guns positioned south of the river and were subject to probing infantry and armour attacks.

On the outskirts of Arnhem, 1st Battalion, which had been joined by Headquarters Company, 3rd Battalion, unsuccessfully attempted to fight through to the bridge, then moved south in an attempt to flank the German line. They eventually ended up beside the river, where after 3rd Battalion advanced 2.5 miles (4.0 km) along the bank until daylight revealed their position to the Germans. Divisional commander Major-General Roy Urquhart and Brigadier Lathbury accompanied 3rd Battalion until Lathbury was shot and wounded. Due to his injuries, they were unable to move him and he was left in the care of a Dutch family. The 1st and 3rd Battalions spent all day trying to force a way through to the bridge. By nightfall they had failed and the strength of both battalions was reduced to around 100 men.

Another attempt to reach the bridge began at 03.45 on the third day, 19th September 1944, when the 1st and 3rd Battalions were joined by the 11th Parachute Battalion and the 2nd Battalion, South Staffordshire Regiment. By dawn, under intense fire from the German defenders, the attack had faltered whereupon the 11th Parachute Battalion, until then held in reserve, was ordered to carry out a left flanking assault on the German line. This last attempt to reach the defenders at the bridge was subsequently stopped on the orders of General Urquhart when he realised the futility of the battle. By this time the 1st Parachute Battalion had been reduced to forty men and the 3rd Parachute Battalion to around the same number.

With no word from division or brigade Lieutenant-Colonel Frost assumed command of the brigade units at the bridge. With their casualties mounting and supplies of food and ammunition running low, a request for the force to surrender was rejected by Frost, who decided they would fight on.

By day four, 20th September, the brigade still holding out at the bridge had been split into two groups during the night by the Germans who had managed to infiltrate close enough to separate them into positions east and west of the bridge road. Any movement was subjected to machine-gun and sniper fire and they were under almost constant mortar and artillery attacks. Added to this were probes by tanks and self-propelled guns, which approached the defenders' buildings and opened fire at point blank range. The brigade, out of anti-tank ammunition, could do nothing to stop them in the east, but the 6 pounders in the west still proved effective deterrent. During the day, Lieutenant John Grayburn of the 2nd Battalion was killed and later posthumously awarded the Victoria Cross for his bravery during the fighting at the bridge. That morning, communications with 1st Airborne Division were established and Frost, on asking for reinforcements and supplies, was informed that the division was surrounded at Oosterbeek and the brigade was on their own. Frost was later wounded and command of the brigade assumed by Major Frederick Gough of the reconnaissance squadron. By midday the brigade position was untenable and the last defenders were withdrawn into what had been the Headquarters Company, 2nd Battalion's position. By nightfall they were still holding out, and in the darkness some of the men tried unsuccessfully to break out. At dawn on day five, what was left of the brigade was forced to surrender.

"When we got on the plane we all said to each other 'how many of us will ever see these parts again?' I had one curl from Graces' hair which I always carried with me. She had given it to me after we got married. I very often took it out to look at it. When the lads saw it they asked if they could look at it so we passed it around. I believe that curl gave me a lot of hope; I still have it to the present day. It is something I treasure very much."

"We were in the air for some time and very little was spoken. All the lads were getting very worked up, me included. The first thing the pilot said was that the sea was calm and it would not be long before we needed to get ready for our task."

"When the time came for the Allied offensive on mainland Europe to begin every soldier expected to be part of it. The 6th Airborne went in; they had been formed after the 1st Airborne. It was their first time in battle. When my Regiment, the Royal Ulster Rifles followed we were with the 1st Airborne and were in gliders."

"Our 'Stick Sergeant' was told to get ready; we all shook each others' hands and got ready for the green light to come on and for our time to jump. All our lot were lucky; we all landed on the ground before the Germans started to fire on the rest of the Paras coming down. All hell was let loose; this was the start of the Battle of Arnhem. It was a battle I shall never forget."

"We advanced quite steadily under a hail of mortar fire; our heavy guns were blasting away. My section kept going until on a bend in the road we were held up in cross fire. It was deadly and we were pinned down for some time. Coming in the other direction were some German prisoners captured by our HQ. We were ordered to get as far as the bridge before nightfall. All that day the Germans fired from every place. Come nightfall they continued to fire but we took some tea, the first drink since we left England."

"Throughout the night the Germans used their heavy guns. We went on a scouting mission to find out how best to secure the bridge. In the morning we could see the German positions around the bridge. We launched an assault and all hell broke loose. It was very sad to see your palls getting killed."

"Our mortar shells got their range and enabled our capture of the bridge. Firing from both sides never let up for long. We were told we would be relieved after two days; to make things worse our ammunition was getting low; supplies were due to come soon. We soon realised the planes were dropping our supplies on German positions instead of on our lines. We were fighting behind German lines which made it very difficult for us. Then we discovered that the 21st Army could not break through. Next the German tanks appeared; two of these were taken out by our gunners. By this time we were getting very tired as well as for the lack of sleep our supplies were getting very short. The Germans tank numbers kept growing. That was the worst aspect of the Para; often dropped behind the lines we would be cut off. We assembled and names taken; quite a few were killed."

"On the fifth day I thought we would be all wiped out. We were hoping the 21st Army would break through; but the German seemed to have more and more troops getting nearer all the time. Word came through in the night that we would be going to Oosterbeek taking the wounded. God, the sight of those poor lads I shall never forget, all our battle dress were in rags, some of the wounded were in terrible pain. When we got to Oosterbeek we were all so bloody tired and we shared what ever food we had and lay down. I thought to myself 'what in the name of god is worth all this suffering'. After a while they told us we were withdrawing and going back. We would have to be very quiet and any old rags we were to wrap around our boots so as not to be heard."

"When we got to where we were to cross the river we followed the white line in single file to the boats. The Germans must have been taken by surprise because they only started firing as the last of the boats was crossing. If they hadn't got us out we would all have been wiped out or taken prisoner. Our heavy guns now fired on the German positions; I hope they did a good job after all we had been through. Most of the 1st Airborne had been killed; it was terrible not having your friends to talk to and have a few jokes when we were together."

"After getting new battle dress we were off to England. I think we had all done our share of the fighting. The pilot in our plane said that the papers were all full of the Battle of Arnhem. Upon landing we had food and showers and debriefed for two days and then were given leave. In Lugwardine the villagers said well done; but my mind was full of sad memories of Arnhem and those of us who did not come back."

*The Battle of Arnhem was one of the most famous Second World War military engagements. It was fought in and around the Dutch towns of Arnhem, Oosterbeek, Wolfheze, Driel and the surrounding countryside from 17-26 September 1944.*

*After sweeping though France and Belgium in the summer of 1944, the Allies were poised to enter the Netherlands. Field Marshall Bernard Montgomery favoured a single thrust north to the River Rhine, allowing the British 2nd Army to bypass the German Siegfried Line and attack the Ruhr. To this end the Allies launched Operation Market Garden on 17 September 1944; Paratroopers were dropped in the Netherlands to secure key bridges and towns along the Allied axis of advance. Furthest north the British 1st Airborne Division, supported by men of the Glider Pilot Regiment and the Polish 1st Independent Parachute Brigade, landed at Arnhem to secure bridges across the Lower Rhine. Initially expecting a walkover, British XXX Corps planned to reach the British airborne forces within two to three days.*

*The British forces landed some distance from the objectives and were quickly hampered by unexpected resistance – especially from elements of the 9th SS and 10th SS Panzer divisions. Only a small force was able to reach the Arnhem road bridge. The main body of the division was halted on the outskirts of the city. Meanwhile XXX Corps was unable to advance north as quickly as anticipated and failed to relieve the airborne troops according to schedule.*

*After four days the small British force at the bridge was overwhelmed and the rest of the division became trapped in a small pocket north of the river where they could not be sufficiently reinforced by the Poles or XXX Corps when they arrived on the southern bank of the river. RAF resupply flights also failed.*

*After nine days of fighting the shattered remains of the airborne forces were withdrawn in Operation Berlin.*

*With no secure bridges the Allies were unable to cross the Rhine and the frontline stabilized south of Arnhem. The 1st Airborne Division had lost nearly three quarters of its strength and did not see combat again.*

"We were given seven days leave; I was looking forward very much to seeing Grace and baby Rosemary. We would spend the time on long walks through the quiet countryside. Sometimes I would help my Father-in-Law cut logs for the fire. Grace' brother Vini was also on leave from the navy. We spent a few hours together in The New Inn exchanging our experiences. He was a good sort."

"When my time was due to go back from leave I didn't like it one bit. When I look back I should have thought myself lucky to have survived to be able to go on leave. I didn't like waving goodbye to Grace at Hereford Railway Station not knowing if I would see her again."

"Getting back to HQ from leave we had to see to all the personal belongings of the lads who did not come back. These we left back at the office. The atmosphere was totally different around the place unlike before we had set off for Arnhem. The Divisional HQ was very quiet; most of the officers who had made it back were on leave."

# 6

# Stores

By early May 1945, the 1$^{st}$ Parachute Brigade had been brought up to strength, albeit mainly with inexperienced replacements and the survivors of the 4$^{th}$ Parachute Brigade, which had been disbanded. On 4$^{th}$ May, the brigade was detached from the 1$^{st}$ Airborne Division and 1$^{st}$ Parachute Battalion transported to Denmark for occupation duties whilst the rest of the brigade remained in Britain as a reserve formation. Without the brigade, the 1$^{st}$ Airborne Division deployed to Norway, but on their return they were disbanded on 15$^{th}$ November 1945.

"My next job was in the stores at HQ in Lincoln. This was to be the best job I was to have in my career in the army. It took a couple of weeks to sort out everything to my way doing things, after this all went quite well. The previous store man had stayed away on leave two days longer than he should have. When he returned he was given fourteen days confined to barracks. I did this job until I left the army. I got on very well with the Quarter Master."

"All the dirty washing was left at the stores labelled with the persons' name and a list of what was in the pile. I would enter this in my receipt book and check the items. The washing had to be at the stores at a certain time or else; it was their own fault. Going to the laundry was great fun, especially after I got to know some women there. Big Mary was the one in charge of the clean clothes. I would count the number of dirty bundles I left and collect the same number from Big Mary. If some items were left out these would be made up from the stores. At the end of each month I would tell the Quarter Master what was needed, from a toothbrush to a battle dress. Each week the lads would have one hour to take their dirty cloths in exchange for new ones. The issue was done by the QM he would call out what was needed and I would hand the items to him. The old kits were sent back to Ordinance Depot. Things sent there were replaced by new. I found 200 old blankets in disused store cupboards. The quarter Master never went around the stores; he came did his paper works and went. I organised things everything in its place in two weeks. Whilst at the stores I could go to the cook house often and get tea and extra food."

"Part of the job involved going to collect items from other depots that we needed. One trip involved going to Selby in Yorkshire to pick up blankets. The driver said he was near his home and would like to go to see his wife. So we did; I slept on the floor; it was a very small house. Following day he realised his fuel was low; calling into an American depot they offered us a fill-up; they said 'buddy pull over and we'll fill you up'; when we told them the forms we had to fill in in a British depot they had a good laugh. Coming back to camp the QM was very pleased with the blanket situation. There should have been a certain number but we left the space blank to be adjusted later. While in stores I did not have to do PE. I did cross country twice a week and really enjoyed that."

"Coming back to camp one evening there had been a heavy fall of snow; we had snowball fights with some RAF who were waiting to go into town. A few days later I was on another long journey to pick up stores of oil and other supplies from Wales. I asked QM if I could stay over night and visit my wife and daughter in Hereford. The driver stayed with some friends near Ross-on-Wye. There were often things like this going on."

"Back in camp everyone from HQ went to the firing ranges not far away for practice. Next day I had to do a parachute jump in the morning but had the rest of the day to myself. Following day there was a big inspection for Major General Urquhart. He also inspected the stores. He came in looked all around; everything was looking smart. He said to the Captain I was a credit and had everything in order. Following this I was told by the Sergeant Major that I had to report to the Captain. I didn't know why. When I appeared before him he said the stores had done him proud so when I went on my next leave I could have two extra days. The soldiers looking after the Canteen were given two extra days as well. I was now established in my job. The officers came in for their new battle dress and berries. In the evening I would often go to the pictures. The QM was a good man; he was off on ten days leave to see his father in Aldershot; I teased him about living so close to British Army Head Quarters. He said quite often to me that the time would not come quickly enough for him to leave the army."

"I received a letter from Grace saying she would like to come to visit. So I booked accommodation for two to stay. She came and stayed for four days. After my duties I would meet her and we would go for walks with the baby. Food was quite short in supply for civilians but the cook house gave me extra for the family; the landlady was kind and gave us extra food. I was not aware that I would not see them for a long time."

"At the time many others were on leave, clerks, officers and drivers. Shortly after this we were very busy preparing stores for a major event. The QM said that a big move was afoot. When ready we were loaded with all supplies onto Lorries and went by road to Newcastle. We were to be transported by ship to Norway. HQ had decided this to be safe from German attack."

*An Irish Boy*

# 7

# Norway

"In Norway we were greeted with very friendly people glad to see us, cheering and waving flags. The Divisional HQ was set up in a large girl's school near the palace of the King of Norway in Oslo."

"The Germans had been well dug in. Their fortifications were strong. Some of them spoke a little English. The ones we met were pleased to see an end to the war as were most of us. They were put on boats bound for their homeland. The QM and I were taken to the German supply depot just outside Oslo; I had never seen so many bottles of Champagne stacked everywhere. There were lots of other drinks and food as well; they obviously had not gone short of anything whilst occupying Norway."

"There were guards on patrol all the time guarding the stores. I had to go to get drinks for the officers' mess and for the sergeants as well. It took me a week to get all the stores organised. I had to go to the docks to arrange supplies. After a few weeks a lot of Norwegian soldiers returned from England to their homeland."

"Norway is a very nice place; around Oslo there are lots of tree covered hills no matter where you look. It was good to be able to go and see the sights. Outside our Girls School base ran many trams to destinations all around Oslo. I often went on these trams sightseeing. A month after our arrival the army hired a large hall for a banquet for the troops to celebrate the end of the war in Europe."

"The last of the Germans had been in Bergen, which is a much forested part of the country. Returning to Oslo was good. Outside the city were based the rest of the 1st Airborne. Everyone was pleased the European conflict was at an end; but the war with Japan was still to conclude."

"The HQ did PE outside the Palace early each morning. The extensive lawns were ideal for the exercises; I have always liked PE. After this the rest of the day was my responsibility; I would have to organising the laundry and stores. The new issues had to be in before 12.30pm. After this many soldiers sun bathed on the school roof it was called the 'naked world'. My time in Norway was very easy and enjoyable. On one of my many trips out of Oslo I went on to the mountain tops and the views were wonderful. Sadly I didn't have a camera or I would have taken some great photos. Sometimes the guards on the trams would take your money, other times not."

"A group of us found out where Sonia Henna lived; she was best ice skater in Norway; we went to have a look at her house. I had seen the ice rink where she had skated and where all the hard work was done. I was a great fan of hers and loved her films especially with Glen Miller."

"A friend of mine who was the driver for an officer suggested that we go for a trip to Sweden. I asked him if we would get in trouble; but he said the officer was away for three days. We left in the morning. We gave the guard on duty on the boarder some fags; he seemed quite pleased. I don't know the name of the small village we went to; but I bought thirteen pairs of silk stockings and a lovely pair of gloves; my friend bought four pairs and some silk underclothes. They were pleased to be dealing with us. If we had more money there was plenty more we could have bought. We stayed there one hour, had a drink and left. We agreed that if we got the chance we would go again; we never did. I bought two pretty pictures in Norway of a boy and a girl in traditional dress. I have them to this day. I thought these presents would be great for family at home. These types of things were not available in England; everything was rationed and needed coupons."

"One evening during dinner it was announced that an atomic bomb had been dropped on Japan. It was not until the following morning that the scale of the devastation became apparent. Within a week of the second bomb being dropped Japan surrendered. All our thoughts were on the poor chaps in the prison camps; they must have been delighted at the end of the war."

"On VJ Day, (Victory of War in Japan), everyone went into the centre of Oslo. Flags were waving and horns blowing. I was shaking hands with everyone. I was thanking the Good Lord that I had come safely through it all. I was laughing my head off when all of a sudden my Brother-in-Law Denis appeared in front of me. His ship had docked in the night. He said he recognised that laugh immediately. It was so good to see him, and a great surprise. He and his mate and I went to the stores and had a few drinks whatever we wanted. I went down to see Denis off at the docks. His ship was on convoy duty; but he was hoping to go back to England soon afterwards."

"Everyone at HQ had a few days doing nothing. There were lots of ships going up and down the coast. I went for a two and a half hour trip on a sailing ship. Mooring on return there were lots of fishing boats unloading their catches. Most of the fish were herrings. We were in Norway five and a half months. The time went very quickly."

"A big party was organised for the officers to celebrate return to England.

It was nice to know we were going home, especially after all the moving around for battles in Europe and Africa. The HQ left for England, I was to follow in Lorries carrying the contents of the stores from Divisional HQ."

"The corporal in charge of the cook house asked if I could conceal a mink coat he had got for his wife. He must have had lots of dealings on the black market. I told him I would see to the coat if he would give me food back in England for me to take on leave.

The crossing was very smooth and took a couple of days. It was great not having to look out for submarines."

"On arrival in England all the transport was lined up on the docks to be inspected by Customs House Officers. Customs officers searched the lorry in front of the lorry with the coat. I had put some drinks aside for the QM as well so I was on the edge of my seat; if they found them I would have been in trouble. These men seemed to have an eye for locating stuff. I was glad to hear the word to get on our way and get away from those men."

"Arriving at our base in the evening I had to remove the items we were most anxious about but left the rest in the Lorries until the morning. The next day was spent running up and down stairs sorting out the supplies and equipment. It was exhausting. The corporal was very pleased that all had gone well with the coat; I kept it in the stores until he needed it. The QM was very pleased with the drink, no bottles had been broken. My things had also not been damaged."

"After one week the majority of HQ was given ten days leave. The Quarter Master said there were to be no new issues given out for a few weeks so I could go on leave as well; anything that came up he would deal with. When I went on leave the QM let me go in the evening and also organised a lift to the station for me. I had my box and kit bag and lots of presents. The driver said I must have all the stores with me. I gave him a new battle dress. At Hereford Station I got into a taxi and avoided being seen by the Red Caps. When I got home all the family were in bed. I made tea for all the family. Rosemary had grown very big and Grace said she was walking well."

"At this time of year most of the villagers were hop picking. Grace would do the washing for all the family. I would get the water boiling in the old fire tub in the back lean-to by 9 am; otherwise it

Chapter 7: Norway

would be midday before she could start. My Mother-in-Law would look after Rosemary to let us go to the cinema. My in-laws were lovely people and everyone you spoke to agreed."

"We went to visit Grace' Grand Parents. Her Grand Father told me all about the war in South Africa. He must have been a very smart man when he was young.

The same day, after leaving them we went to visit Grace' other Grand Parents. It was a very good day."

"Before going back off leave I spent a day with Grace's Mother hop picking which was very enjoyable. I went back to finish my time and this is when I felt most sad. I just looked forward to the time coming to an end. Getting back to camp I found a lot of officers had left to rejoin their own Parachute Battalions. The QM said things had been very quiet whilst I was away. But in the army things never stayed the same for long.

After a few weeks I was instructed to get all the boxes of ammunition ready to go back to Ordinance Depot. My time in the stores was spent packing and unpacking. Next the rifles and mortars were to go. I used to wipe all the guns with an oily cloth. The stores were now quite empty. Only small items like boot lases and toothbrushes were left. The QM left all for me to do; I enjoyed the job and felt pride in the work."

"A few weeks before I was demobbed from the army the MO asked if I would like to join for another term. I replied that I was already three years over my first term and there was no way that I wanted to stay in the army any longer. I told him I was very much looking forward to leaving the army. He was all for soldiering, that was his job. He went through my record of service and after reading it gave it to me. He said he was sorry I was leaving the army and wished me luck in Civi Street. After this all the lads were having tea and having a good chat about signing on for more service. No one had done so. Those who were left to finish their term said they had had enough."

"The Captain organised a farewell dinner party in the dining room for us all before we left. All the parties were good affairs with lots of food and drink. Most of the boys were demobbed from Divisional HQ near Newcastle. I was to be transferred to Taunton for my last few weeks, (which I though was silly as I was due to be demobbed in Hereford). So they gave me additional leave so I did not have to go to Taunton. My friend the QM was looking forward very much to getting out of the army, he had a few months left to do after I left."

"Most of the lads were transferred by lorry. The last few days there was nothing left to do. Reporting to the Officer for the last time to receive my papers I felt on top of the world to be looking after myself and not being looked after by the army. On reflection I can say that I had seen a lot of the World and could talk about so many places I'd been to. Arriving in Hereford Grace met me at the station. She said it was the day she had always looked forward to so very much. Looking back at service it does not fit with family life; if single with no ties it is alright, but it is not good if one is married."

# 8
# Civi Street

"After a few weeks getting used to life outside the army I started my first job. I was to work with a stone mason laying kerbs for the new bus station in Worcester. He was a very nice man to work with and the job lasted seven weeks. Whilst working there I stayed at a good bed and breakfast. I had a nice breakfast and evening meal; all for thirty shillings. I was given an allowance for living away from home as well as a bonus of just over two pounds a week. On the last week I finished a 12pm on Saturday. Returning at the weekends the bus would get to Lugwardine at 3.30pm. The firm employing me wanted me to work on a job the other side of Birmingham. They said I was doing a good job and worked well with the stone mason. When the foreman came around I said that I did not want to work any further away. After just leaving the army and being away all the time I didn't want to be away any longer."

"Grace suggested I try to get a job in Hereford and with luck a job came up for Lloyds Tile Works that very week. It was shift work and paid extra money when on nights. During the days I would help out on local farms."

"My daughter was now quite a big girl by now; she was a little terror getting into all sorts of trouble in one way or another. First of all she broke her arm falling down the stairs. On another occasion Grace found her burning money in the fire which Grace was saving for our holiday to Ireland. She caused us much worry plenty of times. When we were cooking meals she had hers' cooked separately. If you took the food away she would really get annoyed and bang her head on the table or against the doors. What ever Grace did to try to pacify her she wouldn't take any notice. My Father and Mother-in-Laws spoiled her all the time taking her out and giving her things."

"All my in-laws went for walks every Sunday evening. My Mother-in-Law would ask me to get different plants from the gardens of various abandoned houses. She loved her garden; we laughed if we were able to find a certain flower; these were lovely times. She would never join us for a drink after our walks at the local pub. She was against that way; she wouldn't even sit outside the pub on the bench."

"We went to a sale in Ledbury to buy things for our new home, if we were ever to get one. Everything was rationed and all that was new had to be bought with coupons. To buy new furniture would use up all your coupons on one item. So we came away with an iron bed and a small chair and a few mats. These were all delivered next day. A few weeks later we obtained a second hand three piece suite for the bedroom. Working at a nearby large house doing some jobs I used the earnings to buy a good table they were selling. We assembled quite a few household items for our home when ever it might come. We decided it wasn't fair on Grace' parents to have one room full of our things. So the money we saved went into the bank for the big day when we got our own place.

A lot of money had been collected in the village for the troops whilst the war was on. There had been thousands of pounds collected. But because I had not come from the village, even though I had married a local girl from the village, I got nothing. Grace was terribly upset over this, especially as I had served in such combat situations in the war." "Many throughout the country were in my situation and had married local girls. Many of the ex soldiers from the village received £200.00. That would have been very nice to have set up our home. I don't know why people can be so unkind to those who did their share for the country."

"When the county council started building council houses at Barestree we felt sure we would get one. Grace had put our names down on the waiting list shortly after getting married. She was always cycling into town and talking to councillors to remind them we needed housing. We lived with our in-laws for ten years; during this time one room was full of our furniture, we didn't think it was fair on them, but they did not mind, they never complained; it was not our fault, god only knows. When we went to the Town Hall we were always told we were at the bottom of the list; when we said our in-laws had lived in the city for many years that did not cut ice. We found out later that much money changed hands to get a council house. When the houses were built at Bartestree we were not allocated one. After this I never went to the council offices again. Then Grace' two brothers came out of the navy and The Old Manor was quite full; my in-laws tried all the time to make everyone happy."

"Nevertheless I was enjoying working near home and spending time with Grace and the family. I went out with my Father-in-law a lot; we would often go to the bowling alley and play with his team from the Railway Tavern."

*An Irish Boy*

# 9

# Holiday in Ireland

"We went on occasional holidays to Ireland. We would go by train to Scotland and cross from Stranraer to Larne getting to Belfast before ten in the morning. We would go to my friend John Hanna's house in the Falls Road then spend the day looking around Belfast. We had been good friends for a long time; when we were fighting in North Africa we had spent leave together with Grace' parents. Our friendship lasted for a long time. Even after moving to London we would regularly write to each other and he would sent me sporting papers every other week. Eventually we would lose contact."

"We spent the next four days at Newry and Warren Point. The weather was very good. I took Grace to see the Irish Games, Gaelic football and hurling, (both played on the same afternoon). The people we stayed with had hired a bus for the day, we had a great time. The following day we went to the Irish Free State to a town called Dundalk. We bought things that in the North Ireland would need coupons; Grace bought a lovely black Mack, some stockings and underwear; I got two shirts and some food; clothes and food were a little dearer there. We sent meat parcels to my in-laws, which they would have been glad to receive; they were advertised in a shop window. There seemed to be plenty of everything, if you could afford it; they had been neutral during the war.

On the way back to Newry I put the Mack around my waist so as not to pay duty on it.

On the bus we were advised not to sit together in case we were searched. At the boarder crossing Grace was searched down to her under wear. They knew she was English when she spoke. They asked me what was in my bag, I showed them it was a doll and a model bus for my daughter, and they were not interested."

"Next day we went to Warren Point and I showed Grace the place I used to sell ice cream. Then we saw the dairy where I did the milk round. She liked the scenery very much. We crossed the water to Omeath. Here she had a ride on an Irish Jaunting- Cart. We rode to a place where we have the Stations of the Cross, called Calvary. We then went into a quaint old cottage to meet some people I knew. I explained who we were and they immediately recalled and gave us a wonderful welcome. They had been neighbours of the Omeath Taylors who had been so kind to me prior to my leaving for my new life in Warren Point so many years before."

"We were given tea; this was made in a saucepan and boiled on a peat fire. As we had the tea the hens were walking all around us wanting some for them. I asked them if they remembered when I took the turkey away to be sexed, they did. They said to me that the evil people I had lived with on the farm outside the village should have been put in prison for the terrible things they did to me. Their recollections of those outrageous times had remained indelibly within them. We stayed there three and a half hours talking about old times; I don't think Grace could get over how the hens were walking all over the cottage. I said most people in Ireland didn't bother much about those things; it was just their way of life."

"By the time we left the cottage it was late, we had to get to the boat in time to get across to Warren Point before the sea had gone out too far. There is no way you can get back till the tide returns, we got back with half an hour to spare. We spent the following day in Belfast at John Hanna's house and the next day we travelled home. Grace really enjoyed her slim bread and soda food. When we returned home Grace would show her family how they cooked in Ireland. Most of John's family came to see us off on our journey. We had a lovely time. We had a good drink together before leaving. It reminded me of some of the good times past. My friend John said he would like to save up and come over to see us on holiday; but the problem was he had five children. He would write to me regularly after our return and every so often another child would have come along, eventually he had nine including twins. He had two sisters who Grace got on well with. One worked in a linen mill not far away. She would come home for lunch. The girls wore shawls covering their shoulders. Coming home after finishing their shift they would walk in pairs and would sing out loud."

"On leaving the drums of the Orange Men were beating in preparation for their marches. They still perform the same old marches every year to the annoyance of the Catholics. Myself I think these marches don't do any good what so ever and as long as they go on there will always be trouble between the Protestants and the Catholics. I have always said that everyone should live their own way of life. No matter what the other side does one should always work for a better way of life."

"We had travelled via Scotland because there had been some trouble with the boats at Liverpool. The crossing was also only couple of hours instead of the nine from Liverpool. Returning to Hereford after changing at Crew the first person we met was my Father-in-Law having some tea at Hereford Railway Station where he worked. He had a few jobs to do before coming home and was always in demand. Meeting her mother Grace asked if the meat parcel had arrived, which it had and had been gratefully received."

*An Irish Boy*

# 10

# Back to Work

"Going back to work at the tile works it took a few days to get back into things after the holiday. I was an unloader and would have to unload tiles off the Dressler. Like the other unloaders we were always cutting our fingers on the glazed edges of the tiles. The tile works must have spent lots of money on plasters. I worked there two years but didn't like the shift work; many weekends were effected by shifts. I wanted to find another job and kept trying every week different places without luck."

"Eventually I left Lloyd's Tile Works and went to Thynes Tile Works. This was day work not shift work. There didn't seem to be much work in Hereford at the time. As luck would have it shortly after leaving Lloyds it folded. Lots of the men from there were unable to get jobs. After some months at Thynes I was asked by the manager if I could take over the job of firing the kilns as the man who did it had broken his ankle. I was always approaching him to try to get extra money. He was known as the penny man and would not look you in the face. I thought this was a way to ask him for a rise. After this he would often come to me to do odd jobs after hours. I did firing of the kilns for three months but I found it was making my eyes bad. Whilst doing it I had an extra five shillings a week. My doctor gave me a letter so I was able to get off that task.

I now needed glasses for reading. I realised that all the men doing that job wore glasses. But they needed to stay in it for the money."

"My next job would be sorting the tiles into sizes prior to going to the shops. Next I was sent to the workshops where fireplaces were made. I was there for seven months assembling fireplaces and grouting them the assembly was done by 'slabbers', there were fifty 'slabbers' in the works shop. They were supposed to give me one shilling a week for finishing the fire places; some gave me 1/6. Some of them refused so I left their fire places till last. They complained to the manager but when I explained to him that they would not pay or said next week but then forgot he agreed with me that they should either pay or do the grouting themselves and then they would earn less because it would take them longer to finish each fire place. The ones who didn't pay fell behind in their output so after a few weeks they too paid. I had a boy to help me with my work."

"A manager approached me and said there was a job paying extra money in the clay mill. I worked in the mill six days a week and two Sundays a month. The work was hard; the clay was hard to break up and had to be carried in barrows to the plunger. Each mix had five different types of clay. I had to do seven charges a day. Each charge was two ton. Time and motion had just come in, so at the end of the day I had handled twenty eight tons of clay. That was handling each charge twice. My pay was £17 per week; this was very good for Hereford which had very poor pay rates. My Father-in-Law was very poorly paid on the railways even when he worked shifts".

"A few weeks after returning from Ireland Grace found she was pregnant. We were both very pleased. At least we didn't have to get a new pram; Rosemary's pram was as good as new and Grace took great pride in it. We felt we would have a good chance at getting one of the new council houses at Bartestree which were being built as we were having a second child. With the two brothers back at home and another child coming along we wanted to relieve the strain on my in-laws so we decided to become 'Squatters' until we were given a house."

*An Irish Boy*

# 11
# 'Squatters'

"We went up to a place called Madley. There were two camps here ours was in the village of Kingstone. Here there were abandoned RAF huts used as billets during the war. Everyone without a home was living in them; they were known as 'Squatters'. We picked out one for us to move into. It was not far to catch a bus into town. We returned home to tell Grace's Mum that we would be moving to live on the camp. I arranged a day off work to pack for our move. Waking up the day of our move our bed collapsed and we ended up on the floor on top of each other. It was the cheap bed bought in Ledbury. We had a good laugh over it."

"There was much to do to sort out the Nissen-hut. Many panes of glass were broken; so I took glass from windows in unoccupied huts to fix them. When all the officers' rooms had been vacated everyone went to see what they could get. I got a nice stove for our bedroom and a Tilley lamp which provided good light. Also I found some silk parachutes which I thought Grace could use to make dresses. Instead she said they could be used to divide the hut up into rooms. After a while I made a gate and some steps to the door to make it more like a home. Eventually all of the huts were taken up; they were occupied mainly by ex-servicemen who needed homes."

"The journey to work was downhill with the wind in my face cycling and was good but the return journey was hard work. I had been near work when at The Old Manor House; but here the journey was seven miles each way. If I had still been at Lloyd Tile Works the journey would have been five miles further each way and difficult especially in bad weather."

"Grace would go to see her parents most weekends. I spent much of my spare time in the garden and didn't visit much until it was established. The man next door fenced part of his garden to stop people walking over his vegetables. I did the same, like him we both spent much time in the garden and had good vegetable plots. The first day the fence was up it was still dark and we were in bed when a woman got tangled up in the wire. She came to our door and asked why we had put the fence up; she said we had no right to erect it and she would get a letter from the authorities to have it removed. I am still waiting till this day for the letter to come."

"Having fences around the two huts stopped the dogs fouling the gardens. The steps enabled us to go out of our door without passing other huts. Rosemary started school in a village a few miles away called Clehonger. She went on the school bus. Most of the other children went to Madley Village School. Soon after our move the council began work on a new school in the village. This would prove to be of a very high standard."

# 12

# Melvyn's Arrival

"My son Melvyn was born at The Old Manor House. The hospital was full so they asked if Grace could give birth at her Mother's home. When Melvyn arrived my Daughter Rosemary said that he could not stay. I said to her that we could not put him out in the cold. She said that he could only stay for the night and in the morning he must go.

I stayed with my in-laws for a week, Grace stayed for a few weeks before coming home to the camp. He was a fine chap and his Grand Parents doted on him especially the first weeks after his birth that they spent looking after him. I had to go to a council officer to review our rent for the hut which was 7/6 a week. I carefully held onto my rent book as a safe guard so that they could not put us out. After this they started to make improvement, putting a mains water supply to each hut and electricity, also a flushing WC. So moving to Madley was not such a bad idea, it gave us a home of our own. We bought a new three piece suit for our bedroom which we had sent from Cardiff; we were then able to get rid of the old broken bed. I put up a swing in the garden for the children which they enjoyed and Grace did as well. It lasted until we left."

"My brother-in-law Vinny moved to the camp after he was married as well as several families from the Lugwardine Village after they saw how well they could be made homes."

"There was a good bus service into town, one an hour, and they ran much later then other services to other areas. The company was called Morgans and when sold it was said that all the money he made was from the people on the camp."

"As each hut was refurbished the residents were housed temporarily in a spare hut. Our turn to move to a temporary hut whilst ours was refurbished came on Vinny's Wedding Day. We had to get up very early and take what we needed into the temporary hut before going to the wedding. Both of us were not happy going to the wedding as we were up to our necks moving. After lunch we left and had a good wash. We felt quite dirty. It was something we spoke of often to Vinny after all was settled. He said it was bad luck for the two things to happen on the same day. After two weeks the work was finished. The parachuted were replaced by brick walls to make two proper rooms. It was great having running water and a flushing toilet. They soon were to add children's playing fields. Our rent went up to ten shillings a week. The rent collector said several people were behind and if they didn't pay they would be put out. My in-laws came to visit quite often at weekends. We would go for walks around the village and the airdrome. There was often car racing at the airdrome at weekends."

"One Sunday I had a call from the Catholic priest. He wanted to know why I was not attending his church. I told him that I worked most weekends and that my family came first. I also was not going to go to the Catholic Church. My children would be brought up the same religion as my wife. He didn't take this very well. We had many words over it. I told him I wanted my children to have good schooling not just reading the bible like they do a lot in Catholic schools. I asked him if he had been abroad; I had been overseas and had seen what religion had done to the lives of many, particularly in Ireland. The priest said that he was born in Ireland."

"Coming home from works one night I was very cross when I saw Rosemary waiting by the bus stop. I asked what she was doing

*Chapter 12: Melvyn's Arrival*

there as it was getting dark; she said no bus had come for a long time. I waited with her until the bus came. Upon getting home I found that Grace had been very worried at her being so late. She was always getting into mischief. She would often be a cause of anxiety. Rosemary was at school four years when Melvyn started there. He really played up the first few days as Grace tried to get him on the bus. He felt his mum should go with him on the bus as well. The new school was being built at Kingstone and was for all the surrounding villages and also some from families further away."

"At the works we had a savings club 30 shillings a week to put aside for our holiday. When the time came to collect the money we decided to buy a radio gram. We played some records every weekend, Grace and I loved the same sort of music. Another occasion I won money on the football pools at work, (£28.00) so on the way home decided for a present for Grace to buy an electric boiler to do the washing; I paid £7.00 towards it. After a week it had not arrived so I went back to the shop. They said that where we lived people were bad at paying. I said to him that he was classing everybody the same who lived on the camp. He said he would deliver it the following day; I told him that I wanted my money back if he did not deliver as promised. He was surprised that I had the rest of the money in my pocket ready to pay him. It was a great help to Grace as before she had to do the washing on a small priming stove. Every Friday a motor van would come around selling most of the general things people needed. A lot of people received goods then paid next week."

"The council started to build new houses outside the camp. Grace did not want to live at Kingston and would have preferred to have moved to one of the new homes being built a Bartestree. Seeing how these houses were being built really put us off them. But we were told that people on the camp would be first in line for the new houses. Sadly a house at Bartestree was not to be. They had already been allocated and our names were not on the list at the council meeting. Grace's older brother Vinnie was given one and a week later Denis was also given one two doors away from him. We could not see why her brothers were given homes and not their sister even though we had been married prior to them and had been living in Nissen Huts for four years. We wondered when we would get a house especially when people who had left the village years before were given homes."

"I had luck with football pontoon again so Grace and I decided to go to Wembley and see Ireland and England playing. Leaving the children with the in-laws we went to see the match. England won 3 – 1. Grace had been good at sports at school and still liked the same sports as me. A few weeks later we went to see Wales and Ireland playing hockey at Abergaveny. This was not so far from where we lived; Ireland won 6 – 1."

"The two children started at the new school at Kingston and for the first few years the standard of education was very high. We bought two second hand bikes for the children. We could go for cycle rides on Sunday afternoons. On the way back we would stop at the pub. Many people would do this at weekends and lots of children would be playing on the pub lawns."

"Rosemary went to a play at the church hall wearing her new coat. She had only had it a few weeks and it was stolen at the hall. Shortly afterwards I had warned her not to go into a field but she did and cut her leg and knee very badly on barbed wire. I was very cross and got worked up when I noticed the state of her leg. With the rust in the wire she could have lost her leg. I said to her "why don't you go back and do the other leg"."

"Melvyn was to be in the Christmas Play at the new school. My Mother-in-Law was coming to see him and was thrilled when he came on stage. He looked like an angel with his blond curly hair. All the parents remarked on how well he did."

"One occasion we spent three days current picking. The picking was very hard. The first day we only picked currents worth

7/9 and after three days our total was only £1-12-6. After this we never bothered again as it was not worth our while."

During these four years I had great trouble sleeping despite the long hours and heavy nature of the work. Initially when I left the army and moved in with Grace and Rosemary and the family at Old Manor House the joy and relief of the war ending and leaving the army gave me great joy. But as the years went by nightmares became worse and more frequent. Grace helped me so much with my troubled memories; we talked of my childhood much, but of the battles in Africa and Northern Europe I felt I could say nothing and tried my hardest to put them to the back of my mind. This was easier said than done in the darkness of the nights. I would be plagued for many years with these nightmares. On our next house move we were to find these get worse. In modern times this would be known as PTSD, but in those days there was little understanding of these symptoms and certainly no medical assistance.

*An Irish Boy*

# 13

# Weston Beggard

"New houses were being built in the village of Weston Beggard. Grace went to the council offices again. She told them that her parents lived in Lugwardine very near by. For the first time we were added to the list and told to wait to see if we were lucky. Each week I would go to see the progress on the houses. I also went to see regularly a councillor who was on the Parish Council. I told him of all the years of trouble trying to get a home for my family after coming out of the army. This seemed to help and we eventually were allocated one of the houses in the village."

"We already had quite a lot of furniture and items for the house collected whilst at Kingston, enough to fill most of the house. We continued to add to this collection throughout the construction period. It was with great excitement and anticipation that we waited the moving in date to our first proper house. Whilst being erected we would go at weekends and view the progress of the build. It took approximately nine months from initial clearance of that part of the field that had been set aside until completion of the build."

"There were to be erected seven houses and two flats formed as semi-detached dwellings, (the flats being the other half of one pair of semis). They would have good size gardens to the front and rear with car parking facilities to the front of the gardens. This seemed quite advanced for the time as few people owned cars. The building plot for the homes had been a section of field previously used for rotation of arable crops. The soil was clay filled and hard to work initially but was good growing soil. The two storey houses were in local red brick with modern concrete tiled pitched rooves. The front room had an oven in the chimney brest which also heated the water."

"The group of buildings lay in the bottom of a valley midway along Weston Beggard Lane. It was about two miles from Bartestree on the Ledbury Road and one mile from Shucknall Spout which was on the Worcester Road. The small Hamlet of Weston Beggard was just under half a mile away, it was served by The Church of Saint John the Baptist which is c.1200. There was a manor house and sprinkling of farms but was extremely isolated along a winding, steeply climbing lane in either directions bordered by high hedgerow. Being in such a dip in the landscape and also with close proximity to the River Frome the site was cold and damp. In wintery conditions it would be almost inaccessible along an icy dangerous road. At the time of the build there were numerous hop fields around with their frames used for the production beer. This industry was soon to decline. Many believed the houses were placed in that position for the advantage of the local farmers to gain cheap labour. A poorer location for homes would have been difficult to find."

"We had lots of visits to the new house from friends in town. During school holidays lots of friends would drop by. In the summer it was quite idyllic with its good sized gardens surrounded by fields. Grace's family would frequently come to visit and see Melvyn and Rosemary. We would sit in the garden drinking some of homemade drinks and indulging in food parcels from Grace's father's allotment. The walks to the main roads were long, especially if pushing the pram, and then there would be a five mile bus journey into the city."

"One summer holiday we went to Tenby in Wales. We had a short stay in a caravan near the beach. It was in the middle of a field and we had to walk through long grass to get to it. When raining we would get very wet. Each morning I would go and get the bread and milk. The camp shop would only be open a few hours a day. The owners of the camp site were farmers. The camp was just outside Tenby and the beach was very nice. The sands were wide and very deep. We would spend long times on the beach if the day was hot."

"We had a visit from my John Hanna, his sister and niece.

Whilst at work Grace would take them for short trips. At the weekend we left the children with Grace's parents and took them to the hills of Malvern. They enjoyed their stay and said they would like to come back. We received a few letters from them but when the niece got married we never heard from her again. When we had stayed with them in Belfast they had been very nice to us and showed us all the most important sites. Our last holiday in Belfast with them had been wonderful."

"The bus company which took us to work was called Bounds. The son of the owner offered the passengers a weekly payment scheme to go to Glasgow to see England v Scotland. We often had chats about football. The cost of the trip was to be £4-10-0, inclusive of bed and breakfast. It was to leave Friday evening and arrive in Glasgow at 5.30 in the morning. There was only one other chap on the bus from work. On the way back we stayed at Preston. The bus driver had two spare stand tickets which the two of us bought for 15 shillings each. Getting to the stadium we sold them making a good profit for £1 each. The stadium was much bigger than Wembley. The pipe bands marched up and down in lovely colours in their different dress. England won 1 – 0. My friend and I arrived in Preston and went out for some food. In the morning we went for a walk around Preston, all those who had not had too much to drink. The driver said he would put a mark on a tyre of the bus. We would pay a shilling each to guess where the number would end up. My guess was 19 and I won the most money, £7.00 I had a great weekend and came back with more money than I went with."

"After a few months Grace said we could paper the house; after we had papered a few rooms I tiled the Kitchen. The kitchen was very small, hardly enough room to turn around in. The front of the house was very cold, even in the summer.

The sun never got to the front of the house even on the hottest days except for half an hour before the sun set. The first year we were there Grace worked on the hop machines. Most of the women in the new houses were working on the hops. Grace always worked in the fields with the vines as they were growing."

"Our next priority was to get the children into Tupsley School. We went to meet the Head Master and he told us he was only too pleased to take them in as Grace had been a very good pupil of the school and her brothers had been pupils there as well when they all lived at Lugwardine."

"One day Melvyn thought he would take a short cut across fields to get to school. He was part way across the field when he was chased by a bull. This bull was notorious; the man tending the herd was often trapped up a tree trying to get away from the bull. The field had no hiding places to get refuge. We felt sorry for the cows; the bull eventually had to be kept in a special compound."

"After the first year I bought a second hand motor bike to go to work. The bike was only two years old and was very reliable; but in bad weather when the roads were too bad I had to have a lift with a friend in his car. It was a great help having the bike, if we ran out of anything I could go back into town. At weekends we would go together into town to get shopping and visit family. In the summer we would go on trips to Wales joined by Graces' brothers. They organised everything and we enjoyed our outings."

"The side of the house had no path and turned into a quagmire when wet. I made a concrete path and this enabled Grace to put washing out easily. We bought a television, the first in the village. It was good for the children to watch and made up for the lonely evenings in that place. Weston Beggard was a lonely place at the best of times."

"The next shock was that one of the tile works was to close down leaving only one tile works open. So I was sent to work at the other tile factory. I didn't like it there; it was as if a bomb had dropped on it. So I started looking for another job. There was not much work around."

"My next job was working for the council. The wages here were very bad compared to the tile works, just £8-5-0; after tax and other deductions it only left £ 8.00. If I worked Saturday or Sunday morning I could take home £13-0-0, not much for a week's work."

"Grace at the time was working on the hop machines. There was a young girl working there too who had much trouble in home life and she committed suicide. She had always been telling people at work about her home life and this very much upset them. Grace was always trying to get the girl to come home for tea whenever she felt like it. She didn't seem to go to school very much. She was always talking of suicide to Grace which upset her very much."

"After living in Weston Beggard for two years Grace became pregnant. The poor dear had a terrible time all the months she was carrying she was in dreadful pain. This was the time children were being born with missing limbs and other deformities. Grace had terrible pains in her arms and would have injections twice or more a month. Fortunately she never had the tablets to stop the pain and sickness- Thalidomide. It was a god sent the same could have happened to Kevin. Rosemary and Melvyn were at home looking after Grace whilst just before Kevin was born. If they could not be there I would take time off work. A week before he was born Melvyns' school had a trip to Ireland all enjoyed the trip."

"The doctor who looked after Grace was one of the best and we both liked him very much. He told the nurse who was with us that if there was anything she was not sure about to let him know right away. The doctor told us whilst Grace was carrying

Kevin that she had fibrocitus which could give her a lot of trouble. We had to get him when she was about to give birth. The evening before she gave birth she had terrible shaking which did not stop for a long time. I got the water ready very early and had everything ready for the nurse to come. We had wanted for her to have the birth in hospital; the nurse should have rang the doctor and told him how she was feeling. After calling him he sent for the nurse and wanted to know why he had not been informed at the birth. He gave her a huge dressing down. He said Grace was a very sick woman with fibrocitus. He had hoped the fibrocitus might have come away whilst giving birth."

"After Kevin was born the doctor, Doctor Lawson, visited several times. He was to get Grace into hospital to have an operation for the fibrocitus and all should be better.

He said he was going to migrate to Australia; the climate would suit him better as well as the new job. I thanked him for all he had done for Grace; I was pleased I was at home to see him when he came on his last visit. He had filled in the papers for me to sign so Grace could have the operation. Rosemary was a great help after Kevin was born. But it was not long before she decided to go to work in London."

"When he was born we went on a trip to caves in Somerset and Grace kept gripping the ice to ease the pain in her arms. It was a great relief so we stayed in the caves a long time. On the way back from work I would stop at the spring and get cool water for her. I liked it much as well."

"I enquired for work at Wiggins' Factory. They were building a new warehouse and said to come back in a few weeks. The money I was getting on the council was no good. I was on edge hoping I would get the job especially with a new child."

"Rosemary took evening classes at college in town and did very well learning shorthand and typing."

## Chapter 13: Weston Beggard

"One evening I got back from work to find Grace with very bad news her mother had had a stroke. I had been at her house the day before filling her boiler for her to do the washing in the outhouse. Melvyn would call in on the way home from school.

When she came out of hospital if she wanted anything he would be only too pleased to do it for his Nan. I would call in either going to or coming back from work. I would help in any way I could. Grace would try to help as much as possible with Girlie but she was still very weak after carrying Kevin. Vinnie would collect us and take us all to see them at weekends. My Mother-in-Law was recovering from the stroke getting about reasonably well. But she would have confusion with money and any change she was given. She was a wonderful person. We would talk a lot when we sat in her garden."

"At the same time my Father-in-Laws parents had been evicted from their cottage. I helped sort out there house and tidy things. The farmer had loaned me a horse and cart to transport their belongings. They had been awarded an Almshouse within the city walls. They had been living in a tied cottage whilst he worked on a farm; when he could work no more the cottage went with the job so they had to move. Their daughter Minnie Brimfield was living with them she had never married. All her working life she had worked in service. Grace had spent a lot of time with her when she was a girl especially on school holidays."

*An Irish Boy*

# 14

# Wiggins'

"I received a short letter advising me to have a medical prior to starting work there. There were over seventy men waiting for the doctor to give them medical. We all looked around wondering who would be the lucky ones and get jobs. After two hours I was told I could start work next week. It was a huge weight lifted so I could go home and give Grace the good news.

Some of the people who had worked at the tile works also started with me at Wiggins'. When I started the warehouse was not quite finished so for a week we did nothing apart from sweep floors. You can imagine what we thought of that job, with two foremen overlooking twelve men. I was given the job of helping the furnace man to fill the mixed metal to go into the melting pot. Each part of the factory handled a separate part of steel production. I worked in the warehouse as well. Wiggins' was formed in Germany but had been based in Birmingham prior to setting up factory in Hereford. It got much of its copper and other metals from Canada and would make parts for Rolls Royce engines for cars and planes. So it was a big company."

"The part I didn't like was shift work. When on shifts you were mixed with those on day work in each department so it was like being in a prison. I did not sleep well when on night shifts. The slightest noise would wake me up when I tried to sleep in daytime.

Coming off shifts I started to work with my Father-in-Law on a farm owned by Mr. Jack Cook. If I thought Grace was alright before leaving home I would work four hours on the farm. The money from the farm was to buy a new pram. I was pleased Rosemary and Melvyn were at home to look after Grace as she was still very unwell."

"Dear Rosemarys' wages didn't cover what she wanted to do or places she wanted to go to. She had mixed with friends at college in Hereford from wealthier families. She saw what they had and did. Her grand parents had spoiled her. She had stayed of late at The Old Manor House with her Nan and Grand Father during the week to save her long journey from college in Hereford to Weston Beggard. She had not been pleased when my job at the tile works had changed and my working for the council was not to her liking. As for Grace having a baby so late in life, that was bad. We tried to do the best for her. Grace was all the time getting new dresses for her to wear. I got quite upset very often over it, she wanted to wear new clothes all the time."

"She would go out with her friends from college often midweek. Some weekends there were special events or Balls. She would hate to wear the same dress more than one occasion. Her wardrobe was filled to the brim with beautiful dresses; many of these Grace had made herself. She was very talented at dressmaking. One late afternoon on a warm spring Saturday Rosemary started screaming from upstairs that she had nothing to wear. Dear Grace was still very poorly but had even so just completed a new dress the weekend before. I was so angry I went into Rosemary's bedroom opened the wardrobe doors grabbed two armfuls of clothes and threw them out of the bedroom window into the garden below. Both Grace and Rosemary froze and could not react in any way through sheer shock at what I'd done."

"Rosemary had many admirers in the opposite sex. All the time new supposed boyfriends would call at the house. Some would arrive on push bikes, some on foot, some on motor bikes and even some in cars. The most amusing encounter was when she accidentally had two arrive at the same time. One boyfriend was knocking at the front door whilst dear Grace was ferrying another out of the back door discreetly but successfully without either knowing."

"Coming back from his school trip to Ireland, Melvyn was thrilled to see his new brother. Rosemary and Melvyn took Kevin for a few outings in the new pram. If the weather was nice Grace would leave Kevin outside, you didn't know he was born he was so quiet. I would walk as far as my In-Laws each Sunday while Grace got dinner on; there and back took about three hours."

"After Kevin was born I asked the manager if I could have day work for a week so that I could be at home to look after Grace. It was good that he allowed me to because Grace had one of those bad times. Just getting in from work she was in bed and the shaking started. Everything in the bed would tremble. The local doctor came and he said he had never seen anything like it. He had been annoyed to come out after 6 o clock, but he didn't realize how bad she was."

"When I went back onto shift work the man driving the fork-lift truck taught me how to operate it. After a few nights I could go anywhere around the warehouse picking and stacking different metals. The person I was working with would fill the buckets with metal. If the crane was busy I would get the metal in for him with a spare fork-lift. We would finish quickly that way."

"I wanted to use some of the barrels for plant pots at home. I got a ticket from the manager of the ware house. They were just packaging. A friend would put them in his van and take them home for me. One occasion the a Department Manager was looking at the gate with powerful glasses and thought I was taking things away in the barrels. I was stopped at the gate and told to report to him. He asked me who had given me the ticket to remove the barrels. The ware house manager told me later he had no time for the man."

"A lot of the people working in the ware house used to get tickets to take wood or barrels; I don't know why he picked on me. It probably got his nose up when he found I had not stolen anything. It was like a prison working there; everywhere you looked were wire fences. There was a chap who the man stopped and told to empty his bag. He said to him "empty the bag yourself if you want to." What he didn't know was his brother-in-law had given him manure before coming to work. When the bag was emptied out you should have seen their faces. He told them to keep it and clean up the mess themselves. We laughed at the thought of them cleaning up the manure. One day I was moving crates at the end of my shift with the fork-lift. A manager saw me using the truck and asked how long I'd been doing it. I said just two weeks and he was impressed and said a day job was coming up soon driving the fork-lift. He would keep me in mind. I was fed up of shift work, going to work at night. But when you signed you agreed to do it. As new buildings were completed they were taking on lots more people. Our neighbour applied for a job but was turned down; his wife was very upset."

"There was a man who always started work before his shift and did extra work. I said to him he should not do that because if anything happened to him whilst he was outside his shift he would not be covered. He said nothing like that would happen to him. A few weeks later he was working on his own time and a piece of metal flew out of the container and cut his arm and face. He was off sick for six weeks but only received sick pay, no compensation. When he returned to work they put him sweeping floors; whilst I was there he never returned to the cutting machine. I saw him and he had a bad mark on his face and arm. I said that he could have got compensation via the union if he had not been working before his time. He had been with the firm in Birmingham and like others who had come from there many worked before their shift began."

# 15

# Rosemary and Melvyn leave for London

Kevin was coming along fine; he was no trouble in any way to Grace. This was good as she was not in good health. He was a pretty baby with long golden curly hair.

Iris Brimfield following the death one after the other of two husbands early in the war had married Bernard Herd. She stayed with her family at The Old Manor House for much of the war whilst Bernard was on active service. She eventually joined Bernard at his parent's home in Canonbury Park North, near Canonbury Square in Islington, North London. Leaving the army after completing his period of duty he set up in his chosen profession as a jeweller and diamond merchant. They were soon to rent a fine four storey early Victorian semi-detached house along the road from his parents in Canonbury Park North, on the corner of Balls Pond Road.

The house was huge with steps up to a large front door with glass panels either side. The large entrance hall had a conservatory off to the right and elegant staircase to the left with continuous winding banister. There were two large reception rooms on that floor; in the basement there was a further reception room to the front with two windows, a kitchen at the rear and beneath the conservatory some store rooms. The upper two floors contained four bedrooms and a large bathroom. Outside the corner plot retained a good size walled garden until part of it was extracted for widening of the road junction.

The couple were to have two boys whilst in this house; firstly Brian and seven years later Barry. They would spend twenty five years there in great happiness. Iris took secretarial classes at night school and started work in an office locally. She soon realised she had skills in book keeping as well. Being very fond of children she spent several years teaching at a primary school in Islington. Rosemary and Melvyn would often go up to stay with the family and experience the joys and diversity of Central London life. Many parties and get together would take place there.

It was shortly after Rosemary's eighteenth birthday that she took the plunge moved to the city to join Iris and her family. She went to stay for a year with Iris who had plenty of space for her to lodge. She was also in a good position to use her secretarial skill and get a good job in the city. She had developed into an attractive woman. She was quite short, only five feet eight inches tall; but she was somewhat voluptuous. She sported very high heels and in the style popular at the time, a tall bop hair style. Taking after her mother she was very well spoken and elegant in manner as well as being very bright and witty. As I mentioned before she had an obsession with clothes and always looked the part.

She would prove very popular with the more refined and older man. She would soon launch herself onto the West End party scene. She took little time before she started mixing with distinguished people in Knightsbridge and Kensington. Iris and Bernard and the two boys loved having her with them. When they were not having parties or drinks at home they would be frequenting the local Hostelries.

The following year, 1962, Rosemary rented a flat of her own. All through her life she desired independence. She wanted to be close to Iris and her family so the flat she rented was a quarter mile

## Chapter 15: Rosemary and Melvyn leave for London

away on the boarder of Islington and Stock Newington in Sprindale Road. This was the time of rented rooms in large Victorian houses. Purpose build or self-contained refurbishments were a thing of the future. Her flat comprised two large rooms at the top of a tall four floor house which was rented out by the floor. The kitchen was in the smaller room at the back and there was no bathroom, just a shared toilet on the half landing below. Some furniture came with the flat as did the cooker. By modern standards it was extremely basic and lacking facilities. Never-the-less it was the first home of her own and after thoroughly cleaning it she was quite pleased to call it home.

Melvyn and Rosemary have always had a close bond. Melvyn also had done well in his studies at school. He had had the odd fall out with his maths teacher, but still obtained good results. He enjoyed London life and particularly got on very well with Barry. They were both talented musicians and singers. It was not a great surprise that he would join Rosemary in her flat just a couple of months after she had moved into it. He would have great advantages in obtaining work there especially in the line of bookkeeping and then accountancy in the City of London which was less than three miles away.

We were pleased for them but very sad after they left home. It took us some time to get used to not having them at home. I suppose all parents are the same when the children leave home. They would not have got on in life if they had stayed in Hereford. We were very proud of our children; they never caused us any trouble. My In-Laws said they were a credit to have as grandchildren.

"What was nice for both of us we had Kevin to keep us both very happy. We went into town on Saturdays to get our shopping. I had a push chair to take Kevin in while going shopping. We used to go to see our friends who had lived next door to us at Kingston. They said they were to move into one of the new houses almost finished at Kingston. We were pleased for them; Grace and I went along to see their house a few months after they had moved in; they said they had liked our house very much. They came to Weston Beggard a few times to see us; they were great friends of us both. When she was down in the dumps she said Grace was the only person she could tell her troubles to."

"I had been working at Wiggins' for four years on shifts helping the furnace man. While I was helping him I got to know all the different metals. The manager told me he was going to put me on the fork lift and doing day work. There were a lot of new people being taken on in the warehouse. I was over the moon. He said I would be on that job from now on. Going to different sections and collecting different things meant my time went very quick. Outside I would have to unload the Lorries which had wooden pallets with loads of metal. Most of it came from the docks in London. I did this for two hours each day."

"My first day out on the fork-lift I was in the middle of picking up some metal sheets and the fork-lift stopped. The gas bottle was showing half full and to make it worse it was a long way to where the gas bottles were stored. I found out that a lot of gas bottles were faulty. Never got caught again, each day I would get a card to get a new one before starting. All the spare metal was taken and stacked in containers and weighed and entered in my book. These were handed in at end of each day. My day was never dull, I was doing all types of jobs in different departments; you could say 'Jack of all trades, master of none'."

"The next bad news was my Mother-in-Law passed away. Graces' Grand Mother died the next day. Grace went home, (to The Old Manor House), for a few days to help her Father. I stayed to look after Kevin; he was learning to walk quite well. After a while my Father-in-Law had a few days with us. He would come and stay quite a lot at weekends from now on when I was at home. It was a huge shock for all of us. Grace's Mother was a fine and caring woman; Grace's Grand Mother was very much of the same. Grace's

Father seemed to cope much better than we had feared. Having the stroke had been devastating. Trying to cope with the aftermath of the stroke and its debilitating effect can somehow prepare you for the death of the person. This is particularly the case when a severe stroke leaves the person in a great deal of discomfort and confusion."

"The Vicar came to ask me if I would light the stove in the church before the services on Sundays. Grace and I would clean the silver and brass in the church once a month. Each time we cleaned the vases we would put in fresh flowers. The other people who took turn cleaning never left them very clean."

"The Vicar was one of the best at giving a sermon I was never bored while he was speaking. Often when we got back from town our neighbour would say the Vicar had been helping himself to flowers from our garden, even when it was not our turn to do the flowers. He would often take flowers from our garden for the church. He would frequently call in for a beer or some tea. He would talk about anything, it didn't matter what subject; if passing in his car he would often stop for a chat. Before I left he told me he planned to go back to live in Canada where he was from; his mother, though had come from nearby Weston Beggard."

"Melvyn had been an Altar Boy for a short time whilst he was at Tupsley School. Kevin was baptised at the church. It was one of the few decent things one could award to the village. We had very close bond to the church and the vicar. I would go to the church just after six o clock in the morning to get the stove ready for the 8 o clock service in the morning. What I didn't like was that the church warden as soon as he came in would close the old stove down so when I went to light it the following week it was full of old coke. I said to the Vicar why does he do that it was a waste of my time trying to get the church warm especially when the mornings were so cold. He was the one who told me to get out of his field when I was taking a short cut home from my Sister-in-Law Girlies'.

Everyone said he was a law to himself and no one else. When it was our turn to clean the vases in the church, after doing that and then collecting wood for the fire we would do tidying in the cemetery around the church."

"We received a letter from the hospital saying that Grace would be going in for an operation and that it would be a big operation. Everything would be taken away which was causing the trouble. I told everyone that she would be well; they didn't know how bad she felt at times. Minnie said she would look after Kevin whilst Grace was in hospital. To make it easier for her I washed and fed him before taking Grace to hospital."

"Coming back from a walk one evening past the Church Wardens' house his dog jumped through the hedge and bit my jacket into my arm. It bled very badly. I went to see his wife and had a bloody good few words with her over it. She said her dog would not do a thing like that so she was calling me a liar. I said that if my arm didn't get better I would take them to court. Her husband was supposed to be a millionaire so I expect he didn't care. At the time I had been walking past with Kevin. I made sure after that I would have a big stick to attack the dog. It was a good thing that Kevin had been walking the other side of me or else he would have been bitten. Many other people said the dog had tried to bite them and it was a very sly animal."

"Grace would say to Kevin that Dad would be home soon and he would wait at the gate for the sound of the motor bike. I would give him a ride on the bike down the garden path. If it was a nice day I would go round the farms and let him see the different animals; he used to like these walks; if I said I was going out he would be waiting at the door. Coming home from work one night I went to get some coal from the lean-to and saw lots of smoke. The fuse box was on fire. Worst still my motor bike was under it and the wires were melting onto it. It was lucky I'd seen it as the house might have burnt down with us in it. We got hot water from our

## Chapter 15: Rosemary and Melvyn leave for London

next door neighbour and were with out power for a day. They had fitted the fuse box badly and on top of the beam next to lean-to roof."

"Around about the same time, after unloading pallets at work at Wiggins, I went to help another forklift that was stuck. My forklift slipped and the two prongs punctured the water tank of the other forklift. When I explained what had happened the senior manager said I would have a days work without pay. There is no smoke without fire. I thought he was a bit off hand on his part. I believed Wiggins' was like the army; the ones who were charged with sorting things out were the ones who were put on by the ones it didn't affect."

"Grace was to go into hospital the following Tuesday; Minnie had come to look after Kevin; the surgeon was to be Dr. Brown; she would be in for about ten days. What we didn't know about Dr. Brown was that he was to do the operation from a wheel chair; he had lost both his legs. I didn't want to ask how that had come about, he was a brave surgeon doing that kind off work; he came from Ireland."

"Grace actually was in hospital for twelve days. They said everything went well. I thanked one and all. After a day at home the cut where they had operated gave her some trouble. She went to bed for a few days and didn't want to get the doctor out. I was surprised to see a large opening; they said it would take time to seal up. I was afraid she might start to have the shakes again. This would be bad especially in her condition after coming out of hospital. I was hoping they would send a nurse to see if she was alright. I wanted to call the doctor but Grace thought it was unnecessary. I didn't want to do anything she said not to."

*An Irish Boy*

# 16

# We move to London

The winter we left Weston Beggard was very cold; the snow was so deep that snow ploughs could not reach our lane. The water supply to the house froze up. I had to carry water quite a long way from the spring which never froze, Shutnell Spout. This spring was used to give water to the cattle and horses as they made their journey along Worcester Road. The snow blocked many main roads and made them impassable by vehicles. These conditions were the severe winter of 1962/3.

After three months of suffering the extreme cold, trying to get to work, get supplies of food and even the mile or more walk through snowdrifts to get water Grace said would I like to get a job in London; she was fed up living where we were. I made my mind up there and then that we would join Melvyn and Rosemary in London. I gave my notice in at Wiggins' and said I would leave there at the end of the week. I had to go and see the Personnel Manager. Why was I leaving he wanted to know; is it anything someone has said to you. I could have told them quite a lot of what was wrong; but what I was after was for them to give me a good reference for me to have when I went looking for a job. He told me that when I got a job the firm should request a reference from him; they did not give references to a person who left. I thought I might have got one after all the years

I had been there. I worked at Wiggins' metal works for just over five years.

The extreme winter of 1962/3 was the final blow to us to make us leave Hereford. We had close family bond there; Vinnie and Betty and family were at Bartestree, Girlie, Horace and Keith were also in Bartestree and were now joined by Grace's Father; Dennis and Glenda and family were in Lugwardine; Leslie, Bernes and family were in The City of Hereford; Ronnie Brenda and family had moved many times all around the country and also abroad to Germany, (he had remained in the armed forces).

Throughout our married life we had struggled to get a place to call our own; when we obtained it there were many shortcomings. Work had been difficult to find and usually involved unsocial hours and poor pay. Dear Grace had worked on the land and this no doubt affected her health. She was now making great progress in her recovery. Kevin was in his third year. With her Mother now gone and her Father in the care of Girlie and Horace; also with Melvyn and Rosemary and Iris ensconced in London it was time for us to join them. We would move in with Melvyn and Rosemary temporarily until I found work to provide for us and then a home of our own. It was a totally new start for us. A big gamble one might say.

**End of Part Two**

*An Irish Boy*

*Joining the Paratroops as a 28 year old*

*An Irish Boy*

*Grace Brimfield aged 20, 1942*

*An Irish Boy*

*Preparation for Operation Market Garden*

*Hamilcar and Horsa Gliders being towed by Halifax Bombers*

*An Irish Boy*

*Wedding party in garden of Old Manor House, 1942*

*An Irish Boy*

*Left to Right: Africa Star, WW2 Medal, Defence Medal*

*Statue commemorating Paratroop Regiment at Arnhem*

v

*An Irish Boy*

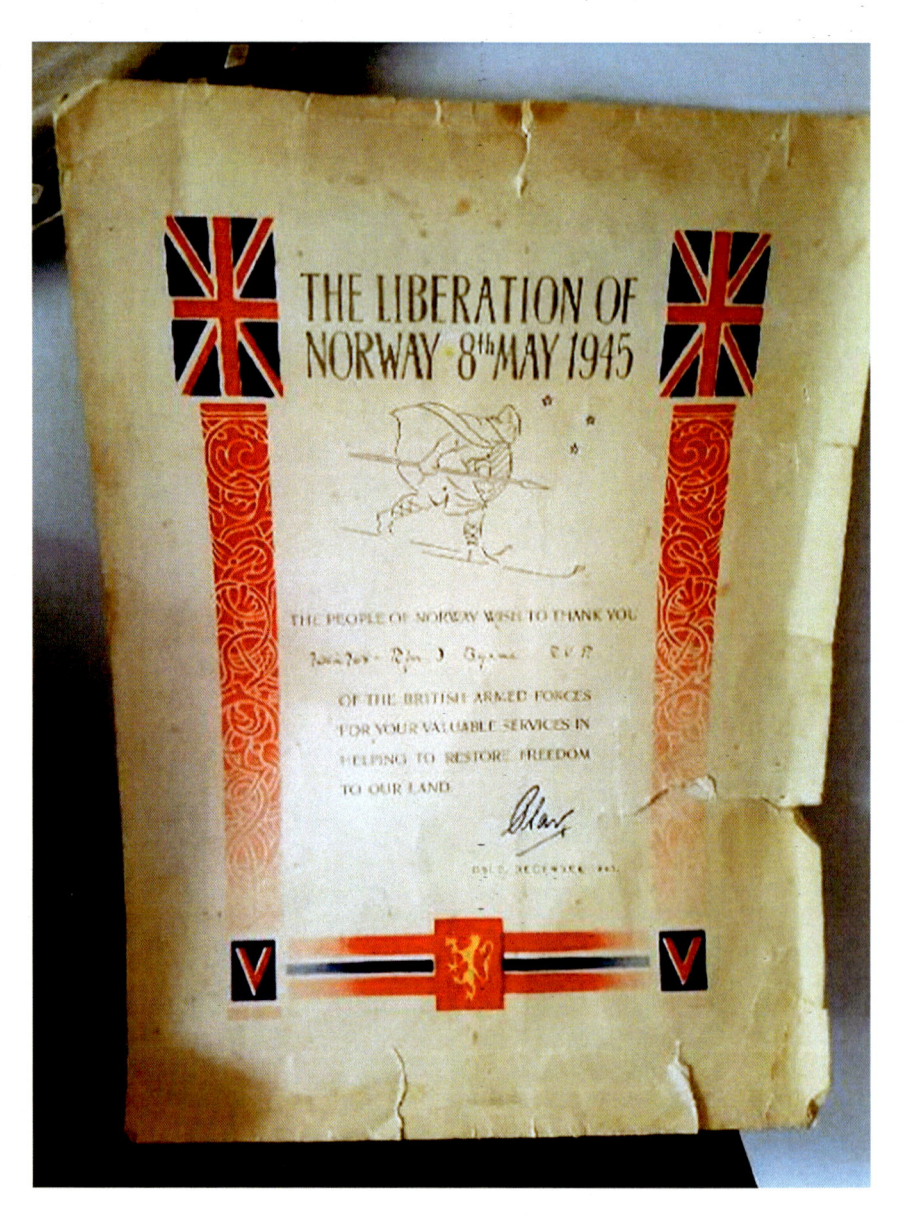

*Commemoration Certificate from King Olav of Norway, 1945*

# *An Irish Boy*
Part 3

# 1

# Moving to London

After the worst winter for decades and Melvyn and Rosemary having already taken the plunge John decided to go in search of work in the big city leaving his secure job and home and Grace looking after three year old Kevin back in Weston Beggard.

Grace said Girlie would have the furniture until we got a place or until we could find storage for it. Girlie and Horace had rented one half of a semi-detached pair of stone cottages at the end of a narrow and winding lane in Bartestree. Luck would have it that they would purchase the two semi-detached cottages and with the help of Keith their son would convert them into a substantial detached house in a good square plot of ground adjacent meadows. Grace and Girlie were extremely close to each other and spent lots of time together. Girlie was most upset that her second sister was going to London to start a new life. They had lived only two miles apart and the journey to London by road or train in those days took hours. She had had much better fortune with Horace being a Welshman whose family were less than twenty miles away in Monmouth just outside the border of Herefordshire. Almost immediately after the war they had been awarded a council house at Withington, not far from Bartestree. Horace had a knack of finding unusual employment as well as in his part time assisting the hunting and fishing brigade on nearby estates. He also had a lot of luck at the 'bookies'. Horace and Girlie made available a large room in their home for all our furniture and helped us pack and install our things with them for as long as we needed. They were always very generous and our close relationship would continue until our deaths. We would frequently go to stay with them and Girlie would likewise come to visit us. Horace would always be working so rarely would come to London likewise Keith was a self-employed plumber so also could not come.

"A friend at work said his wife was having a baby, it was their first. I told him we had a nearly new pram if he would like to come and see it. He and his wife loved the pram and they took it away in their van along with some baby clothes; they gave us £13-0-0 for it. Grace was pleased to know the pram was off our hands before leaving. Some neighbours three doors away bought my motor bike for £60-0-0, so I left the village in good spirits after all my dealings. I had originally bought the bike for £100-0-0 but was pleased to get it off my hands. At least we had a little money between the two of us for the time we were to be parted."

"During my last week at work many of the men said I was mad to go to London not having a job to go to. I took no notice of them. When I look back it was the best thing I could have done; luck was to be on our side we would get to have our own house, which is what everyone would like to have."

"So off to the big city to live with Rosemary and Melvyn in the flat they had rented from an Irish couple called Mr and Mrs May. Melvyn met me at Paddington Station after the long rail journey still the old steam trains. It was great to see him after such a time. We got the underground to Highbury and Islington then walked about twenty minutes to their flat. Rosemary met us at the front door, she had seen us coming and was thrilled to see me. Coming up the forth flight of stairs and into the two rooms at the top of the house I was a bit surprised. I had expected a slightly more cheerful place and a bit more space, bearing in mind Grace and Kevin were also joining Melvyn and Rosemary here. It was like a time warp from the war years, I am sure little had changed since then."

"The first week the weather was not very good. I had a good look around. There was plenty of snow and ice on the roads this turned to black sludge. The buildings in those days were blackened by soot from the thousands of chimneys both domestic and industrial. North London where we were to settle was not as smart then as it is now; but it did retain some of the charm from yesteryear. The area near our flat was almost entirely residential with large buildings on tree lined roads. There were many open spaces to get away from our cramp quarters; Newington Green was at the end of the road; Clissold Park was five minutes' walk; Highbury Fields was half a mile."

"I went with Rosemary to where she worked to see if there was anything doing for a job, but there was nothing in regards to work. They said to come back later on. On the way back we went to see Iris; she said that the tea lady at the printing works was away sick and if I wanted I could make tea for the 16 people. I thought that was alright until I got a job and ended up there five weeks."

"I saw an advertisement for men wanted at a paint works. I got a job there spraying the lids of the paint pots with a small gun. After a week I decided I didn't like the job. It was also quite a long way from where we lived, it was near Hackney Marshes. The first Saturday they asked me to work and I had to be there for 6am. There were no buses to get me there for that time so I had to get up at three o'clock in the morning to walk there. I got home at 2pm. I was done in."

"I stayed working at the paint works for six weeks. Then I got a job in a metal works drilling hoardings which were supplied to Marks and Spencer Stores. After a few days they left me to work on my own. I discovered that there were lots of different pay levels and lots of immigrant workers working there. So after a month I asked if I could have a few pence more per hour. They said they would look into it for me."

"The firm was in Old Street EC1, (on the edge of the City of London), not far from where we lived. I got there on the 73 bus. Now we were more established Grace decided to come to London to live with us all. She didn't like being away from the rest of the family."

The week before the move had seen the removal of the furniture from Weston Beggard to Bartestree. Grace had stayed with her sister for the final week having taken the keys back to the Town Hall and settling any account with the utilities and council. The evening of the move Grace and Kevin stayed with Leslie and Bernes at The Old Manor House; they had recently moved there and taken over the tenancy following their Father's move to live with Girlie and Horace. The mood was sombre as everyone was sad Grace was leaving them to move to London. Leslie and Bernes had a two year old boy, Stephen, and were expecting soon to arrive, Janet and later Richard. It would have been nice for the two boys Stephen and Kevin to play together as all their other cousins were much older.

Leslie had a saloon car with plenty of room. He offered to take Grace and Kevin up to London. The next morning they had sweet porridge for breakfast sat around a big wooden table in the central room of the house in front a roaring wood fire. It was extremely dark and cold and still very icy. As was normal for that time of year in Lugwardine the wind tore up the Ledbury Road up from the marshes below.

The road looked precarious. The car had been loaded the evening before and was very full. Apart from child paraphernalia and four large suit cases of clothes there was a wooden clothes horse which somehow managed to fit over their heads inside the car and various boxes and bags of pots and pans and personal effects. When I had joined the children in London, about two months

*Chapter 1: Moving to London*

before, I had carried just a small suitcase on the train; enough for myself to get by.

Setting off from Lugwardine they had a long and slow journey. A snow plough had been out an hour before and the main Ledbury Road was passable but with great care. Some of the bends were steep and bore a thin layer of black ice not obvious to the eye. Many years later Grace and Kevin would have a bad accident in similar conditions near Dormington luckily escaping with their lives after demolishing fifty yards of fence and hedge and ending up in a field.

From Ledbury through to Tewkesbury the conditions deteriorated and they were forced to stop in the Town Centre at Tewkesbury until the snow stopped and the light improved. By this time the young Kevin who had not been any great distance in a car before was violently sick. Grace had opened the door just in time for him to vomit in the gutter. On through the Cotswolds to Stow-on-the-Wold they had to stop twice more. The up and down momentum along the undulating roads had bad effect on the porridge. After managing the steep hill in Burford they joined the Oxford Road passing through Witney and eventually into The City of Oxford. They had been forced to stop three more times for this delicate child. In those days before motorways and dual carriageways all traffic passed through the towns and cities. Next along the A40 over another steep range of wooded hills and weaving their way along the meandering road through many small villages they passed Highwycombe. A further twenty miles and the A40 entered the sprawling western fringes of London. Mile after mile of semi-detached house with little to distinguish from the next these dispersed with large factory and storage facilities; occasional green spaces broke the symmetry.

The buildings became more period and greater in stature. The road had widened considerably and was punctuated by large intersections. Lots of underground stations were dotted along these junctions. Coming into Euston Road after passing the corner of

Regents Park a huge demolition site lay to the left of the road. This had been the site of the Doric Euston Arch which had been the entrance to the terminus. It had been controversially demolished after years of wrangling between politicians, architects and rail officials. Harold MacMillan and the Conservative Prime Minister had been among the many who desperately wanted to save the building. Next they passed St. Pancras Station the fate of which would lie in the balance for decades to come. How such a beautiful, fairy tale gothic cathedral-like building could face demolition was impossible to understand. Kings Cross, its neighbour was the only edifice in this group to be unthreatened by the philistine planners of the sixties and seventies.

The snow now a distant memory they headed up Pentonville Road, left into Angel Islington and through Upper Street to Highbury Corner thence the short hop to Newington Green and Springdale Road.

"I was very pleased to see young Kevin again and it was wonderful to be united with Grace. The weeks apart seemed interminable. I had the new experiences of work in London but I was not unduly concerned about Grace's recovery and how young Kevin was getting on because we had kept in touch regularly."

"There was a lovely park only a few minutes away from where we were living, Clissold Park. There was a safe children's area with a splash around shallow paddling pool. I would go there when off work with the family. In the park there were deer, ducks and swans on the lakes. A mansion was set within the grounds this was now tea rooms. It had been a former estate and the house and grounds had been saved from development and had become a sanctuary for those living nearby. There was a miniature railway which children could have rides on."

"The other park we would go to at weekends was Finsbury Park. This was about one and half miles away. We would go there Sunday evenings. The flower beds were very well set out with lots

*Chapter 1: Moving to London*

of different arrangements. The bus services were very good. We visited most of the Parks in London whilst we lived there. It was good to see people off work having fun playing games; we often would join others in football games or cricket. People were very open then and would invite you to join them in a game."

"Rosemary was desperate to get a flat of her own and after a couple of months was to move out into similar rented rooms nearby. We had been living in the top two rooms of the house for the best part of ten months. In these two rooms were myself, Grace, Melvyn, Rosemary, Kevin and we had frequent visits from Auntie Minnie who loved to come and see us in London. The Kitchen was in the rear room and we had to share a WC situated on a half landing below with three other households, (The May's had their own facilities in the basement); it had a toilet but no sink and any personal hygiene had to be undertaken in our Kitchen. Where we all slept I cannot remember. Kevin had boxes of toy cars all over the floor. To make it worst Mrs. May expected Grace to clean and polish the hallway and stairs throughout the four storey building and outside the flats of all the other residents living below us."

"The Mays' were to go on holiday to USA for a month and they asked Grace to collect the rent from the rest of the tenants while they were on holiday. While they were away there was a terrible thunder storm and the drains got blocked. Their kitchen was in the basement and I was in my pants up to my knees in water from the drains trying to unblock them. It took us a long time to clean up their rooms."

"The rent Grace collected amounted to £80-0-0 which was a lot of money then. As soon as they got back they were up the stairs after the rent money. They didn't even give Kevin as much as the price of a packet of sweets as a little present. You would have thought they would at least have offered us one week rent free, especially after what we had done for them whilst they were away."

"I went to Mrs. May to complain about the springs in our mattress. When I lay in a certain way they would cut my leg. She did nothing and was the type of person who did not care. Another occasion Grace was making us pan cakes, Mrs. May asked if she could make them some as well. All she contributed was a lemon. Grace said to her there were other ingredients but that's all she gave. Irish people are renowned for giving and taking and their generosity; but the Mays would take blood from a stone if it was possible."

"Mrs. May said to Grace that no one would give us rooms with all of us and our furniture. We were lucky that they had let us move in; also she was told that she put too much washing out on the line. As luck would have it Grace made a friend of the local green grocers' wife. Grace often told her of the cramp conditions we were living in; she said she'd keep her in mind if something became available. Shortly afterwards she told Grace that she knew a landlord who had a place to let; so she introduced us to him and we took the place."

The maisonette was the top two floors of a three storey early Victorian house in Mildmay Grove on the boarders of Canonbury and Newington Green. Mildmay Grove would have once been a good road of quality houses. Our home was near a now redundant station Mildmay Park Station on the old main line to Broadstreet Station in The City. In the days of Victorian railway fever it was not thought bad position to be next to a railway line. Mildmay Grove was on either side of a wide railway cutting with at least four railway lines. This meant lots of noise from trains. Like many older houses at that time it had been poorly divided up into badly served rented accommodation. There were two rooms on each floor, the larger at the front and smaller at rear. There was a front door positioned at the bottom of the staircase in the front hallway to section off the maisonette. There was no bathroom and the only toilet for the house was in the back garden accessed by going through the ground floor flat. Nevertheless there was a great deal more space for us to live in and the opportunity to bring our furniture up from Hereford to make life more comfortable. We were also only a quarter mile from Iris and family; Melvyn and Barry being very close friends and on verge of starting up a group- The Blue Saints.

"Needless to say the place needed a lot of cleaning. We were so pleased to be leaving the Mays and their place. It would be lovely to have our own furniture around us instead of cleaning other peoples tat especially as they were telling Grace to do this and that and getting on our nerves. We sent for our furniture from Girlies' and all went very well until the three piece suit would not fit through the door at the bottom of the stairs. So I got a small saw and cut the middle rail out of the sitting room window on the first floor and we pulled them up on rope."

"Just before we told Mrs. May we were leaving she said to Grace that she had bought some new wall paper and would she decorate the front room for her. It was such a surprise to her when we said we were leaving at the weekend. You should have seen her face. As we left the rooms we had a good laugh to ourselves knowing we had got one back on her."

"I had been at the metal works for three months then bad news the metal works were to move to the North Circular Road. They offered me an extra sixpence an hour pay if I would go there. I said to them why they not given me the extra money when I had asked for it. I did not want to travel that far to work. It would have been about ten miles and difficult on buses. The last few weeks they put some people with me to learn the job; the first one lasted half a day the next two days."

"I'd seen a job advertised in a tobacco works near Clerkenwell cleaning machines and collecting loose tobacco after the shifts finished. I went there at the hour they said and there were four other men beside myself. A few days later I'd got the job. It was enjoyable working there but it was to close and relocate to Ireland.

I worked there two and a half years. Each day I was allowed one pint of milk, an ounce of tobacco, and each week twenty cigarettes. As I've never smoked in my life I saved them up and gave them to my Father-in-Law when we went on trips to Hereford."

"I started at 12pm and worked till 9 in the evening. I worked most Saturday mornings and every other Sunday. The other employees were good to get along with. There would be a good bonus every six months, the first I missed by one month. I was also responsible for locking the doors at lunchtime. They had their own security all the time these were ex-Scotland Yard. You were warned not to take anything. Whilst I was there lots were caught steeling tobacco. You were searched as you went home randomly so you didn't know when they would search you. I was stopped a few times. If you were a smoker, if the wrappers on the cigarettes were broken and some missing they would let you through as you could not sell these. If you were found with goods the police were called and cigarettes taken as evidence."

"The charge hand who issued me with my wages was a woman who was in charge of lots of machines. She had worked there many years but was caught with fifty ounces of tobacco. If she had been selling this amount for all those years she must have made a lot of money. When I came in the following day and heard the news I felt quite sorry for her."

"If I worked Sunday my wages were for the week £19-10-0; I was very happy there. A year before they closed the factory I got a job cleaning a butchers shop in Smithfield Market. I had to be there at 7am finishing at 11am. It wasn't very far from the tobacco works so I earned an extra £5-10-0. You could order your meat for the weekend whatever you wanted by Tuesday. It would be a lot cheaper than the normal butchers shops. Grace would sometimes come to meet me in between jobs and have a cup of tea and a walk around. It was a long day. I would order my dinner at the tobacco works and get it half price. We'd have it at 4pm. The food was very good. I liked to earn a little extra when I could I never liked being short of money."

"When the firm relocated some of the Irish girls who came from that part of Ireland went as well. They said there was a job at Wills Tobacco if I wanted it. I didn't want to be out of work so took the job. The job was to clean all the office lights, when I had finished cleaning all of them they would need to be cleaned again. I didn't like the job; the foreman was very mean. If you asked for more cleaning materials he would say "what did you do with the ones I gave you". I would have some words with him. Eventually I went to a manager and he said he would have a word with him. I said to Grace I wouldn't be there very long."

"I had a 3.30 dentist appointment one Friday and the works closed at 4.30pm. This foreman said to me "make sure you come back after the dentist appointment". Leaving the dentist it was not worth going back to work. On the Monday morning arriving at work I didn't have time to say anything and the foreman laid into me before I could say anything. I said my piece to him and told him he was a little Hitler. I went up stairs to ask who was above him; after waiting some time his manager appeared and I explained what had happened and what I thought of the foreman. I could not stand the sight of him. The manager didn't seem to be surprised but did not take side and dismissed the incident."

"Another occasion on my tea break he came over to me and said I was five minutes over my break. What annoyed me was I was not on machines and was just cleaning lamp shades so what did it matter if I was five minutes over on my tea break. Once again I went upstairs to give my notice in. I said to them if they didn't keep him away from me I would not be responsible for my actions. For the rest of the week I did anything to kill time. Others told me that he had behaved the same to people doing that job. I told him he was a little tin god. They must have had a word with him, but the last few days I didn't ask him for anything. I was never so pleased to get away from that sort of work."

"Meanwhile Grace and I thoroughly cleaned the flat. She papered all through and I replaced some panes of broken glass in bedroom window and hall door. Grace was very professional with her papering the flat looked very good. People would say they could get her plenty of work if she took up decorating."

"The flat now decorated and comfortable with our furniture Melvyn and his girlfriend and Rosemary and her friends and Barry had a party. We had a great time. It was good to reciprocate for all the parties we had been to at Iris and Bernard's.

It was at this time that Melvyn and Barry and some friend started their band- The Blue Saints. They played in local pubs and in some West End clubs as backing group. They played at the 100 Club in Oxford Street. I would love to go and watch them. They were very talented and they made a recording. Melvyn would take Kevin to the pictures on Saturday morning when he was playing in the band before the film came on. After their gigs the group would come back to our flat and have bacon sandwiches then fall asleep on the floor, all over the living room and kitchen. It was great to have them there with us."

# 2

# Highbury Fields

"After the party we had a long lay-in and then went to the park with all family and friends. In the park we met a friend we had often spoken to, John Grant. I told him I was out of work and looking for a job. He said he would take me to see his Manager in the Parks Dept. at GLC. It was Monday and his day off so he took me to the office which was in West End. They gave me a short interview and then I had to fill in some papers these to take to the Superintendent in charge of Highbury Fields. I went home to tell Grace who was delighted. Next I went to see the Superintendent in the office in Highbury Fields. I gave him the papers to read. He signed them and said I would start there next week, but first there were some things he needed to explain as to the way they did things at Highbury Fields.

He asked me if I had any driving experience. I said all I had driven was a motorbike. Leaving there I thought if he thinks I am going to drive anything he can think again. I discovered that he drove the tractor and there was no one else working there who could drive. So I could understand why he would have hoped for another driver. His day off was Monday so my first day he was not on duty. It turned out that he was on a week holiday, so I didn't see him in my first week. My first job was cleaning around the road and football field."

"Little did I know after the first few days that this would be the best job in my working life. I only wish that I could have gone to work there when I first moved to London."

"At the same time we were getting the landing papered and painted, the flat had been empty for some time. The only trouble was we had to share the toilet with the couple who lived downstairs. Very often they would use daily news paper rather than toilet paper. When we saw the roll was coming to an end we would make sure the proper ones were used. They would often have rows and fights and I felt like telling them to keep the noise down. All the time we were there we did not know whether they were married or not; they had one child, a little girl. He used to collect scrap metal and old clothes and rags in his hand cart. I don't think he made very much money. Neither of them seemed very clean when I saw them."

"All my time at Highbury Fields I never had much high regards for the Superintendent. The second in charge was Jack Crawley. He was a very fine person to work with and became a lifelong friend. When the Superintendent was off duty Jack would be in charge of all the parks which came under control of Highbury Fields. There were seven parks in all."

"He came along with the tractor and trailer and said to me to come and empty all the bins full of rubbish. After this was done he took the tractor into the big field and said for me to sit in the seat and drive around. He stood on the back and told me what to do. I was ok until he said to back the trailer between two trees. The trailer went one way the tractor the other. After a few tries I got a little better. He said I had done well in the few hours he had taught me. The rest of the week I drove it on my own and felt rather proud. After five days I was shown how to connect the triple gang mower to the tractor and cut the grass. I was competent with much of the manoeuvres by then. Jack said he would send me for a test and if I passed it would cover me for driving a car of my own. Sadly the following week they recruited a tractor driver who also had a car

*Chapter 2: Highbury Fields*

and I was not put on the tractor anymore. On the tractor drivers days off I would be able to use the tractor. They were pleased I could do the job, there was much work to be done going from one park to another. I spent much time with Jack and he showed me how many things were done. He had been in charge of Springfield Park before coming to Highbury. The Superintendent had arrived just after he took over. His name was Elmer and he mainly stayed in the office doing paper work, wages for the various parks. I didn't have much to do with him. He seemed to want to keep himself to himself; I would say good morning and give him a cup of tea and that would be it. I accompanied Jack all the time and he issued instructions for the others. Going to other parks Jack would drive the tractor if the tractor driver was off."

"While we worked together we had some good times and plenty of laughs. When managers from the GLC Parks Dept. visited they would come to talk to Jack, I don't think the Superintendent liked that very much. I told him he was a 'Man for All Seasons'."

"We paid the rent each Monday morning to the local Rent Office in Green Lanes, the other side of Newington Green. When the Manager came to see the flat he was very surprised how well we had decorated it and what a lot of money we had spent getting it so nice. He said to Grace that he only wished the people living downstairs would pay their rent in time like we did. His name was Mr. Brunston, he was an extremely good man; his partner in the business was Mrs. Enright. She was a no-nonsense sort of person. If she took a dislike to you, you'd be put to one side. One day Grace saw her telling off a woman who was behind with her rent. Grace was uneasy when she was in one of her moods. The rent office moved to a new branch near where I worked and it was from here we had news from the landlord that we would have to move the landlord was selling the house."

"It was terrible news after all the work we had done making the place look so nice. We were given two weeks notice. The landlord had lots of property but was a serious drinker and had to keep selling them. Mr. Brunston was very concerned and said he would do everything he could to find us a home. We had only been there ten months."

"As luck had it he owned a house which was becoming vacant in a few days time. He would give us the keys if we wanted to go and see it. A young couple were living in a few rooms downstairs but were going to move abroad. We went to see the house."

It was a small terraced house in a quiet road, Kynaston Road, in Stoke Newington. With a road directly opposite going downhill, it seemed in a nice open location. The High Street was couple hundred yards away and Church Street with its shops and Church and restaurants, (even then,) ran parallel, a good infant and primary school, (William Patten), was one block away. Buses to The City and West End were a few minutes walk. The house had three bedrooms upstairs, one permanently locked as Mr. Brunston wanted to keep it should he ever need to move back there. The bedroom at the front of the house was large with two windows and a stone Victorian fire place. The middle bedroom was much smaller with a pretty metal fireplace. Two rooms on the ground floor had big pair of interconnecting panelled doors and a pair of large but simple fireplaces. The larger front reception room had a well-proportioned bay window.

Five steps down led to a room used as a kitchen with sink and fireplace with an old range. A further flight of stairs behind a door led to the cellar. Two rooms were in the basement one had been the original scullery and had a stone butler type sink in one recess, a fireplace in the middle which probably was where a range had been and the other recess had a round stone boiler housing a copper which would have had a small fire within heating the copper that would have been for laundry. Through a low door was a storage cellar in bare brick with a coal chute coming from outside the front door. It housed an Anderson Shelter, (bomb shelter left over from World

## Chapter 2: Highbury Fields

War II). The atmosphere in that room was heavy and threatening as if something terrible had happened there. A concrete reinforcement supported the front external wall. There was no bathroom in the house and the WC was in the back garden. There were sinks in four of the rooms suggesting multiple occupations for many years. Despite bay windows to rear and front ground floor rooms and small columns either side the front door most of the period feature had gone; we were told that it had suffered bomb damage in the war; which would account for this and possibly other things too! Needless to say that the eerie atmosphere in the basement could have suggested some tragedy had taken place there. Nevertheless it was to be a lovely family house. Rosemary was to move back in with us for a while and Melvyn would be with us together for a few years. The neighbours were good and friendly. The area was a great place for Kevin to grow up. The year was 1964 and we would not leave the house for twenty years.

"Looking around there was as usual much dust and ingrained dirt. The upper floor rooms and stairs were black. I don't know how long they must have been empty. After moving in it took us a week just to clean. We thanked Mr. Brunston so much for letting us live in his house. He said he knew it would be clean and well looked after if we were there. He said that he would probably use the little bedroom at the back to stay over occasionally when he was late getting from his Club. As it happened he never came to stay once all the time we lived there. He kept a bed and some furniture in the room and Grace kept it clean for him in case he needed to stay. Just before leaving the Mildmay flat the landlord said he had changed his mind and that we could stay. Mr. Brunston told him that we already had a place, but he didn't say it was his own house. A man like that you would never know when he would change his mind. Mr. Brunston said we could stay there and he would never turn us out which was good news after all we had been through since moving to London. As it happened the house in Mildmay Grove was sold within two months, very lucky we had not stayed. He sold it for £4000-0-0 only a few weeks later the new owners resold it for £8000-0-0 which shows how desperate he must have been for money to get drink."

"So it was starting all over again painting and papering. We had done quite a lot of this throughout our married lives. Mr. Brunston was very pleased with the way we decorated the house. After two years we would have loved to have tried to buy the house but sadly Mr. Brunston did not want to sell it. We were very happy living in Kynaston Road. He would come for the rent money each Monday morning; he was well pleased to see the hedge trimmed and the garden neat. When we arrived the hedge had been covering the whole of the front bay window as well as the footpath. Grace planted a flower boarder and it looked very attractive."

"The first few years we spent much time decorating, I often said Grace was born with a paint brush in her hand. Whilst doing up her own house she would often go and do some decorating for Iris and Girlie. She was so kind to everyone."

"Kevin had just stated nursery school at Newington Green School when we had been given notice to leave. So for the first few weeks Grace took him on the 73 bus to Newington Green until we got a place for him in William Patten School literally two roads away two hundred yards. This was a lovely school with a very good reputation. Kevin was to have three years in the infants and four years in the junior school."

"Working at Highbury Fields was very enjoyable. Alongside Jack we would plant flowers in many places including in front of the Town Hall, in front of banks, schools, and other parks. The flowers were collected from Finsbury Park, there was a large nursery there. Jack and I would choose the flowers for the jobs as well as lots for our own gardens. I would work on my own at Highbury Grove Boys School. There I would cut the grass and attend flower boarders."

*Chapter 2: Highbury Fields*

"It was at this time that Melvyn and his girlfriend Josie went on holiday to Ireland in their first car, 'Buttercup', a very old Ford Popular. Whilst they were there they made great efforts to locate a birth certificate for me. I had never been in receipt of a birth certificate from childhood. When I had joined the British Army I had not required one and after leaving the army I had not been out of the British Isles at any time. They were to bring back from Ireland three birth certificates one of which I would need to agree was mine. I decided to choose the one with the name 'John Joseph Byrne' with date of birth 25$^{th}$ March 1913. This as far as I knew was the nearest to what I remember from childhood at the Work House in Newry more than fifty years before when my name and its spelling had been emphasised upon me. The reason that no concrete information was available was that the Records Office in Dublin had been burned in the troubles in the 1920's. I needed a passport at this stage in life to enable foreign travel with my family now we were more established. Until this time and until I had chosen my most appropriate birth certificate we had only guest at my date of birth and celebrated my birthdays on a day picked out of the air. It was like being a man without a birthday and without any childhood family."

"A few months later we joined Melvyn on a trip to Belgium. He was playing for his firm's team against a Belgium branch team. His team won 1-0. We enjoyed ourselves; it was the first time Grace had been outside British Isles. We went on several trips. Our next trip was to Holland, we had wanted to see the daffodils but on arrival we found bad weather had made the flowering weeks late. It was very bad weather with high winds and cold. We visited a beer garden and were shocked when our first round of drinks came to £5-0-0. Little did we know the beers were in jugs like Wellington Boots which you drank with the heel away from you? You would try not to get the beer up your nose. The ladies glasses were very big. When I look back it was quite cheap, with the size of the measures and the live music on stage. The hall was filled with people singing and dancing. Melvyn with his girlfriend Josie and us had a great trip. The bus driver was a jolly man. It was no trouble for him to take us to see other cities if we requested. He had been in the Navy at the end of the war. He had often ended up in the Guard House. He lived near Highbury and came to see me several times at the park."

"I was working at Highbury Grove School attending the flower boarders when lots of chalk came flying out of a window. Looking up I recognised the boy throwing the chalk. I could have caught it in my eye. So I went to see the Head Master, I knew him well; he would come and discuss the planting with me. He took me to the class room and I pointed out the boy. The Head Master got him to pick all the chalk up. Then he said he must help me for two hours. The boy laughed."

"Next day I had two tons of manure delivered. The boy had to wheel-barrow it to the flower boarders then shovel it out for me to the amusement of the other boys looking out of the windows. He never said nor did anything more and I had no trouble from any of the boys after that. The manure came at a good time and I didn't have to move it. Jack laughed his head off. The Head Master became a Conservative MP for Brent. That was under The Iron Lady."

"I did lots of different jobs; I never had a problem getting up early so all the time at Highbury I opened the gates. All the men previously had opened them late. I would open them at 6.30 Jack would come in at 8am if he was a little late I would take the bookings for tennis. I would have a quiet couple of hours reading the paper before the rest arrived and extra pay too. The people with a card for bookings paid extra but could book three days in advance. Some always wanted the same court to play on and would get steam up if they could not have it."

"When not working at the school I had a little motor-buggie to ride on and carry tools around. Jack would ride on the back. We would fix fences and do lot of jobs. When the tractor driver was off we would use the tractor to cut the grass and also fix a heavy roller on the back to flatten the lawns after heavy of rain or if the boys had been having lots football matches. The boundaries also had to be marked for the girl's field games and the grass tennis courts."

"In the summer the boys would lie on the grass even if you were cutting. One boy had his radio on loud and wouldn't move so I drove over it. He went to the office to complain but it was Jack in the office and he said it was the boy's own fault. Jack said there would be no comebacks and the boy had wanted me to pay for the radio. In future the boys stayed well clear of the tractor when I was grass cutting. I'd got my way twice with the boys from Highbury Grove School."

"After starting at the park and leaving Wills Tobacco I had to give up my part time job cleaning the shop at Smithfield Market. When I told them I had to stop the morning cleaning they said why don't I come and do cleaning in the evening. I was only opening the gates in the morning so after finishing at the park at 4pm I would go to Smithfield for a few hours in the evening. Shortly afterwards the park introduced floodlit football in the evenings for which I was to do two nights a week. I then had to stop work at the butchers and it was much nicer staying on at the park and not having to go on to Smithfield. The pay for it and for the opening of the gates in the morning was good too."

"I also locked the children's bathing pool at the end of the day and regularly cleaned it. Last time I went to Highbury it had been demolished and the site filled in. The woman who looked after the pool in the daytime was strange; Jack and I agreed you couldn't tell whether she was a man or a woman. Her name was Joyce Brown. Her voice was very rough and she would walk like a man. We never saw her in anything other than trousers. She often had two or three other women with her chatting and having tea. We always got on well despite her hostile appearance. The drivers making deliveries would laugh at the way she would strut about."

"In the winter I often had to open the pool at 7am and shut it at midday. Parts of it were often iced up but swimmers would still come in all weathers. Warning one person that the side of the pool was iced up so not to dive in I went for some tea only to see him with a cut on his face. Lucky there was a first aid kit handy. Joyce came in next day and I showed her the report I'd written to cover myself; she said he should have done a better bloody job. Jack and I often had tea with her; her hours were very long in high season."

"Mum came to see me one day I was closing the pool so I could show her inside. It was an icy windy day so I asked if she wanted a dip. She declined, next there were three men running around the pool naked; I don't know who was more embarrassed, Mum or the men. They came over and apologised but we all had a laugh together."

"Some years later when Kevin was at Upton House Comprehensive School in Hackney, he was twelve and not keen on sports, He often would get out of Sports afternoons and come to the park to meet me. Jack and I would take him to the local café and buy him lunch with us. Jack thought he was a very smart boy and would always be asking how he was doing in his studies. Later when he was at college locally he would do the same."

"In my first year they started having a huge bonfire party. Wood was collected from all over Islington and Jack and I erected the bonfire. We spent three weeks building it then yobboes set fire to it and we had to start again. After this there were two men guarding it until bonfire night. I enjoyed the first few years but after Jack retired got fed up doing it. The wood had to be pulled up on ropes. Lorries delivering wood if it was wet could not come onto the field because they would get stuck; so the wood had to be carried a long way. Before being lit 24 gallons paraffin were used. It would be smouldering for three weeks afterwards. A canteen for the staff serving hot soup was made available on the night. It was during one of the constructions that I had a hernia. I had the operation

*Chapter 2: Highbury Fields*

in Manor House Hospital at Golders Green. I never got involved in another bonfire after this I just showed them how to construct them."

"The Lord Major of London would be the person to light the bonfire which I felt made building such a big bonfire a waste of time. Day of the event I started 5.30 am and didn't finish till one in the morning. These were very long day. That was the only job I didn't like at Highbury Fields."

"Jack was now retired; he came to the park to see everyone. I rang Grace for him to speak to her; she said "why don't we all go on an evening out to see a show in West End". It didn't happen; that was the last time I saw him; he had an operation for cancer which he did not recover from. His wife phoned the office and as the Superintendent was not in I answered the phone. She phoned to tell his friends and those who knew him at the park that he had passed away. He was such a nice man. He was buried in a cemetery not far from where Melvyn now lives in Hertfordshire, near Goff's Oak."

"Jack had come to our home several times for dinner and said my wife was such a lovely person. She put a wonderful spread on for him. She would dress the table in the Dining Room with nice crockery, she was a good cook. We all got along very well and had lots to talk about. Grace was a good hostess. Our guests would always say what an attractive lady she was."

"I found my time working on my own went very quickly raking leaves then finishing planting the bulbs before Christmas. If I needed help I would ask some of the other and they would help; but generally they were a very lazy lot; all they wanted to do was sit and drink tea in the cabin."

"I would in my lunch break go and do some planting for an old lady nearby who was going blind. I did it without pay. Her daughter would get the flowers. One such time the Superintendent over all Parks visited and saw me working in the garden near the park and reported me to my Superintendent. Going back after lunch he told me what had been said and I assured him I had taken no flowers from the park and it was my lunch break and what had the world come to if you could not do such a thing for an old blind lady. My superintendent phoned his superior and he was saddened and said that I could take any flowers I wanted to plant in her garden. I didn't take up his offer."

"This superintendent would come often to the parks and I got to know him. He would often visit just after my opening of the gates. I would make him some tea and he said the range of jobs I did was very good, no one else had done such good service. When it came for time for my retirement I asked if I could have an extra year. No one else had been granted this but they asked me to stay for an extra year. The letter arrived when I was on holiday and others asked why I'd been given it when others wanted an extra year but were refused. It is dreadful what people do behind your back. If I'd not been given it I would have just accepted it."

# 3

# Finsbury Park

"The only period I can complain about during my time at the Parks Department was when I was sent to work at Finsbury Park. I should never have agreed to go there. On the first morning I realised it was like being in the army. A man came into the staff room and said stand up. I just sat where I was and he repeated stand up. There were fifteen of us in the room so I laughed out loud. I was sent to see the Superintendent. In the yard he told me I should have done what he said. I said it was bull shit."

"I was to work there for a month after that I swore I would go back to Highbury. In the mornings I would get my flask and sandwiches ready if I was to be sent to another park. But if I thought I was to be working at Finsbury I wouldn't need to. I found out that first thing in the morning you could be issued with a job anywhere. This meant on several occasions I had no food or drink all day."

"There was another man from another park who like me had been sent there and we both hated the job and the people over us. We both planned to get away from there as soon as we could. I phoned the Superintendent at Highbury and explained what the conditions were like and Elmer said to come to see him within two weeks. I saw him and got the papers signed by him and sent them to Cavil House. If I hadn't got back to Highbury I would have quit the job it was that bad. While I was there four men quit. They were always fighting with each other."

"Another morning they loaded all the grass cutting machines onto the truck without tying them. They said to get on; the tail gate was open as well. I jumped off and said I was not going to the job like that. They should know the rules. If they pulled up quickly the machines may have moved forward and broken my legs. They said they weren't going very far."

"On the third week the weather was terrible and we were not able to cut the grass. We also had nowhere to keep dry."

"My day was from 7am-4.30pm. If you were two minutes late you lost 15 minutes pay. You had to put your marker on a time board to say you were on time, coming in from the rain you had to wait till they gave you the marker back before you could go home. The superintendent would be in front of a fire holding the markers. You had to wait for him before going. Looking at my watch one evening there was two minutes to go so I left. The following day I was called in to see him and told I'd left before my time. I said to him that he had been warming himself before a fire and we were all very wet. I told him the sooner I get away from this place the better I will be. He said you will never get away from here until we give you the sack. Little did he know that the paperwork was done and it had been agreed that after I had completed the four weeks I would be going back to Highbury Fields. At the end of the month to my joy I could tell him where to go in no uncertain terms."

"My last year at the park was spent setting out and planting new trees all over the big field. They came from a nursery in Hereford and my thoughts were that at least when I go back there in the future there will some of my work to see. Since I've retired I have only been back twice. There are a lot of new faces in all the places I went to see. There is no one who opens the gate every morning; different men are detailed for each morning. I used to plant lots of shrubs in the girls school but the boxes are now empty. One man locked all the gates before he should have; a man had to try and climb over the railings and slipped and a spike went through his leg. He was found calling for help; the case is continuing."

"In my last year my Superintendent Mr. Elmer had been talking to me about the new tennis courts replacing the grass courts. That evening he died while having his tea. People had rarely seen him; he had a bungalow provided for him to live in on the park and he rarely ventured out of it or the office. He was very careful with money yet had no close relatives. It was discovered that he left assets of over £100,000.00. For the week until they found a replacement I looked after things; the money from the tennis courts I put in his safe."

"Before retiring Jack had said I should apply for the post of Superintendent and be in charge. But I believed my written and mathematical skills were not adequate. I often wished my education had been much better. To me it is like grasping in the darkness wondering where I was and was I going to make a fool of myself. I am very pleased my children have all had a good education; they have all got quite good jobs; I feel very proud of them. My extra year to me went very quickly; at least I had a bit more added to my pension. Working the extra year was also a great help with Grace working as well while Kevin was now at North London Polytechnic."

*An Irish Boy*

# 4

# Kynaston Road, London N16

"During my early years at Highbury Fields we had moved to our first proper home in London. The twenty years at that address were to see the family evolve and benefit from living in that location. Personally as I've already shown I was to have a long and secure period of employment at Highbury fields for eighteen years until I officially retired and started pension; much different from those working for local authorities in more recent times. With the mornings, evenings and Saturday morning overtime, my earnings were very good even compared to 'white collar' workers."

"Living in London was a lot more expensive than Hereford. That is why we received the London Waiting Allowance. Property had always been dearer and became increasingly so during the late seventies and beyond. Rents were likewise. There was much more variety in the shops, especially food wise. Families in the 1970's developed a taste for eating out more often and for regular take away food, especially fish and chips and Indian. With three children now back at home we would enjoy the many things available. We would also go to concerts, some West End Theatre and obviously the local Pub."

"Both Minnie and Grace's Father would be regular visitors along with most of my other family members. It was tragically in 1966 that Minnie past away the same age as her Sister, (Grace's Mother), only sixty two years of age. She had been deeply fond of Kevin and loved taking him to Clissold Park. She left him an upright piano in her Will which we arranged to be brought home. He was six years old at the time. Kevin later began to teach himself to play, but sadly never managed to get lessons to go further. 1969 saw the death of Grace's Father."

"Kevin started his holidays in Hereford at the age of eight. We would put him on the train at Paddington and ask the guard to make sure he got off in Hereford; they would get his suit case down from the rack and put it on the platform. Girlie would meet him at Hereford Railway Station and take him to Bartestree on the bus. On his first holiday he would have many long walks across the fields with his Grand Father. This would be the last time spent with his Grand Father but every year following he would join Girlie and Horace for at least three weeks playing in their garden, often with Caroline who lived down the lane, daughter of Ray and Gwen. He loved Hereford very much and often did not want to come back to London, so Grace would go down spend some time with her family and then bring him back."

"Because of the extra money needed to live in London especially with a young child at school Grace almost always had to work. She was none too pleased with having to do this. She started as soon as we moved to Kynaston road working for a while at the local Woolworth and then Marks and Spencer. This was very handy as Kevin was often being sent home from school with some sickness or other problem. When he went to Upton House he had to travel an hour or more to the school and was much stronger so Grace worked for two years several days a week at Harrods in Knightsbridge, she was very good at customer services and dealing with problematic customers."

"Now at Parmiter's in Bethnal Green even further away Kevin would go to work with his Mum on the bus to St. Paul's Cathedral where she worked in the book department opposite at W.H.Smith. He would then catch the Central Line to Bethnal Green."

"Grace was to join Iris in 1974 in a small book keeping business. This lasted four years. They would drive between six businesses in Central London doing the book keeping for each. Iris's son Barry had started a Real Ale Pub in Walthamstow and also a small chain of Off-Licences, including one in Camden Town; so Iris and Grace would do the book keeping for these as well. Iris's other son Brian would manage the Camden Town shop."

"As Kevin grew up Iris and Grace taught him book keeping and he would later help Iris in between school and college."

"By the time Kevin was nineteen and going to Wimbledon School of Art Grace was working in the Accountancy Department of a small firm in Old Street in The City of London. This would be her last job."

*An Irish Boy*

# 5

# Kevin

"Kevin's time at William Pattern was lovely. He was so close to school he could take himself. Most of the pupils were nice and the area was comparatively safe to let a child play out with friends. Unfortunately the move to secondary education was not good."

"Kevin had hated Upton House Comprehensive School in Hackney. It was in a very rough area and there was much violence and intimidation there. Kevin fortunately was six feet tall and able to stand up for himself. He was top of his class in all subjects with triple A's. The only thing he didn't excel in was sport. His Head of House, Mr. Luder in Kevin's second year at the school was about to retire. Mr. Luder had met Grace and me many times at parent's evenings and open days. He had a very high opinion of my wife as well as my son. He said that he did not want to leave Kevin at that school after he left."

"The London County Council had been reorganizing the school system for some years. Grammar schools were being abolished in favour of these multi-layered comprehensive schools which abhorred grading. Many of these were failing with standards of education falling and crime with anti-social behaviour proliferating. Teachers were subject of abuse and even rape; vandalism was widespread. Upton House was an appalling school housed in an eight storey 1960s block. The pupils would had to walk the full height of the building for some lessons. The sports halls were the setting for much bullying and vandalism. The corridors on the lower floors were a labyrinth of violence. Furniture and other objects were regularly thrown out of upper floor windows."

"There were just a handful of Grammar Schools left in Central London. Mr. Luder knew the Head Master of Parmiter's Foundation Grammar School in Bethnal Green. He explained that he would have great opportunities if he were to transfer to that school. He organized interviews for Kevin and his best friend Stephen Clarke and also Prakash Patel who was also a clever boy and mutual friend. All passed the interview with Parmiter's Head Master as well as English, Maths and some General Tests set at the interview."

"It was spring 1973 and the three boys were ensconced in their new school."

"Parmiter's school occupied a prominent corner plot on Approach Road, the approach to Victoria Park. It was a rambling Gothic edifice with a pointed arch front door up steps for teachers and prefects to enter; a much smaller door to the right of the building was the entrance for all the other pupils; to the left of the main entrance a huge stained glass window stood three storeys high lighting the great assembly hall. The older part of the building was on three floors and donned many pointed glazed windows of classrooms. A modern sports block was set to the rear of the plot. The Head Master and teachers wore mortar boards and gowns, the Head Master's dog followed him about the school; the teachers sat on small stages at the front of the classrooms."

"The atmosphere was exceedingly friendly with the masters speaking to pupils in very informal way despite their attire. The smartly dressed boys ran up the wide oak staircase to the various floors in a free manner. It was so unlike the intense threatening atmosphere at Upton House."

"Kevin exceeded expectations and did very well firstly in 'O' levels then 'A' levels. He particularly enjoyed art. Not joining the sports classes he spent all spare periods in the art room. Becoming a Prefect he left the school in 1978 with many qualifications. To this end He felt he wanted to go into some art profession. To help decide his vocation he found a placement on Foundation Course at Wimbledon School of Art. The year at Wimbledon was the most enjoyable of all his education. He would drive his Mum to her office near Old Street in the City, and then drive down through South London- Balham, Tooting and onwards to Wimbledon. At the end of the year it was clear that he wanted to be an Interior Designer."

"The journey from North London to Wimbledon had been a little arduous so despite being offered a placement at Kingston Polytechnic, which was well respected in the field, he decided to go to North London Polytechnic in Holloway Road, very near Highbury Fields and not a huge distance to walk from home."

"I made sure Kevin had plenty of pocket money. Grace would pay for his books which were many. It must have been a nightmare for some parents while their children were at college. When I went up to see Kevin doing his college works in his room I thought then how hard it was. For weeks preparing his final presentation he never left his room. He would work most of the night and only have an hour or two sleep. Sometimes I would stay and just look through his work and give him tea or coffee. Grace would like looking at his work as well as seeing if there was something she could do. When the time came to know if he had passed I was on tender hooks all day; when Grace rang the office just after 4pm and said he had passed I was over the moon with joy. When I got home Kevin was in bed and stayed there the rest of the following day."

"The next day the three of us went to The Prince of Wales Pub in Kynaston Road and celebrated his big day. He was the first person in all our extended families to get a Degree. The last celebration at The Prince of Wales had been when he passed his driving test just before his eighteenth birthday some six years before."

"It was the following March 1984 when he got his degree. It was nice seeing him getting his papers and passing out at The Barbican. He was presented the roll by the Chairman of Pilkington Glass. There were hundreds of graduates at the award ceremony. We had a group photograph taken afterwards. It was a very special day."

"He had finished college in the July of 1983. He had many part time jobs during the holiday's whist at college in the West End for Prime Appointments Agency and at the Polytechnic of North London in the Admissions Department. He set up his own Interior Design business 'Leon Paris Interiors' two months before finishing his course. Within weeks of leaving college he had his time filled by Authentic Interiors who specialised in traditional pubs, restaurants and domestic interiors. They needed someone young to do their modern commissions. His first job was 'Charlie's Bar' in Poole, Dorset. It was a great success, increasing turnover from £2000.00 per week to more than £6000.00 per week. His style was very much of the 1980's, extravagant furnishings, disco lighting systems and Terrazzo dance floors with video screens. Many more were to follow during the next three years. His first interior design scheme featured in 'Disco International Magazine' with photographs and impressive article in three columns."

"He had a lovely apartment near Stoke Newington Common, this was just a five minute walk from home. Later in the eighty's he moved to 'Blanchards' in Sloane Street in the West End dealing with mainly Middle Eastern clients, but also embassy work and designs for members of the Royal Family and some Middle Eastern aristocracy. From there he became Senior Designer at 'Norland Interiors' in Holland Park. Following the crash in 1988 He and his partner Stephen McLachlan set up a much smaller, but successful 'Home Makeover' business in East Sussex which would last twenty five years until their retirement in their fifties. They started with small projects but within a few years were doing schemes for complete interiors with kitchens, bathrooms and furnishing often around £100,000 in value. They complemented this with a property portfolio, buying and selling and also residential lettings.

*An Irish Boy*

# 6

# Melvyn

"Melvyn already loved London life well before moving to the city. Rosemary and He had stayed with Iris, Bernard and family on many occasions throughout their teens. They loved concerts and music in the many local public houses. As previously mentioned Melvyn, Barry and three other friends formed the 'Blue saints'. They were the backing group to famous bands in the late sixties, also playing The 100 Club and Ronnie Scott's. Café Bars were the preferred meeting places of the day; also the place to meet girls. Coffee was generally partaken of rather than alcohol; I believe they did not partake of the mild drugs that were very popular at the time, like purple hearts and LSD. This was to prove a great credit to them and benefit their futures. The band continued for three or four years until Melvyn left to pursue his carrier more thoroughly. A tour in Germany had created a problem with his visa."

"He worked for a large firm in Finsbury Square near Moorgate. He studied hard at night school to obtain accountancy qualifications."

"He later moved to an oil company in Victoria and developed financial management skills which took him further to work for a large national oil company where he commuted to Aberdeen on a regular basis. During this time he also worked in Brussels and Zurich."

"Eventually as a completely different career move he became Financial Director of McNicholas Construction, a large company specialising in telecommunication and later fibre optic installations as well as gas and other infrastructure projects."

"Melvyn and Rosemary re-joined the family when they moved to Kynaston Road.

Rosemary would have the top rear bedroom and Melvyn and Kevin would share the rear ground floor reception as their bedroom until Rosemary again moved to her own flat. He quite magically could turn the lights on and off without getting out of bed. He would take Kevin to football practice near River Lea on Saturdays and Kevin would go off on rambles through the woods."

"Melvyn met Josie Bradley in 1966 and married in 1968 at St. Mary's Stoke Newington Church Street. Their reception was at Beale's Banqueting Hall on Holloway Road. Kevin was the eight year old Page Boy. At the reception some very naughty uncles gave pints of beer to the toddler who was crawling around under the long tables."

"Melvyn and Josie moved into three rented rooms in Lordship Road nearby the family in Kynaston road. On one visit Kevin stayed over and brock a glass and upset the sugar. Josie was most annoyed."

"They moved to a good flat in Chingford and then to a new development in 1974 in Claremont, Goff's Oak Hertfordshire. Melvyn was never very keen on the particular estate; Emma his first daughter had arrived followed two years later by Vikki; so they moved back to Kynaston Road in 1977 whilst they had a purpose-built house constructed in Bury Green, Hertfordshire. Four years later they progressed even further and had major alterations and additions made to a house in Tolmers Road, Cuffley, in Hertfordshire."

"The rail connections were very good from Stock Newington to Hertfordshire. Grace and Kevin and I would go to visit very often. Whilst Melvyn worked in Central London the whole family would come to stay most weekends with us as there were many office parties and other functions like Eighteen Plus and Organised Events. We would have Sunday lunch together at home most weekends and Grace would make a roast meal followed by home-made apple pie."

"Kevin would also cycle out to Hertfordshire to babysit with one or two of his school friends on a regular basis along The Great Cambridge Road; something one probably would not do now."

"Grace and I would join Melvyn and Josie and sometimes some of their friends on outings and on some lovely foreign trips. We went with them to Belgium, Holland, Italy and Switzerland. Kevin loved Hereford and would go for long holidays staying with Girlie and Horace rather than joining us. One exception to this was in 1973 when the three of us went to Yugoslavia. We stayed at The Materada Hotel in Porec. The scenery was beautiful and the Roman remains at Pula were fascinating for Kevin."

*An Irish Boy*

*Chapter 7: Rosemary*

# 7

# Rosemary

"Rosemary had been a driving force for the family moving to London. I have mentioned her many admirers in Hereford and more so on her arrival on the exploding and very glamorous London scene in 1963. The West End and in particular the restaurants, bars and clubs as well as the party set of Knightsbridge and South Kensington and Maida Vale, was a spring board to transcend class boarders that in the previous decade would have been almost insurmountable. Rosemary was attractive, intelligent but also, being a Leo, very gregarious. She would be the centre of attention and intrigue at any social gathering."

"She was very much at home in the smoky atmosphere of the upmarket bars or public houses of the era filled with executives downing large brandy after finishing work or those who were also finishing large whiskies who did not have to work."

"She met many and various older gentlemen and the occasional younger one too. After some brief relationships she had the misfortune to end up moving in with Michael Neale."

"He was younger son from a prominent Bristol family who made lots of money in tobacco amongst other less desirable products. He had had a privileged upbringing and had inherited a lot of money. When they met he was married with family. By the end of the 1960's he had spent most of his inheritance with the exception of a Trust Fund which provided a small annual income."

"Rosemary was a secretary at The London Bible Society in Queen Victoria Street. She enjoyed her work and stayed in that employ for several years meeting major figures in the Anglican Church. Leaving the family home in Kynaston Road within a year or two of the family moving there she rented the top floor of a three storey Victorian house in Carysfort Road, Stoke Newington, again within half a mile of her parents. Kevin would often go to stay with her and they got on very well."

"Meeting Michael Neale the couple formed an inseparable bond despite her being twenty five and him being fifty eight years of age. He was tall, well dressed in tweedy Noel Coward, sort of way. He wore expensive clothes, beautiful leather shoes and had a thick moustache. He smoked cigars incessantly and was rarely without a malt whisky in his hand. The two moved into a purpose built pre-war flat which they were to rent for fourteen years together. The flat was in a block that before the Second World War would have been a pied-à-terre for a professional man to stay in during the week whilst working in London."

"Rosemary made the flat very homely; she had a good eye for decoration and accessories. Sadly there was a bad condensation problem. She developed her love for animals, especially cats and was soon to have four interlopers indoors and a further twenty five in high-rise cardboard box living in her garage. Michael's habitual smoking, added to the damp problems and the presences of so many animals were to cause the onslaught of life-long respiratory illness. Initially she was diagnosed with under-active thyroid; but later fibrocitus of the lungs, diabetes and finally stomach cancer."

"Rosemary was to find her aptitude for Human Resources soon to get an appointment in HR at Ernst and Young in the City, mostly based at Waterloo. Working later for Whinney Murray Limited, (the Middle Eastern Branch of Ernst and Young), she was Department

Head of recruitment and organised all aspects of Human Resources for accountants, management consultants and banking posts. She also looked afters domestic arrangements for Partners including accommodation and schooling for their children. She attended Annual General Meetings in Middle East including Beirut."

"Michael was to prove unreliable both in their relationship but also financially. He had very little income all the time they were together. Initially on secretarial salary but later on much improved professional income she supported him for fourteen years. She bought all his clothes. He loved restoring classic cars, especially Jaguars. This she also subsidised. During their time together Michael lost his licence three times for drinking and driving. During his bans he still refused to allow Rosemary to drive when they were out together. Many times they visited us and she would try to insist she drive the car home but he would grab the car keys and demand to drive sometimes barely able to stand."

"This would not have been so bad if he had not returned to his wife three times and temporarily deserted Rosemary. On two occasions I stopped seeing her, firstly for one year then the next occasion for two years. Melvyn was to get us back together on both these times."

"Eventually he agreed to marry Rosemary and divorce his wife. The wedding was arranged but he disappeared three weeks before and went off with a widow who owned a bungalow somewhere or other."

"Six months later in the summer of 1982 Rosemary met a pleasant young man who was a film extra and model, his name was Kit and he lived in Hampstead. They had a lot of fun for a few months. One occasion Kit and Rosemary and Kevin and a friend in a second sports car took a group of children including Kit's boss's son dirt track riding in the car park of Alexandra Palace. After tearing around the tarmac for half an hour the children threw Rosemary's entire picnic at the two cars; she was none too pleased. The children before disappearing stole a bag of money which was on the floor of Kit's car. The three went on lots of trips and also came to Grace and Mine for meals. She somehow ended up washing dozens of shirts for him on a weekly basis; needless to say Grace helped her wash and iron them; I don't know what he did with them all; they would be hung up all over the house. Another problem was he seemed a little too fond of her younger brother who he said ought to do a modelling career."

"Approaching Christmas of that year Grace and I were despairing regarding Rosemary's relationships. One weekend she phoned to say she had been meeting with a young man who she had met on the tube on her commute from The City to Burnt Oak. She was now thirty nine years old; the young man whose name was William was almost the same age as Kevin twenty two."

"We invited her and her new interest home to meet us. He was a very likeable chap; a little bit like an East End Barrow Boy but well dressed with a big pointed nose and long greasy hair. Kevin and he consumed lots of Martini. We were all delighted to meet someone relatively normal; added to that He had his own house in Ashford in Kent which his Father had given a substantial deposit to purchase. He was employed as A Law Cost Draughtsman. Better still his Father was a diamond merchant and appeared to be loaded and worked for De Beers."

"The wedding followed in March. It was to take a very similar format to the one that didn't happen the previous summer. After the wedding Rosemary and William went to live together in his modern house in Ashford and Rosemary would begin what would be twenty years of commuting by train to London."

"Later in 1983 the couple moved to Bexhill-on-Sea after William had obtained promotion to a firm in Hastings, East Sussex. They bought a detached house on the outskirts of the town."

# 8

# My Retirement

"I was now retired approaching sixty nine years of age. So I helped Grace by doing the washing and other jobs about the house. I would have her dinner ready for her when she came home. She was still at work in Old Street in the accountancy dept. of the small firm in The City. She enjoyed her job, it was quite interesting, but I could tell she would not be disappointed if she were to stop."

"It was 1981, Kevin was in his second year of his degree at North London; Melvyn was now well ensconced and doing extremely well at McNicholas Construction and enjoying the work; the company was growing well. Financially and domestically all was looking good. The children Emma and Vikki were in good schools local to them. Hertfordshire has an excellent reputation for its education standards."

"Melvyn asked if I would like to do some work for McNicholas. He got me a job at the works depot near Edgware. I was in charge of booking in the Lorries and writing down what they had taken from the depot for the jobs they would be doing the following day. I was there for at least seven months and got on very well with all the men as they were mostly Irish. The company was Irish and owned by the family. They had given Melvyn a good share in the business as he had helped them become very successful and grow very big."

"The only one I had no time for was the foreman. He was in command of the yard and he thought he was god. He told me no one was to use the fork lift truck only him. If the men came for a pallet of bricks they would have to load it by hand. When the men came for more bricks they said to ignore him and give them the key to the fork lift truck, so I did and the job was done in five minutes. When he came back he made a terrible row over it, I thought it was very silly. He was going to do this and that and report me. On my first day he totally ignored me so I asked a lorry driver who he was and he said no one likes him everyone is always having arguments with him. I was very pleased when he took the low loader off to another site and I didn't have to see him for a while. He made everything very unpleasant."

"My day was spent cleaning the yard; after I got it as I wanted there were lots of other tasks as well as booking in the Lorries. They would sometimes come in during the day if they needed to shift materials to other sites. The only problem was getting there. It was a long way from where we lived. I would catch 73 Bus to Kings Cross then the Northern Line underground to Edgware then a long walk to the yard. I worked from 11am to 6.30pm. I was always pleased to have the job thanks to my son Melvyn whatever money I earned was a big help as I only had my pension."

"After working there a few weeks one of the directors asked if I would like to clean up his mothers' garden and cut the grass. I was only too pleased to do so. I went there a few times his Mum was a very nice person."

# 9

# Home Owners at Last

"We had been living at Kynaston Road for fourteen years when very sadly Mr. Brunston died. He died quite suddenly; when Grace had last seen him she said she didn't like his colour. Kevin drove us to his funeral but he stayed outside. It was held a long way out of London on the Great Cambridge Road. He was very upset because he had seen Mr. Brunston a lot, he would cycle to the office and pay the rent each fortnight and Mr. Brunston would give him a small present each time of some silver.

Kevin took us in our little car. Melvyn had got it from his friend in Epping. It was a black Austin. It had been very good to have a car for him to take us around as I never took my driving test. We had use of it for three years, but when Kevin went to Polytechnic we sold it and he was back to his bicycle to go to college. Unfortunately the car was prone to stopping. We didn't realize that an optional extra to the engine was a plastic cover to protect the electricals which were inside the front grille. If you were stopped at traffic light and it started to pour with rain the engine would stop. Many times when Grace was out with Kevin she would have to get out and push the car. When you started the engine a cloud of smoke bellowed out of the exhaust. For this reason Kevin parked it two blocks away from Parmiter's."

"It was not long before we received a letter saying the house was to be sold. It was owned now by his sister, his father didn't want anything to do with it as he was quite old. Mr. Brunston's partner Mrs. Enright said not to go over £6000.00. They wanted £10,000.00 for it; we knew Mrs. Enright had told us not to pay that so she could buy it herself. We knew the house was worth £10,000.00 so we offered the full price and got it for ourselves. We went to the building society and they gave us the full loan. Despite my age they knew that it was worth much more than the loan. Mrs. Enright was very upset and told us we could have got the house for much less. I said that their solicitor had written to us telling us what price they wanted; she said it was too much to pay. If she had bought it we would have been homeless again."

"We were very happy at last to have the papers saying we had a home of our own; it was something we had always wanted."

"While we lived at Kynaston Road Grace was mugged three times. Twice she was pushed over on the pavement and her purse snatched; then she was walking through the alley, Kynaston Avenue, and three black teenagers asked her for the time then ripped her necklace from her. That was always on her mind and she was always afraid of going out in the evening. We went to the police but didn't get any satisfaction. They just fill in lots of forms and talk a lot."

"Whilst we had the little Austin it was stolen. The police didn't find it but a friend of Kevin's saw it the other side of Hackney Downs. We were pleased to get it back. Whoever stole it had travelled sixty miles"

"We were also burgled whilst there. One night we had forgotten to lock the Kitchen window and thieves broke in put our crockery sets out side so they could climb in and stole watches and some electrical items and some jewellery. They took these things and went out the front door whilst we were still in bed asleep. They left the front door open. Again the police did nothing apart from more forms. They said five houses had been burgled that same night. I screwed closed the ground floor windows after this."

## Chapter 9: Home Owners at Last

"Grace was very proud to be a home owner after all these years. We loved our home and it had served as a very good home to all the family; Rosemary, Melvyn, Melvyn's family, Kevin, had enjoyed living there; and many members of Grace's family had been to stay with us on holiday or for other reasons. Denis had stayed with us whilst he was attending hospital in London."

"Kevin was studying Interior Design and was quite good with his hands. Because so many people came to stay with us we were often short of accommodation. Mr. Brunston had his private room at the rear of the house converted into a large bathroom and WC in 1970. So we only had two bedrooms. When Melvyn and Josie and the children came the four of them used our bedroom, when other relatives came to stay they were given Kevin's bedroom, (at the rear top floor). So Kevin dry lined and damp proofed the old scullery in the basement, levelled the floor. Melvyn and Josie gave him their old shag-pile carpet and with two large TV and HiFi it was quite luxurious and made an extra bedroom and a play room to bring home friends from collage."

"Next we removed the hall wall to make the kitchen larger and we fitted a nice kitchen with doors from Melvyn and Josie's Claremont house. This was a big improvement. We then removed the wall between the inter-connecting reception rooms making a very good sized room. Kevin organized two feature fireplaces, one Victorian brick arch, the other wood and marble."

"In our bedroom I got a lot of old goal posts and drove them home from the park on the tractor and trailer; Kevin and I made these into a split level platform for the bed with wooden wardrobes either side. At the lower section of the room we used a row of mirrored wardrobes to make the room look very large."

"We fitted a new porch and front door. I would do the sawing and help fit things together and we worked well as a team."

"Kevin built fitted wardrobes in his bedroom; the doors he carried down from B and Q at Stamford Hill. He had a lot of clothes. His Mum was always buying him new clothes. I think he had thirty five pairs of shoes and one hundred ties and shirts. The house was looking very good. We bought new carpets throughout and new sofas for the lounge."

"As a final touch Kevin organized a central heating system. For us in 1982 this was sheer luxury."

# 10

# Miscellaneous Events

"One very good event we hosted was the Wedding Reception for a friend of my Daughter-in-Law Josie. It was great to be able to help people in those circumstances on their big day. I stayed home from work so I could help Grace. They had a ceremony at Stoke Newington Registry Office. At least we had enough crockery for the table. We opened the double doors up between the rooms and put a table front to back. It went very well. I've seen them a few times since and still get Christmas cards."

"A couple of months afterwards Grace' brother Vinnie and his wife came to stay with us for a week. We took them to see The Sound of Music on stage in West End. We enjoyed it so much Grace went again with her friend Babs to see it. We went to lots of shows and films whilst we lived in London."

"Most of our relatives came to stay with us there. I think they liked to go to see all the sights which were near to us and the shows. It was also good for them to spend time with Grace. She loved her phone; it was there when we moved in, we had never had one before."

"Our doctor came to see us and asked if I could plant some fruit trees and do some pruning. He knew I liked that kind of work. He had done a lot for me; it was he who had got me into hospital quickly for my hernia operation. I would often get him some bulbs to thank him. He always walked strangely, when I asked him what was wrong he said he had arthritis and soon after retired, he was quite young."

"In the same period of time Grace' legs became very bad with varicose veins from standing so much doing shop work in her earlier years; also all the work on the land in Hereford probably did not help. The doctor arranged for them to be operated on and after this she had to walk three miles a day. She had suffered ill health although her life. The waiting lists for operations were very short then compared to now, I feel sorry for people waiting for operations now."

"When Kevin was fourteen he didn't have to wait long for the operation on his teeth, only a few months. I took him to The Royal Dental Hospital in Leicester Square and waited two hours whilst he had the operation. He had eight teeth out, milk teeth and the four wisdom teeth under them. They said if it had been private it would have cost £1000.00 He was 14 years that was in 1974. For the next two years he would have metal rings on each tooth connected with wire and elastic bands to eventually make them uniform. It was painful but the end result very good."

"Many years before when Minnie died Grace went back to Hereford to help with arrangements and I looked after Kevin. We both spent a couple of weekends down there and Rosemary joined us now and again. I would take Girlie and Horace's dog Buttons for three mile walks it was the only time he'd have a long walk was with me. He would collapse when he got back; later if I tried to put his lead on he would refuse to come. Whilst in Hereford Grace and I would take flowers to the family graves at St. Peters' Church Lugwardine. It started a tradition we keep till today. Every year Kevin drives Grace and me to Hereford; we stay at Girlie and Horace's at Bartestree and we go to The Butter Market in High Town Herford and then to the grave yard and put flowers on all the family graves."

# 11

# Moving to Hastings 1984

"Rosemary and William were now in Bexhill-on-Sea. Kevin had just setup his own business as an Interior Designer and had recently moved into his apartment near Stoke Newington Common. He was working at the time for Authentic Interiors five minutes away in Dalston Lane on the borders of Hackney and Islington."

"Rosemary had suggested to her Mum that it might be a good idea to join her and William on the coast. Property was less than half the price of that in Stoke Newington and we could pay off our mortgage and I could give up work as could Grace.

I said to Grace if that is what you want it would be alright with me. At the time there were a lot of people getting their houses broken into and being held up with knives. She never got over the three times she was mugged."

"Rosemary and William had moved from the small 1960's Ashford home to a detached 1930's house on the outskirts of Bexhill-on-Sea. In theory this was a great advance on the home front; but the draw back was that the house was on the A259, a busy trunk road which would later see much redevelopment as well as a round-a-bout outside their home."

"Grace would get the train from Charing Cross meet with William and look at houses. She visited half a dozen times; he was very good taking time off work and driving her around. The coastal properties were much cheaper than those in our area. They also benefited from being larger most having double glazing and central heating. Grace fell in love with a semi-detached Victorian house about one mile from Rosemary and William in West St. Leonards."

"Our home in Kynaston Road took very little time to sell. Eventually two teachers moved in with their son. We also got four times the price we had paid for it. Nowadays the prices seem unbelievable compared to what we sold for."

"Our new home was just a few hundred yards from the sea and shingle beach. Shops were nearby and despite being again on the A259 trunk road it was opposite open fields."

"It had a good sized entrance Vestibule with inner front door to Hall much wider than Kynaston Road with attractive glass surround; this protected it from the weather. On the ground floor there were two reception rooms; behind these was the Breakfast Room and Utility Room and behind that the Kitchen, down stairs WC and porch to garden. Upstairs to the front was a very large bedroom with bay window, behind that a good sized bedroom which Kevin moved into, to the rear were a further bedroom and bathroom and separate WC. To My delight the rear garden had a lawn and greenhouse."

"The downside was that the whole house needed completely refurbishing. We moved in in late April and for the next two months we stripped all the wallpaper throughout. Kevin came to stay every weekend and refitted the Kitchen and Bathroom. For the first time ever we could buy all new; we even had our first dishwasher. Grace and I papered all the rooms and finally had the house carpeted throughout. Kevin found a beautiful wrought iron fireplace in Bexhill for the front reception room."

"Kevin had tried to live in his own place several years before when he went to Wimbledon School of Art; he had managed one month then moved back home and commuted for the rest of the year. Similarly this time within four weeks of us moving to St. Leonards he moved back in with us. He would leave early to get to London before the worst of the rush hour and try to leave Authentic Interiors after 6pm to miss the traffic. When managing the building schemes on public houses and disco in Poole in Dorset he would rent a Studio Flat in Bournemouth to cut down on the travelling."

"By July of 1984 Kevin bought a small cottage as an investment on the outskirts of St. Leonards. It was in a dirt-track lane; little did we know but it was not a good area and it needed work. Kevin was working long hours so I painted the outside of the cottage and replaced some broken panes of glass; Grace decorated the main Bedroom in a lovely light blue paint. Needless to say he hardly stayed at the cottage but instead slept in his bedroom at our home."

"The five of us would go out most weekends to the many beautiful country pubs for lunch or just a drink. We found the countryside very attractive and the people extremely friendly. I would go to Rosemary's and help them out with the garden and other jobs."

"Since I have retired and living in these parts I find the time goes very fast. It is nice to know that my daughter and young Kevin don't live very far away from me, they see me quite often and I go to stay with them very often it makes a nice change. Like everywhere else I've seen some changes with new places getting built."

"After one year in Hastings we had a letter from our next door neighbours from Hereford saying they were coming here for a holiday. Grace was pleased they were coming; they had had trouble with their in-laws and family problems. Tragically a week later we were told by the Salvation Army, they knocked on our door, that she had committed suicide and drowned herself in the river. It was a big shock to both of us; her brother had done the same two years before. When we lived in Hereford Grace was often visiting her in hospital trying to console her, she was often in a terrible state. I just feel that if they had come down to stay with us this might not have happened."

"When in Hereford we used to take her to the cinema if she was down in the dumps her husband never took her anywhere. It was too late to go to the funeral, she was already buried; but we were very hurt that the husband and daughter did not phone us, they had our telephone number."

# 12

# Trip to Irish Free State

"We were delighted when Melvyn and Josie said they were going to take us to Irish Free State. We travelled and saw a lot. We went down to Cork but didn't even kiss the Blarney Stone. A lot of Americans were in the castle kissing the stone. The only bad thing was Grace had her handbag stolen. It happened so quickly there was no one around while we were walking along the road. The thief must have hid behind a car. A security man in the shop heard me call out and ran out and saw the man running away and called the police. They knew where to find the man as he must have offended before. The police went to his house and his wife had already spent the money. At least we got our pension books back which saved us applying for new ones."

"When we were back in England the police kept ringing to get a date from Grace for her to appear in court to give evidence. When she eventually returned to Ireland the security guard did not turn up so they said there was insufficient evidence for a conviction. The police said that the stolen money would be returned to her in a few days; it took seven months to get it back. Each time Grace phoned about the stolen money the police said the officer was on leave. He must have been on leave more than he was doing police work. Eventually Rosemary had a candidate who she was sending to Middle East, he knew a solicitor in Ireland. The solicitor went to the police station and demanded the money and we got it in a few days. But the exchange rate had altered so we lost £19.00."

"We saw many places in Ireland and Melvyn paid for everything which was great. The food and clothes were much dearer there than in England. The retired people there have higher pensions and much higher standard of living than in many countries."

"What I really would have liked was a car to be able to go places when I was not doing much. I could not drive; I suppose I always thought I would not be able to afford to run a car on my wages. I would rather pay my bills than get in debt. Since all my children have cars and are only too pleased to take us out with them when they go out, it's not a problem. My wife is very understanding about these things so we go a lot of places by public transport."

"We often went to stay with Melvyn and Josie at their new home in Tolmers Road. They have a very nice home. They bought a smaller house and had extensions built around it including a terrace to the rear garden. We were very proud of how well they had got on. They would occasionally have parties at the house, especially in the summer. On one occasion there was a West Indian steel drum band. We would go to see Emma and Vikki perform in school concerts and later in Hertford Youth Orchestra. They are very talented children Vikki plays cello and Emma Violin and piano."

"Three years after moving to Hastings we went on a short holiday to Holland to see the bulb fields. We stayed five nights and saw a lot of the country. It was only three months since Grace had had her operation for cancer. It was discovered that she had stomach cancer. In an operation she had half her stomach removed. It took much time to recover. She could not eat very much because of having a much smaller stomach. She lost lots of weight which she believed made her look much younger. But the feeling within she compared to being pregnant."

"It was very nice to be able to go there and take her mind off it. She was such a lovely person all through it all. To make it worse three of her brothers died from cancer at very young ages."

"In the September we went to Scotland with my Daughter and young son Kevin. It was nice having a car to travel around in. We hired a car so Rosemary and Kevin shared the driving. We rented a caravan in a Cumbrian Village called Silloth. We saw quite a lot of The Lake District. We had holidayed there back in 1982. At that time Melvyn and Josie had loaned us their Vauxhall Chevette which was very kind of them. We had driven out of London on the day Charles and Diana had married so there was no traffic travelling north. On that holiday we had stayed in various bed and breakfast in Kendal then Fort William in Scotland, Aberdeen, Inverness and Edinburgh. We had enjoyed that holiday so much we were so pleased to return now in 1987 and hopefully help Grace on her recovery."

"While in Silloth I had two dances with Grace at the holiday camp we were staying in. Grace said I hope I don't suffer after this dancing. We were very glad we could take her we looked forward to that holiday very much. I was very pleased when it all seemed to go well. Travelling through to Scotland is very similar to the countryside in Ireland. On the Thursday of that week Grace felt great discomfort so Rosemary stayed with her in the caravan and I went with Kevin to Edinburgh for a trip."

"I was very pleased that we were able to go to a few places whilst we were living in this part of the country. Kevin and Rosemary were always taking us out we had some fun on these outings. Apart from country pubs we went to castles and historical places such as Arundel, Brighton and Dover. Every Saturday Grace and Kevin would go into Hastings shopping for clothes. They both were very fond of shopping. Grace found a hair dresser in Bulverhythe Road, five minutes from us and she would go every week to have her hair done."

"Grace loved living by the sea, she would do the short walk to the beach almost every day to enjoy the air and sit on the beach. It was such a contrast to Stoke Newington and the worry of being attacked walking to the shops on Stoke Newington High Street. At weekends we would sometimes go on longer walks through the fields opposite into open countryside beyond."

"It was four weeks since we returned to St. Leonards from The Lake District. Grace was never one to dwell on her problems but she seemed in constant discomfort. Meal times were particularly distressing. We had been in contact through our doctor with the specialist who had performed the operation in February. I had noticed big changes in my wife when I was trying to help dress her. She never complained all she would say is it felt like she was having a baby the way in which her inside was rolling around. I took her to see her specialist and he said she would receive a letter as to when she would be going into hospital. Ten days later we received a letter saying Grace would be going into hospital on the following Monday morning. We talked it over some tea. I could see a change in her. That morning I phoned Rosemary about going shopping in the country stores. I asked her to get a loaf. Grace said why don't you go and get one in the shop yourself. I didn't want to be very far from her seeing how she was looking. I phoned my Daughter-in-Law Josie to say that Grace would be going into hospital Monday morning. The grand children were going on a short break from school she said they would phone and have a talk with their Nan. Little did we know she would pass away that evening. It was nice that she had a few words with Grand Children before she went. In the afternoon Rosemary came with some new slippers for Grace to go into hospital. Grace asked me to go and get the dressing gown which I had washed to put on. After getting the gown I washed her face and legs and brushed her hair. She must have known why in herself with the changes coming over her. I was sitting with her holding her hand when she said to me I am dying. Then I was holding her in my arms when the ambulance came. It came quite fast, I was glad she never suffered very much pain. It is terrible when the person you love passes away from your life I haven't got over it in the two years since she has gone. I don't think I ever will."

"Grace died on 19th October two days after the great storm of 1987. There was massive damage all around the country but all we lost was a TV aerial. I was very grateful to Melvyn who took me away for a few days to help get over the shock. I wanted to put my wife's ashes along with her parents on their grave. The Vicar said there were new rules so we could not. So to make things easy I put them where I first met her, my children agreed with me. So her ashes lye opposite the gate to The Old Manor House in Lugwardine where I first saw her sitting on the fence reading her magazine."

"It was a huge shock to all the family. Only I had been truly aware of Grace's swift deteriorating health over the past few weeks. Kevin had driven to London to open Norland Interiors that day because the trains had not been running due to the Great Storm. He worked long hours and always arrived home late so he was unaware that his Mum was so ill. He came home and had dinner, then was going clubbing as was the norm as it was the weekend. Grace said to him before he went out, "have you got enough money?" He went back to his own house that night to find a note on the front door mat from Rosemary saying to come home, something terrible has happened. On arrival he was met by the ambulance crew carrying Grace out of the front door in a black body bag. The shock took many years to come to terms with. It was the worst thing that happened in his whole life; they had been so close and he had never properly left home."

"The Christmas after Grace had died Kevin and I were invited to stay with Mel and his family in Hertfordshire. They made us very welcome. It was good not to be alone so soon after loosing her. We went up by train as Kevin's car had broken down. After Christmas we all went to see where Kevin worked at Norland Interiors in

Holland Park. The shop was closed but he had the keys so we were able to have a good look around and choose some things to buy. Melvyn and Josie chose some furniture they liked. The Grand Daughters had a good look around I think they liked the shop."

"I am pleased to have my daughter and son living not far from me. I go and see them a lot they come and see me as well. I suppose when I painted the house for the second time after I lost my wife this caused me to have my first heart attack. My Son-in-Law was going to take me to America for a holiday when I was taken bad. Perhaps it was a good thing it happened before we left. The week they went on holiday I came out of hospital and stayed with Kevin for a while till I was better and took things easy."

"It is nice to go and do some gardening in my Son-in-Law and daughters garden it gets me out of the house. They are very good to me as is my other son Mel. I pay all my bills as soon as I get them; I used to leave them to my wife. It took me a while to get them sorted out. My monthly pension from Islington is a big help. It is a pity some have to live only on their old age pension especially if they have to pay rent for where they live."

# 13

# Trying to Cope with Life without Grace

"In the February of 1985 Kevin had sold the cottage he disliked so much and had moved to a nice three storey house on West Hill in Hastings. Needless to say he continued to sleep in his old room at our home and rented his own house out. As he had never properly left home I was very worried about him. No one had really known how ill Grace was and no one expected her to pass away so suddenly and so young. The shock would take years to come to terms with. One month after Grace died he met Stephen at a night club in Hastings. Six months later on April 11$^{th}$ 1988 the two decided to move into the Vicarage Road house and later move across the road to a larger four storey home with sea views, so eventually leaving the family home."

"Every Thursday evening I would join the boys for dinner and then watch Question Time on TV. I would stay over every week. At weekends we would go over to Kent on Sundays and meet some old laddies whom Stephen had adopted years before. We would go out for a pub lunch with Jane Cockell or Francis Smith. Sometimes we would stay the weekend at Stephen's beautiful country house The Old Rectory, Burmarsh in Kent. This was situated in a pretty village set just below Aspinall's Wild Life Park, 'Port Lympne Reserve'.

One such weekend some years in the future, in the mid-1990s, Melvyn and his new wife Janet Butterfield joined us. We had great fun driving the tractor around the garden. I liked Janet very much. She was so easy to get along with and a nice looking girl. Janet's family were lovely too. I would go to stay with them on many occasions in the future at their new home in Little Berkhamsted near Hertford."

"It was nice when I went on a day trip to France with Stephen and Kevin and some friends of theirs's. They were Kitty and Arthur Peerless. Kitty was a large very friendly German lady who had met Arthur when he was on National Service in Germany. It was the first time I had been to France. I will be going again and I hope to see some of the countryside. Going by car I will be able to know more what the country is like. They have fresh bread baked twice a day for the people, I think that is a good thing to do.

All the people coming back were loaded with bottles of wine. They do a good trade with English people crossing every day to buy wines and spirits. One of my son's friends said they bought a bottle for £14.00 which would have cost £30.00 in England. I got some cheese and a bottle of wine for myself. The day out was what I needed and the crossing was very interesting."

"When we got off the ferry Stephen drove us to a large white country house near Deal in Kent. Winston Churchill had stayed here on occasions during the war. It was now The Don Medi Restaurant. You drove up and four men opened your car doors. You went into a foyer and saw the car being parked on a bank of TV. The restaurant was huge with sofas to sit on before going to table. The meal was very good Italian but the five of us only paid £35.00 for the lot. The meal was to celebrate Kevin's 30th birthday."

"My Son-in-Law and daughter are going over to France to see about a house. I think that will be a good idea; it will be nice for them when they go together on holiday. They will be taking me with them; I will be looking forward to that stay very much. They say that there is much more land attached to houses there than in England. Living here on the coast it won't be such a long journey over to France. Some of the goods are much in line with our own, others are more expensive."

"It is hard for those like me to loose a dear one. To make it worse I had been left alone throughout childhood. Life can be cruel at times since I lost my wife it is like starting over again. I get out quite a lot and the people I know are very nice. I go for walks and see people I know; I still have a bike so at least I have my own transport."

*An Irish Boy*

# 14

# France

"My Son-in-Law and Daughter took me over to see their new house in France. The place is very nice also quiet. We all hope to be staying in France for their first Christmas. I am hoping as I write this that my Grand Daughters and Son and Wife will be able to come and stay. The country is very big you do need your own transport. There are miles of countryside without seeing any houses. Many of the railways seem to have closed down. The road signs are very confusing two signs in different directions pointing to the same place. The road lighting along the sides of the road I like it is better than England. I now know where all the forest fire on TV are especially the part we came through. There are lots of rabbits everywhere. The foxes are many and they won't go short of food."

"During the four days over in France we had a good clear out of the sheds and out buildings. There was plenty of old wood and rubbish. We had some big bonfires on the lawn. The people who had lived in the house had moved to live on south coast, French Riviera. They had lived and worked in Paris which was about two hours' drive away; this had been their holiday home which they had lived in for many years."

*We had travelled over from Newhaven with Kevin driving Rosemary and William in a Luton Van full of beds and furniture. Rosemary* insisted that she had been told no documentation was needed for these. Stephen and I were following behind with more things in Volvo estate. The Duane at Dieppe took a dislike to Rosemary and impounded the goods until we persuaded her to give goods in transit certificate. Rosemary insisted on stopping at the first supermarket and spending one and a half hours buying food and wine. When we got out all was pitch black. We preceded with no map though the huge town of Rouen. Circling it twice eventually found the road to Gace. We broke into and stayed at the cottage the night, despite not having taken procession of it. The cottage had been unused for a long time and as well as dust and cobwebs we had frequent sound of rats within the rooms gnawing. Following day we met the Vendors and the property purchase was concluded in Hotel de Ville with the Notary. Customarily Rosemary and William then took the couple plus, Stephen and Kevin and me to lunch in a busy Gace restaurant. Needless to say the only person who spoke any French and that was not too good was Kevin. We had a very difficult meal and then went to the cottage where the French couple handed over the keys. They had a few discourteous comments about Kevin's translation skills and pleasantly left, never to be heard from again. They had sold their apartment in Paris along with this, their holiday home which they had spent several months a year and had retired to Cannes. They had left everything, family photos, books, furniture, everything. Needless to say the 200 year old converted barn on rolling hillside was idyllic. It had an overhanging gable to one side sheltering the outside staircase to upper floor; this is quite common in Normandy country architecture. The roof had felt tiles and three pretty windows protruded from it. It was some sixty feet long and steeply pitched. The ground floor walls were of stone and the upper floor on external staircase gable end brown and white; the other gable end was of stone punctuated with four small window openings. The windows had pretty wooden shutters. There were two front doors, wooden with four glazed panels in *each, one entered the sitting room, the other was the entrance to the dining room, and both were on the façade facing the meadow, which was just eight feet or so from the house. Down stairs there was a large room with timber ceiling which would have housed the animals, it had a huge stone Normandy fireplace with overhanging mantelpiece; and then there were three other rooms which the farmers would have lived in when the building was an agricultural dwelling. These formed a Dining Room, again with a substantial fireplace, this one in metal, Kitchen and Bathroom. On the upper floor the whole area went up to the pitch of the roof and had huge timbers as its structure partly dividing it into three areas. But apart from these timbers it was completely open. The walls and ceiling were covered in richly patterned fabric. The cottage was on a long narrow plot with lawns both ends and sheds and out buildings to the rear and a Bewl Putong Area to the north end. A garage was inside the garden's five bar gate. The plot nestled beside a narrow lane with tall hedges and to its front façade past its garden hedgerow and gate the field dropped away steeply sloping merging with a valley full of meadows and woods with lots of cows and a fierce bull at close proximity. The valley led up to wide escarpment in the distance. No other buildings were in view. The other side of the lane was a farm with farm house and outbuildings. The farmer and his wife were extremely friendly and gave us a ton of logs, dropped over our hedge next to our wood store, for Christmas. This wonderful new home for Rosemary and William was called: 'La Ronflette'; The Snoring, or Slumber.*

"I hope to go back to the cottage soon. Next time I go I would like to see Paris and some of the other famous parts. My son Kevin is going to go over to do some work to the house. His friend Stephen is a builder. My son does all the design drawings which have to be done. They are both good at their own jobs. Kevin passed with high honours from Polytechnic; I heard someone speaking on the radio that the ones who come out of polytechnics are better than those who come out of Oxford or Cambridge. It was nice seeing him passing with full honours. We were both very proud of him getting his scroll he worked very hard for his degree."

"My Sister-in-Law had her 50th Wedding Anniversary in the village hall in Bartestree. We all went down for the celebration. Melvyn, Josie and Grandchildren stayed in the new part of Longworth Hall, I had my own room, Daughter and Son-in-Law had The Bridle Suite, Kevin and Stephen had a smaller room. It was great to see all the family and my own together; I only wish I had some of my own brothers and sisters to have been there. Girlie and Horace had a great time with music and dancing. The village hall was soon after demolished to make way for new houses. It has been replaced by a purpose built hall with sports facilities on the edge of the village. The old hall had been there since the war and with it go many memories of happy times. We met Mrs. Pantile the wife of Horace's boss. She was young for him and a good looking woman. She knew where Kevin had worked in London. They soon after got divorced. We were all very sad that Grace was not with us. Kevin and I shed tears thinking about it."

"Whilst staying in Bartestree I went with my Daughter and Son-in-Law to Hereford Cathedral to see Mappa Mundey. We also saw the Chained Library with some of the oldest books in the World. The books appeared not to have been out of their shelves for many years."

"While in Hereford we went to put flowers on my wife's grave. I felt a little lost at the time it would have been nice if she had been at the party, I would have enjoyed it much more."

"A few weeks after the 50th Anniversary Party in Hereford I went over to France with my Daughter and Kevin and his friend. They were to do some work in the house. She had the Kitchen floor ripped up and a new brick floor laid, (*In herringbone design*). We had taken some flat pack kitchen units over from B&Q to make a fitted kitchen. I worked in the garden planting lots of bulbs to make a good show of flowers in the spring. It took a few days getting to grips with the weeds. There seemed to be plenty of rabbits there were holes everywhere. Under the sheds there were signs of other inhabitants. Trouble was they had kept chickens so this attracted all sorts. We all slept in the top floor. We put velvet curtains on the beams to divide the room into three bedrooms. It was very cosy. There was lots of wildlife and birds sang early in the morning. The cows would come to the hedge by the front doors every evening to watch us. They probably thought we had food for them."

"The oven the people had left for us in the kitchen was difficult to control and my Daughter burnt all the pizza. She didn't like pizza anyway. She cleaned thoroughly all the old kitchen units and all the plates and other things they left, it took her hours, and then Kevin and his friend Stephen took them out side onto the lawn and burnt them."

"Before we left for home we booked up to have our Christmas Dinner at one of the hotels in the village which was not very far from where we were living. (*Les Hostelries des Champs, in Gace; a beautiful Napoleonic former country chateau*). Coming back on the boat we lost my car rug which I had given to Rosemary for the crossing, it was bought by my wife. In the morning we found it in a baby's cot I don't know why they had to take it, but I was pleased to get it back. The crossing from Caen to Portsmouth was very rough; the boat was six decks but it was like being in a lift going up and down. It took seven hours. They turned the lights down and closed the shops and restaurants for the journey because of the storm."

*An Irish Boy*

# 15

# Arnhem Visit

"For my next trip I booked myself on an excursion to Holland. The car picked me up at Warrior Square and took me to Flimwell some fifteen miles north where the coaches went from. We went on the ferry and then over to Arnhem. I met some chaps who had been fighting there when I was there. It was good to meet with some people who knew what I'd been through. We went to the Museum and then to Arnhem Bridge, which was what all the trouble had been over. We stayed over two hours looking around the site of the battle. The place was very much as I remember it from when I was there in the closing months of the Second World War. As I've described earlier the battle was fierce and long lasting. Many of my mates were killed and it rekindled the great sadness of losing them. I had many thoughts of all those brave men who didn't make it. When I look back I wonder how I managed to come through it. I even saw the place where I had my first drink of tea when we were rescued after swimming across the river. They kept the grave yard very nice and tidy, very respectful of that tragic battle and the huge waste of human life. Whilst we were there many Germans were visiting as well. They looked as if they had been at the battle the way they were looking around the roads surrounding the bridge. It took us seven and a half hours to get there and a little longer to get back. The night was very cold, they said they would push on to get back as the heating was not working, but they never did. I was in the no smoking section at the top. We got back at 12am to the bus yard. I didn't get in until 12.50 and was very cold; I went straight to bed and put the electric blanket on. On the ferry I'd got talking to a woman who was from the same part of Ireland as me. She was a nurse and worked in a hospital in Kent. In her years of working in England she has only been back to Ireland twice. We talked about Ireland and how long I'd been here and all the different types of work I'd done. Her cousin was Michael Collins; he was the one who had been shot in the 1922 uprising. I have read that he was quite a leader of men. There are lots of songs about his life and death. I feel sorry for all those men who give there lives for what they believe in. No one seems to want to sit down and see what can be done for the troubles. Michael Collins seems to have been quite a hero in Ireland. Many of the things he wanted to sort out then are still wrong today. You would think by now the issues could have been resolved."

# 16

# Christmas in France

"My Daughter and Son-in-Law and young son Kevin with his friend Stephen all went over to spend Christmas in France. We all enjoyed it. We went to Midnight Mass at the church in our village, *(The village church in Resenlieu, just outside Gace)*. It was a lovely service, but all in French. It was a pretty church with a small pointed wooden spire, not very large and on its own outside the village. The inside was lined with wooden pews with doors on."

"Following day we drove the two hours to Paris in Stephen's old Volvo car. It was about 110 miles from Rose and Bills' house. We stayed in a hotel in the centre not far from Eiffel Tower, *(Hotel Vaugirard, off Avenue Vaugirard)*. We went up the Eiffel Tower and saw lots of the famous buildings including Notre Dame. The people were very friendly. Quite a lot of the food and drink is more expensive than in England. I expect the people get better wages than we do in our country."

"The roads in France are very good; as well as being straight you can see for miles ahead. We had a trip on the Paris Metro. The underground trains run on rubber wheels so there is not much noise in the stations. The stations were very clean as are the streets."

"What took my breath away was Versailles. The size of the palace buildings and gardens, they are the best I have ever seen. The size of the man made lakes is incredible they must have had a huge labour force working there for a long time. I should have liked to have seen all the rooms. Some were closed off; the paintings and statues were amazing works of art to me. Just after our return from France Versailles was on the TV; it was nice to think that I'd seen the place and been there recently myself."

"In Paris there were different buses from all over Germany, Holland, Spain as well as from England. The weather was good and it was sunny and warm while we were there. The night we stayed at the hotel in Paris we were watching TV after getting in from our meal and it showed Chowchesco and his wife being shot in the revolution in Rumania. On the journey back the fog was bad. Paris seemed much smaller than London; we were soon on the circular road and then out of the city into the countryside. Kevin said they raise the level of the water from underground so as to clean the street. It is a good idea we should do it here."

"We will all be going back to France in a short time. I will be looking forward to seeing the Daffodils in bloom that I planted as well as other things. When they have got all the building work finished they can go there for their holidays and enjoy their stay. I expect my son Melvyn and his wife and children will be going there sometime for a stay. They are always going away to different parts of the World when the children are on holiday. My Grand Children have seen more parts of the World than I have. It is nice that they have good parents and a happy home life."

"When I was out for a walk a few days ago I was talking to an old friend who I often see about and he told me about his troubles at home. He lost his wife and then had to leave his house. I felt very sorry for him."

"When I'm not busy in my Daughter's garden or my own I often go to see castles and other sites. I still get up early I have never been one to lie in bed. All my working life I have been one step ahead of my alarm clock. I would turn it off so it would not wake Grace up. Opening the gates at the park I sometimes had to light paper to melt the frost around the locks; I was only caught out once not able to unlock them."

"Since retiring and living in Sussex my daughter often takes me out in her car for rides in the country and shopping at the farm shop. My young son Kevin when he has time does as well. Sadly He and Stephen have to work on jobs for customers during the week, often commuting to Brighton or Folkestone or even London. At weekend they have to maintain their properties and do the gardens. I still go and stay with The Boys on Thursday evenings we have a meal and then watch Question Time. We still on occasion at weekends go over to Stephen's house in Burmarsh in Kent. It has a lovely garden and the lawn needs cutting each weekend. Because of the housing situation he has not been able to sell it. But I enjoy helping cut the grass; they use a tractor and gang mower like I used at Highbury. I have seen most of Sussex. The county is very beautiful with plenty of different trees. We go to Rye quite a lot, strolling around the shops. When we were there last time I got some things in the Kitchen Shop that they wanted for their house in France. When they go over again they should have most of the things they need for the house. The agency where they bought their house is in Rye and last time we went to Rye we went into the agency and they were talking about property they said since they had bought the cottage a lot of the house prices had gone up."

"Kevin and his friend will be going over again to do some more jobs they want done. Both of them are quite busy since the recent bad storms there are lots of houses with chimneys blown over and roofs to repair. In the first storm two years ago my chimney got damaged; Melvyn arranged for it to be taken down. I was very glad as it could have caused a lot of damage to my bedroom and kitchen. Walking around there is much damage everywhere to walls and fences. Talking to some fishermen they said that their nets had been ruined, they had not seen anything like it for years. This had been the more recent storm of 1990."

"One of the fishermen I know said he would take me out in his boat. I hope the weather will be good. These fishermen on the high seas have hard lives in the winter. The boats in Hastings are small and have to be pulled up onto the beach out of the water. I haven't seen him for a while because I've had a cold. Because of this I was not able to go with Kevin and his friend Stephen to France while they were doing the work. I was going to go with Rose and Bill next time they go, but they asked if I could look after the cats and rabbits. They have their house on the market, they want to sell it and move away. A lot of things have changed where they live. They have built a shopping centre opposite them and a big roundabout in front of their house. To make things worse a large McDonalds has opened over the road from them, a drive-in. Rosemary is in a very bad way; I worry about her having a nervous breakdown. They would like me to buy a house with them. Since I put my house on the market I have only a few come to look. Some say they will call or ring but never do. I read in the papers that houses are not selling and people are getting in trouble because of the high interest rates. Some are loosing their homes."

"I went to Hereford for one night with Kevin to put flowers on my wife's grave and on the family graves. Grace's memorial plaque is now on the family grave. It was Grace's birthday on the 24th August we went the day after on the 25th. It was good to see old friends and family. There are lots of new houses being built around Les and Berne's house. The town of Hereford has been through some changes since I went there for the first time in the war years. I went down with Kevin to Weston Beggard to see the place he was born and to see the places I'd taken him around, the farmyards to see all the farm animals. It's the other way now he takes me when he has time. He and his friend are working long hours at this present time. They took me to Brighton where they were working and I spent a day going around all the famous sites while they were at work. I go to Eastbourne quite a lot with Rosemary and Kevin.

Melvyn took me to Hereford just before Christmas and also Easter time. Both times was to see about a violin which his daughter has always wanted. It was laying in a case for a long time and will need much restoration before she can play it. He is a very good provider managing to get everything they want as well as pay school fees."

"Emma has won a scholarship at Haileybury College. I've seen it from the outside it is quite some place. She must be doing very well. I love to hear her playing; she takes everything in her stride. I feel very proud of both my Grand Daughters. I only wish my dear wife could have seen the way she plays now. The rest of the family went up to London to see the Youth Orchestra playing at The Royal Albert Hall on 8th April 1991. I really enjoyed my night; more so it was the first time I had been in the Royal Albert Hall. I was amazed how large it was. I had passed by the hall many times whilst living in London."

"In London there are lots of places to see if one had the time or the money. When I was not working weekends my wife and I and Kevin would go to see lots of different places as well as go on boat trips on the River Thames. We would go at weekends to Melvyn's to see his family in Hertfordshire and they would often come to stay with us, especially if there was a firm's party in the West End. The Grand Children would stay over and we would look after them and Melvyn and Josie would come back and stay after having a great night out. Kevin would get in later after going to one of his parties at college or in West End. We often had Grace's family coming to stay with us and we would show them all the sites of London."

"I look back and believe that moving to London was the best thing Grace and I could have done. It was good for us and for all the family."

*After April 1991 Dad's collection of memories ceased to be added to. Many things were to happen to the family starting very shortly afterwards which would probably distract him from* reflecting back to earlier days. What is clear is how vividly he had recorded the life so very rich in experiences and emotions that he had had up to that date.

Ten years subsequently to the last entries in Dad's collection of memories he would sell his family home and move to a gorgeous luxury garden flat in a Victorian Mansion in Markwick Terrace, St. Leonards-on-Sea. It would have huge living space, two bedrooms and two bathrooms and keys to a communal private square. He would be very proud of his apartment; it was a great achievement giving his torturous and very hard childhood in Ireland. Sadly he would pass away March 2003 aged 89 years followed in 2010 by Rosemary at a similar age to her Mother 67 years.

Many years later in 2017 Melvyn was gifted an Ancestry Pack which involved him sending away a saliva sample. Incredibly he was to discover that John's sister had survived childhood and from her adopted family in Northern Ireland she had moved to Dublin and later to Canada. This revealed a large extended family with many relatives, cousins and second cousins, existing which we had no knowledge of prior to this. John would have been delighted to have known that his sister had survived as had he and he had not been the last sole member of his Irish family.

The End